SHADES
OF GRAY

SHADES OF GRAY

Perspectives on Campaign Ethics

CANDICE J. NELSON

DAVID A. DULIO

STEPHEN K. MEDVIC

BROOKINGS INSTITUTION PRESS
Washington, D.C.

ABOUT BROOKINGS

The Brookings Institution is a private nonprofit organization devoted to research, education, and publication on important issues of domestic and foreign policy. Its principal purpose is to bring knowledge to bear on current and emerging policy problems. The Institution maintains a position of neutrality on issues of public policy. Interpretations or conclusions in Brookings publications should be understood to be solely those of the authors.

Copyright © 2002
THE BROOKINGS INSTITUTION
1775 Massachusetts Avenue, N.W., Washington, D.C. 20036
www.brookings.edu

Library of Congress Cataloging-in-Publication data

Shades of gray : perspectives on campaign ethics / Candice J. Nelson, David A. Dulio, and Stephen K. Medvic, editors.
    p.   cm.
Includes bibliographical references and index.
   ISBN 0-8157-0618-9 (cloth : alk. paper)
   ISBN 0-8157-0617-0 (pbk. : alk. paper)
   1. Political campaigns—United States. 2. Political ethics—United States.
3. Elections—United States. I. Nelson, Candice J., 1949– II. Dulio, David A.
III. Medvic, Stephen K.
   JK2281 .S489 2002   2002008639
   172—dc21   CIP

9 8 7 6 5 4 3 2 1

The paper used in this publication meets minimum requirements of the
American National Standard for Information Sciences—Permanence of Paper for
Printed Library Materials: ANSI Z39.48-1992.

Typeset in Sabon

Composition by Stephen D. McDougal
Mechanicsville, Maryland

Printed by R. R. Donnelley and Sons
Harrisonburg, Virginia

Contents

Foreword

Elections are arguably the single most important event in American democratic life, as they are an opportunity for Americans both to give their consent to be governed and to hold their representatives accountable for past performance. Importantly, the quality of election campaigns has a direct impact on the health of democracy. Democratic elections are, or should be, competitive events. Yet while we expect vigorous campaigning focused on securing victory, we also expect campaigns and candidates to conduct themselves in a manner befitting the high offices they pursue.

Unfortunately, the feast of democracy is no longer so nourishing. Some scholars and journalists have argued that the modern competitive rough-and-tumble campaigns in the United States are, at the very least, undermining civility in politics and government, and at worst are damaging deliberative democracy. Others maintain that recent trends in "negative" campaign tactics misinform and mislead citizens and discourage political participation of both voters and quality candidates, as well as leading to excessive partisanship and deadlock in policymaking.

Rightly or not, a great many woes in American democracy have been blamed on the way in which modern campaigns are run; many observers go so far as to consider tactics of today's campaigns to be "unethical." To know whether such a charge is accurate requires an understanding both of how campaigns operate and of the ethical principles that can be applied to those campaigns. Examining these issues is an essential first step in moving campaigns in a more positive direction.

Shades of Gray: Perspectives on Campaign Ethics is a key contribution to the Center for Congressional and Presidential Studies' Improving Campaign Conduct project at American University, a six-year study supported by The Pew Charitable Trusts. In 1997 the center was awarded the first of two three-year grants from The Trusts to work with leaders of the campaign consulting industry to try to improve the conduct of election campaigns. One goal of the overall study is to develop an industrywide set of standards of practice that encourages the consulting industry to produce high-quality, informative, and ethical campaigns. Some of the original research that serves as a basis for this goal is captured in this book. However, the book goes beyond simply a discussion of what professional political consultants should and should not do. *Shades of Gray* is a unique compilation of perspectives from various scholars and practitioners who are intimately involved in the everyday aspects of campaigning.

While the Improving Campaign Conduct project has a focus on professional political consultants, it is not the only Pew-funded project charged with investigating and assessing the health of democratic elections; its funding has a much wider view of elections—and of ethics. *Shades of Gray* mirrors the concerns of The Trusts in its comprehensive assessment of the ethical challenges facing the major actors in elections: candidates, professional political consultants, political parties, organized interest groups, the media, and citizens. Campaigning in competitive elections always has been a rough "contact sport" in American politics, but deciding what actions are in fact "ethical" in today's campaigns varies depending on the perspective one takes to examine this question. Therefore, this book describes ethical standards and establishes a framework within which to understand the responsibilities of different campaign actors, discussing how they grapple with the dilemmas that confront them.

Other activities of the Improving Campaign Conduct project include on-the-record and off-the-record discussions with campaign professionals, journalists, citizens, and candidates; research about and discussions with political consultants to form consensus around useful codes and standards of campaign conduct; an effort to organize campaign training schools and educators into an informal association to share teaching materials and research about campaign management for the purpose of developing and disseminating "best practices" in election campaigns to the students who will be tomorrow's campaign professionals, candidates, party staffers, and citizen activists; opportunities for members of the consulting industry to discuss issues of campaign ethics among themselves; and the periodic recognition and celebration of campaign professionals who have run consistently high-quality campaigns through a lifetime achievement award.

Shades of Gray is the fourth in a series of books published by the Brookings Institution Press about the world of campaigns and elections; it is a companion to *Campaign Warriors: Political Consultants in Elections*; *Crowded Airwaves: Campaign Advertising in Elections*; and *The Battle for Congress: Consultants, Candidates, and Voters*. All of these works originated from the Improving Campaign Conduct project.

The scholarship and activities generated from this project would not have been possible without the support and leadership of Sean Treglia, program director, Michael Delli Carpini, public policy division director, and Rebecca Rimel, president, of The Pew Charitable Trusts. Special thanks also go to Cornelius M. Kerwin, provost at American University, who has played a special role in sustaining the initial support of the Improving Campaign Conduct project.

James A. Thurber

Acknowledgments

This book would not have been possible without the support and assistance of a number of people. First, we would like to thank Christopher Kelaher, the acquisitions editor at Brookings Institution Press, for his support of this project as well for the three previous books in this series. We would also like to thank at Brookings Robert L. Faherty, the director of the press, Janet Walker, the managing editor, Robin DuBlanc, who copyedited the text, Carlotta Ribar who proofread the pages, and Sherry Smith, who provided the index.

Thanks also go to our colleagues at American University who provided assistance at various stages of this project: Jennifer Arnold, Nathaniel Kraft, Leslie McNaugher, Sam Garrett, and Katy White.

Finally, we would like to thank Sean Treglia, program director, Michael Delli Carpini, public policy division director, and Rebecca Rimel, president, of The Pew Charitable Trusts, for their support of the Improving Campaign Conduct project.

SHADES
OF GRAY

CHAPTER ONE

CAMPAIGN ETHICS

Approaching the Issue

DAVID A. DULIO

STEPHEN K. MEDVIC

CANDICE J. NELSON

Many people snicker when they read or hear the words *campaign* and *ethics* in the same sentence. It is difficult to blame those who think that *campaign ethics* is an oxymoron when one thinks about all the activities that occur during campaigns that can appear to be unethical—or at the very least questionable. One need only look to the last presidential campaign to see numerous campaign practices described as such.

One of the lasting images of the battle between Vice President Albert Gore and Texas governor George W. Bush is the infamous "RATS ad." The television advertisement in question, sponsored by the Republican National Committee (RNC), contrasted the prescription drug plans offered by both candidates. Contrast ads like this are a common campaign technique designed to set one candidate's record, proposals, or stances on issues apart from his or her opponent's. However, in this particular case, the ad used some creative film-making techniques that included flashing the phrase "Bureaucrats Decide" across the screen to help depict Gore's proposed plan. The controversy over the ad began when someone realized that as "Bureaucrats Decide" scrolled across the screen, the word "RATS" was isolated momentarily (see figure 1-1).

While the RNC and the creator of the ad said that the inclusion of the word "RATS" was purely an accident and that the techniques were used "so the ad would look more interesting" and have a "visual drumbeat," Democrats and the Gore campaign characterized the incident as some-

Figure 1-1. *Segments of the Republican National Committee's "Priority" Ad (also known as the "RATS" Ad)*

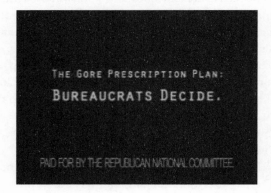

Source: www.cnn.com (January 4, 2002).

thing more, even going so far as to say that it was an intentional act to manipulate voters.[1] Was this an attempt at subliminal advertising, something considered to be unethical by experts in the field, or was it simply an oversight on the part of the creators of the ad, who were quick to point out that "the word 'rats' flashes across [only] one of the 900 video frames that make up the ad"?[2]

Before the first debate of the 2000 presidential campaign, a videotape of Governor Bush's debate preparation found its way into the hands of a Gore supporter and adviser.[3] Was this a conspiracy on the part of the Gore campaign to infiltrate the Bush campaign and gain an advantage for the debates, even though the vice president was reported to be the superior debater? Was Yvette Lozano, a Bush campaign worker who was photographed by the FBI sending a package that looked similar to the one delivered to the Gore supporter, a spy for the Gore team? Or was a fake videotape sent by the Bush campaign in order to spur accusations against the Gore campaign of dirty tricks, or at least disrupt the vice president's debate preparation?

There are plenty of other examples of questionable campaign conduct from the 2000 presidential election. For example, early in the Republican primary a pro-Bush organization ran radio advertisements in New York State claming that Senator John McCain, Bush's chief primary rival, had voted against breast cancer research. The ad highlighted a few items that McCain had voted against, which "were included in more than $13 billion in what [McCain] characterized as pork-barrel spending requested by lawmakers."[4] Many, including the McCain campaign team, challenged the legitimacy and truthfulness of the ad, pointing to the large number of other bills that McCain had supported over his career. Was it unethical for the pro-Bush organization and its professional consultants to make this ad, which can be characterized as misleading at best and false at worst? The ad was technically true—McCain did vote against the bills in question—but was it ethical?

Questions about the ethical purity of a campaign advertisement lie not only in what is said in the ad but in the implications the ad makes about the candidate(s) featured in it. The NAACP ran an ad entitled "James Byrd" on behalf of Al Gore's campaign during the 2000 campaign. James Byrd, one will recall, was the Texas man who had been dragged to his death behind a pickup truck while George W. Bush was governor; the story of those responsible spurred calls for hate crime legislation in the state of Texas. The ad featured the following audio:

I'm Rene Mullings, James Byrd's daughter. On June 7, 1998, in Texas my father was killed. He was beaten, chained, and then dragged three miles to his death, all because he was black. So when Governor George W. Bush refused to support hate crimes legislation, it was like my father was killed all over again. Call George W. Bush and tell him to support hate crimes legislation. We won't be dragged away from our future.

The text of the ad's script is all very likely true. James Byrd was killed on June 7, 1998; it is difficult to quarrel with the feelings of Mr. Byrd's daughter; and Bush, the sitting governor, did oppose the hate crimes legislation that was introduced. However, this ad also implies something that may be totally different. One observer stated, "the real ethical question surrounding this ad arises from the implied message, which is clearly something along the lines of: George W. Bush doesn't care if black people get dragged to their death behind pickup trucks."[5] Were the facts in the "James Byrd" ad correct? Yes. Was the implication in the spot accurate? No. What, then, are we to conclude about the ethical nature of the ad? Whatever the real answers are to the questions surrounding the ads discussed above, the appearance of unethical behavior and dastardly deeds is undeniable, and in the current context of elections in the United States, replete as it is with cynicism, citizens are not likely to give those in question the benefit of the doubt.

These examples from the 2000 presidential campaign are surely the tip of the iceberg. In fact, some would argue that unethical acts are omnipresent in campaigns at all levels today. For instance, that billions of dollars are spent on campaigns each election cycle raises questions for many.[6] For some, the simple act of a candidate taking a contribution from a corporation's political action committee or an individual donor is an unethical act because it can lead to access to legislators—and potentially to influence in government—that nondonors do not have.[7] However, others do not see as clear a link between contributions and corruption. As one citizen in Ohio put it, "How [do people] think campaigns are funded? Would [they] rather have only the wealthy in office, [or] those who can afford to run without taking campaign contributions?"[8]

Accusations of unethical behavior in campaigns raise serious questions about the health of our democracy. In fact, each campaign actor in modern elections—candidates, professional political consultants, political parties, organized interest groups, the media, and even citizens—can be associated with specific behavior that might be considered unethical. Professional consultants, for example, have been accused of purposely manipulating the American electorate through their tactics, especially in television commercials.[9] Most of the time these criticisms are focused on "negative" advertisements that consultants are blamed for creating.[10] One example of a very questionable act on the part of campaign consultants occurred in the 1996 Virginia Senate race between incumbent senator John Warner and challenger Mark Warner. The John Warner campaign aired a commercial that tried to define his opponent as a "liberal" by showing him shaking hands with former Virginia governor Douglas Wilder as Bill Clinton, then president, looked on. While Mark Warner was at that event, he was not where the photograph suggested he was. The creators of the ad had doctored the photograph by electronically placing Mark Warner's head on the body of Senator Robb, who had originally been in the photo. Was altering Mark Warner's position at the event—he was just out of the frame used in the picture—unethical? Or was the ad essentially true because Mark Warner had been at the event?

Changes in the context of elections in the United States have forced political parties to rely more and more on the campaign finance loophole that allows them to raise and spend unlimited amounts of money—so-called soft money.[11] As noted above, for some observers the mere existence of such huge and unregulated amounts of money is enough to render the practice unethical because of the ties it creates between donors, parties, and candidates. There is an implication of a quid pro quo between donors and the recipients. In other instances, similar appearances of corruption have caused the U.S. Supreme Court to uphold campaign contribution limits from individual donors first outlined in the 1974 Federal Election Campaign Act.[12] At this point, however, raising and spending soft money is legal: but is it ethical?[13] Many critics also consider the activity of interest groups and especially their electioneering components—political action committees (PACs)—to be unethical, because the money they spend on "issue advocacy" campaigns is thought to skirt campaign finance regulations.

Modern media outlets have also been criticized for actions that hamper campaigns. For instance, in nearly every election cycle the media are criticized for focusing on the "horse race" aspect of campaigns—who is ahead and who is behind in the polls—or that they cover only sensational and startling events, such as Gary Bauer's fall from a platform at a campaign stop in 2000 or Senator Robert Dole's tumble from a stage during a

1996 campaign, rather than meaningful issues. We can hardly discount these criticisms when we think of the time and column inches devoted to discussion of Vice President Al Gore's makeup and perspiration during the presidential debates. Critics may consider the lack of issue coverage to be unethical because stories about polls, candidates' balance, or makeup do not contribute much information to the electorate during a campaign. The question then becomes: Do the media have a responsibility to convey information to the electorate during a campaign?

Finally, even citizens can be accused of unethical actions during campaigns. In its ideal form, democracy requires citizens to actively take part in the electoral process during elections as well as to become informed about candidates and issues. As long ago as Berelson, Lazarsfeld, and McPhee's classic study, *Voting*, scholars saw that the "requirements commonly assumed for the successful operation of democracy are not met by the behavior of the 'average' citizen."[14] The evidence of sliding electoral turnout levels since the 1960s and surveys showing that the American electorate is not well informed about politics or issues in elections only reaffirm the belief that we should "temper some of the requirements set by our traditional normative theory for the typical citizen" and that the electorate is not meeting its responsibility.[15]

Questions of unethical acts or lapses in ethical responsibilities are by no means limited to elections at the federal level; many actions similar to those outlined above have been seen in elections at the state and local level in races for mayor, state representative, and even the judiciary.[16]

The kinds of questions posed above are not easily answered. For example, what constitutes an unethical act? The question of campaign ethics goes beyond mere "ethical dilemmas" or trying to decide if a particular questionable act is aboveboard or not. Questions of campaign ethics are broader and go to the obligations of those who take part in election campaigns.

The chapters in this book are an effort to examine broad questions of ethics in campaigns from the perspective of the actors who play critical roles in modern elections—candidates, political consultants, parties, interest groups, the media, and citizens. They are an effort to outline, understand, assess, and critique the role and responsibilities of each of these actors. Academicians who have conducted research and taught courses on the different electoral actors contribute, as do several practitioners from the world of campaigning and campaign reform. The contributors in this volume take on the difficult task of differentiating between acceptable and unacceptable behavior, rather than assuming that all campaign tactics are corrosive. Each electoral actor is considered in a chapter by a scholar; a shorter chapter written by a practitioner follows immediately. The practitioners' chapters are not responses to the scholarly chapter per se, but are a way to ground the discussion of campaign ethics in the "real world" of campaign politics. For example, Professor Robert E. Denton's chapter on the media precedes a chapter by Paul Taylor, a former *Washington Post* reporter and the current executive director of the Alliance for Better Campaigns, who provides a practical perspective on campaign ethics with a focus on the media.

Before the discussion of campaign ethics from the standpoint of different electoral actors, Dale Miller and Stephen Medvic, in chapter 2, provide a theoretical foundation from which to begin. Making evaluations about what is in fact ethical in campaigning requires some standard against which actual campaign activity can be judged. Before creating a framework that can be applied in just this sort of way, Miller and Medvic explain what is meant by the term *ethics*. They note that the term is used differently by philosophers than by the rest of us. For philosophers, ethics is concerned with the question of how we are to lead our lives; morality, or the evaluation of actions as right or wrong, is simply part of the broader field of ethics. In everyday life, however, ethics means something different—specifically, the rules and standards that are used to judge individuals' actions.

This is an important distinction because the use and applicability of the term in politics generally, and especially in campaigns, is closer to the everyday definition than to the philosophers' perspective. For example, many legislatures have ethics committees that hold their members accountable for their specific actions. Two of the most well known are the ethics committees in the U.S. House of Representatives (the Committee on Standards of Official Conduct) and the U.S. Senate (Select Committee on Ethics). Both bodies have ethical guidelines that members must follow, but they deal with issues that are more tangible than what philosophers are typically concerned about. For example, former Speaker of the House Newt Gingrich was formally reprimanded and fined $300,000 by the U.S. House of Representatives' ethics committee for activities surrounding a course he taught at two Georgia colleges between 1993 and 1995; and Senator Hillary Rodham Clinton, after congressional watchdog groups raised concerns, sought and received approval from the Senate committee for the

$8 million advance she received for a book deal.[17] Most of the questions these and other ethics committees deal with are specific and narrow judgments about what is and is not appropriate. However, to fully understand ethics one must look not only to these specific questions but also to what ethics means on a broader scale.

Having clarified the term *ethics,* Miller and Medvic proceed with a discussion of a framework for evaluating campaign activity. They identify two schools of thought with respect to the obligations of campaign actors. The "self-interest" perspective holds that, beyond following universal moral rules that apply to everyone in nearly all situations, individuals and groups are obligated only to advocate on behalf of their own interests in the campaign. In other words, candidates are ethically free to consider their own victory—and consultants their clients, parties their agendas, and so on—before thinking of the public interest. Indeed, according to this argument, a system in which people guard their own interests may very well be the best system for achieving the common good.

The "civic responsibility" perspective, however, argues that campaign actors have a duty to enhance democracy. The democratic ideal that this camp embraces includes the classical notions of an informed electorate and a debate-like campaign. Some version of a deliberative campaign, then, would be the ultimate goal, and anything campaign actors do to hinder the realization of that goal would be considered unethical. In practice, this means that civic responsibility proponents will be more willing, for instance, to label a television ad misleading or untruthful than would those adopting the campaign advocacy perspective.

Not surprisingly, nearly all of the authors in this book can be easily placed in one of these schools of thought. Though they do not always use the specific phrases found in chapter 2, they do use terminology that makes clear their adherence to one perspective on campaign ethics or the other.

The chapters that follow the theoretical foundation in chapter 2 address common questions about ethics in political campaigns with a focus on a particular electoral actor—candidates, citizens, the media, professional consultants, political parties, or interest groups. For each electoral actor, each chapter written by an academic addresses the following questions:

—What role does the actor play in fostering ethical election campaigns, if any?

—How well is this actor currently fulfilling that role?

—Does the presence of money in elections help or hinder the actor's ability to fulfill this role?

—How do the other electoral actors influence that actor's ability to fulfill this role?

The chapters written by practitioners also deal with campaign ethics from the perspective of a particular campaign actor, but they do so from a slightly different perspective. These chapters were designed to provide the reader with a view of campaign ethics from those who are currently, or who have recently been, "in the field" dealing with the different campaign actors. Each of these chapters deals with the same central questions found in the academic chapters, although the final question is replaced by:

—Assuming that actor could do a better job of fostering campaign ethics, what solutions would you offer?

Chapters at the beginning of the book deal with the most prominent actors in campaigns—candidates, consultants, parties, and interest groups—and later chapters focus on "reactors" in campaigns—the media and voters. Sandy Maisel leads off the consideration of individual campaign actors with his examination of candidates in chapter 3. He begins with the assumption that most of those seeking public office are ethical, by which he means they seek "to advance policies that they believe will benefit the polity as a whole." Maisel turns to democratic theory in an attempt to establish some ethical standard by which to judge candidate activity. Campaigns, he argues, must help voters make choices and citizens must then hold elected officials accountable. In order to accomplish this, "candidates should act in such a way that allows the electoral system to operate as it should within the framework of our polity. Further, they should be compelled to act in a manner that does no harm to the polity as a whole."

Maisel examines two aspects of candidate activity in campaigns—making promises and persuading voters. In the case of making promises, Maisel suggests that candidates tell voters what they plan to do in office with as much detail as possible, without exaggerating what they are capable of delivering. Indeed, the problem of overpromising is a serious one and, to the extent that it occurs in campaigns, it "undermines the electoral system by giving citizens reasons to be cynical." With respect to persuading voters to support them, candidates must be accurate in their claims and truthful in the implications they make. While hard-hitting, comparative campaigning is acceptable, and even desirable, candidates should focus on policy differences between themselves and their opponents. The use of negative personal attacks that are irrelevant to serving in public office "disregards the impact on the polity" and as such is unethical. In the end, Maisel argues that a system that accepts unfettered actions deemed clearly detrimental to the process as a whole because legal language cannot be found to draw what are obviously fuzzy lines contains within it the seeds of its own destruction. And those who participate in such a system have an ethical obligation to observe self-restraint in order to preserve the democratic process.

Like few other authors, Dale Lawton and William Wood (chapter 4) have one foot in the theoretical world and one in the practical. As part of the Sorensen Institute's Project on Campaign Conduct at the University of Virginia, Lawton and Wood help train candidates "on the nuts and bolts of running a political campaign within a framework of campaign ethics and public responsibility." For these authors, unethical campaign tactics are those that "do not help citizens make informed choices . . . [and add] to the environment of public distrust that already surrounds candidates and campaigns." While they note that there has been little empirical research on the ethical conduct of candidates, they also point to the overwhelming evidence that the public perceives candidate behavior to be abysmal. In order to alter that perception and to ensure that candidates run ethical campaigns, the Sorensen Institute asks candidates to start their campaigns by developing "a personal code of campaign ethics." Only after they have done so should they proceed to draft blueprints for campaign strategy and tactics. In this way, "strategy is developed within the framework of ethics rather than the other way around." Indeed, as individuals who are working to transform the way campaigns are run, Lawton and Wood make the practical point that ethical campaigns may have a strategic advantage over unethical ones. Yet even if one might not benefit from making the ethically appropriate decision in the heat of the campaign, a candidate has an obligation to follow that route. As Lawton and Wood put it: "The candidate's desire to win must be firmly placed in the context of the public good."

Our own chapter (chapter 5) on political consultants takes an almost clinical approach to the subject, examining consultant behavior from a largely empirical point of view. Applying the framework established in chapter 2, we suggest that consultants view their obligations according to the self-interest perspective, while critics of consultants are clearly in the civic responsibility camp. In practice, the vast majority of consultants believe that unethical practices occur only sometimes in campaigns. Consultants tend to resist the enforcement of a formal code of ethics and prefer to be guided by their own consciences and the presumed consequences of acting in unacceptable ways (for example, being blacklisted by parties or candidates). Nevertheless, consultants do recognize various practices they have witnessed as unethical. Lying, of course, tops the list. However, without a framework to help clearly identify when a statement is a lie and when it is not, any such interpretation of a specific piece of campaign communication is likely to be contentious. We conclude by noting that it is difficult to enforce an ethical standard on consultants (or any campaign actor, for that matter). Nevertheless, informal pressure from parties, candidates, voters, the media, and even other consultants has the potential to keep political professionals in line.

In writing about the ethics of political consulting from a practitioner's perspective in chapter 6, Carol Whitney identifies a central question of this book when she asks, "Does the consultant owe his or her first responsibility to the client or to the public?" Her answer might very well be "neither." Whitney has a great deal of confidence in the individual consultant's personal moral compass and the desire to be guided by it. Noting that many of the difficult questions in this area have "no one right answer," she argues that "the majority [of consultants] do have standards," though these may differ from person to person. In discussing the standards of direct mail consultants, a field where some of "today's most bothersome ethical questions arise," she further expounds a sort of ethical relativism: "Some of us may disagree with [the direct mail consultants'] standards, but who has the right to judge?"

Robin Kolodny's approach to evaluating the conduct of the political parties in chapter 7 is unique. Rather than judge them according to one of the two standards, she notes a distinction between the parties' activities and the incentives that are embedded in the larger political system. Kolodny also highlights a difficulty in analyzing party behavior that stems from the confusion over which actors the parties as agents are to serve: are parties responsible for assisting voters or candidates? In fact, argues Kolodny, our political parties serve the state. As such, "we must ask ourselves if the entire system of electoral competition created by the political parties as agents of the state is consistent with our conception of democracy, and if it is not, whether the two parties' domination of electoral politics in the United States is itself ethical." Thus if one hopes to improve the campaign behavior of parties, it is the electoral system that would have to be redesigned.

Kolodny details a number of paradoxes in which the demands of voters or candidates conflict with the interests of the state. In every case, it is the interests of the state—of which the most fundamental is the desire for stability—that hold sway. As a result, for example, voters are given limited choice at election time in exchange for a two-party system that is thought to be more stable than a multiparty system. In the end, Kolodny argues, "Political parties appear to behave ethically within an unethical system." That is, the parties' primary goal of winning elections is not unethical, nor is the way they go about reaching that goal. But the system itself leaves much to be desired.

Mark Siegel, a former executive director of the Democratic National Committee (DNC) is a proponent of what he calls "ethical pragmatism." In chapter 8, Siegel maintains that voter disenchantment with the two major political parties has less to do with public policy than with the parties' lack of ethical behavior. Indeed, he argues that while the parties have become increasingly differentiated in terms of ideology, they are "indistinguishable where political ethics, or the lack thereof, is concerned." In particular, the parties have "deliberately . . . sought to circumvent the spirit and letter of the law" with respect to fund-raising. The "huge sums of corporate and union treasury sums, and the public outrage at the scope and methods by which they were raised," according to Siegel, "have accelerated the erosion in the trust and confidence Americans have in their political system."

One way out of this morass would be for parties to give their operatives and candidates ethical training. While such training should avoid "moralizing about what should or should not be done in specific situations," it would sensitize campaigners so that "in times of ethical crisis, decisionmakers will pause and think before committing themselves." As he discusses a curriculum used by the Democratic Party to educate its operatives about ethics, Siegel is most taken with its emphasis on the practical consequences of questionable behavior—the attention it garners throws campaigns "off-message" and it "damages reputations, destroys careers, and can cost huge amounts in legal fees."

Yet Siegel also mentions the consequences for the democratic process, pointing out that unethical activity discourages citizen participation and threatens "the legitimacy of the electoral and representational process." In the end, even this pragmatic practitioner is concerned with "democracy's infrastructure" and hopes that campaign actors will work to increase political participation and restore "the public's faith in our political system" to "expand our civic culture and relegitimize the foundations of our American democracy."

In chapter 9, James Thurber discusses interest groups and the myriad ways their activity raises questions of ethical importance. He notes that while much of the concern about interest group involvement in campaigns focuses on how such groups raise and spend money, the wide array of campaign activities they engage in deserves scrutiny as well. Among the potential problems Thurber enumerates are the huge sums of money pumped into campaigns from interest groups, the issue advertising and independent expenditures they use to frame debates according to their interests (and to skirt campaign finance laws), the role they play in creating the "permanent campaign," and the real or perceived reciprocity that exists between campaign contributions and access to, or influence with, legislators. Thurber also highlights a practice that has previously been given very little attention—that individuals who advise candidates during campaigns often become lobbyists after the election. One major consequence of this and other interest group activities is that the public becomes increasingly cynical. Unfortunately, Thurber concludes, codes of ethics governing interest group activity have proven to be unenforceable and therefore cannot be relied upon to prevent unethical behavior.

In his examination of interest groups' role in fostering ethical campaigns, Larry Makinson (chapter 10) attacks a campaign finance system that allows questionable activity to occur without any of the participants actively—or perhaps even consciously—making unethical decisions. As he notes, "the way the system is structured, clear-cut ethical questions may only rarely arise." Instead, more subtle issues of fairness are raised by current campaign finance practices—do politicians make "equitable decisions" for all groups; does money "shift the likelihood of a favorable outcome" for contributors; who is really being represented, constituents or contributors; and "what implications does this have for the public's perception of how government works"? We could just as easily question, as Makinson does, the motivations of the interest groups that make the contributions. Do they expect favorable treatment, in the form of either access or actual supportive votes, in return for their money? Do they consider the interests of a representative's constituents when they contribute to that representative? These are questions that go beyond considerations of one's own interests and are rarely if ever entertained by interest groups and candidates because the current system creates "ethical blind spot[s]."

Only "ethical entrepreneurs" would dwell upon these matters and few of those can be expected to actually alter their behavior.

In detailing the media's role in democracy, Robert Denton (chapter 11) summarizes the civic responsibility argument laid out in chapter 2 in one sentence: "Ethical journalism serves the public interest and facilitates the democratic process." His review of the current state of media coverage indicates that it falls far short of that ideal. The problems include limited access to mass media outlets afforded to some voices in our political process; "sound bite" journalism that covers campaign strategy more than policy pronouncements and emphasizes conflict over consensus; and an overreliance on the medium of television, the logic of which makes politics "an activity of style over substance, image over reality, melodrama over analysis, belief over knowing, awareness over understanding." The primary cause of these problems, Denton argues, lies in "contemporary news values." As a business, the media must maintain high circulation (or ratings) in order to make a profit by selling advertising. The incentive to make the news entertaining is overwhelming. But information that is most useful in a democratic system may often be subtle and complex—boring, to some.

"By my lights," argues Paul Taylor (chapter 12), "political campaigns perform their highest function when they frame public life as something larger than the sum of private interests." He sees the media's role in ensuring ethical campaigns as threefold—they are to be watchdogs, guides, and soapboxes for candidates. While the media are currently doing a decent job of scrutinizing the records and lives of candidates (serving as watchdogs), they perform less admirably in the "civic-minded" roles of guide and soapbox. The media as guide "consists of helping citizens to understand who the candidates are, what the issues are, and how their Election Day choices will impact their lives." The goal here is not high ratings for the media; it is an informed electorate. That is also the goal of the media as soapbox. Here, the media would provide candidates, and perhaps parties, with a forum for explaining their issue positions and ideas. It requires allowing candidates to speak directly to the public with little or no editing, as would be the case if networks offered candidates free airtime rather than charging them for advertising space. In the end, financial considerations (that is, self-interest) keep the media from performing the last two roles adequately. As Taylor maintains, current practice "enriches the broadcasters while it impoverishes democracy."

In his chapter on citizens (chapter 13), Michael Traugott explicitly recognizes the distinction between a self-interest perspective and one of civic responsibility. "Citizens sometimes face complex issues," he argues, "about how to choose between satisfying their own self-interest and the greater social good." Furthermore, citizens clearly have obligations that require a great deal more effort than the typical citizen exercises. For instance, individuals have a duty to monitor the activities not only of candidates, but of the media and interest groups. With respect to the media, citizens must demand balanced coverage for all candidates, according to Traugott, even if it means their preferred candidate will lose the advantage of a favorable press. The justification for such behavior is that "the preservation of balanced campaign coverage is an important democratic value."

In addition to making the decision about whether to vote, citizens must also decide whether to cast an informed vote. Traugott maintains that one should be informed and vote according to policy preferences, rather than simply use party identification as a voting cue. While he defends the informed voter (as opposed to the party loyalist) by suggesting that being informed best protects one's self-interest, the knowledgeable voter could also be viewed as necessary from a civic responsibility perspective while the party loyalist is the embodiment of self-interest. Finally, citizens ought to stay informed and keep in contact with representatives between elections. They may even have an obligation to avoid acting as free riders in interest groups (though Traugott only implies the latter point).

Brad Rourke brings practical experience to bear on his discussion of the ethics of citizenship in chapter 14. Though "things are not so good" with respect to citizens' attitudes toward politics and politicians, Rourke insists that there "are positive signs of a citizenry that knows things can and should be better." Based on his work at the Institute for Global Ethics, Rourke believes that certain universally recognized core values can help guide the behavior of citizens in our political system. These values—respect, responsibility, fairness, compassion, and honesty—form an outline for a "code of ethics for citizens." So what, according to Rourke, are citizens to do? The answer is complicated because, as Rourke acknowledges, the real ethical dilemmas faced by citizens are not questions of right versus wrong but of right versus right. That is, when two courses of action are equally justifiable ethically, citizens have to choose one desirable course of action over another. There are philosophical theories that can guide the decisionmaking process, but Rourke places his trust in "a broad-based and thoughtful approach to civic education in general." Certainly, citizens can demand good conduct from candidates by "refusing to support unethical campaigning." But they must also recognize that the role of the citizen extends beyond that of mere voter. Indeed, one of the results of a solid civics education would be to remind citizens that more is required of them than an occasional vote, which is all too often uninformed. In addition, it would make citizens "comfortable with the idea that it is appropriate to discuss morality in the public sphere." At that point, argues Rourke, we would be on the verge of creating the sort of "robust" citizenry required for a healthy democracy.

The contributors to this volume vary in their approaches to the issues and in the conclusions they reach. While there is no consensus among the authors, we hope this book will help to start a discussion of the difficult questions of ethics in campaigning. There are no absolute answers in the chapters that follow, but the contributors do offer different perspectives and ways of thinking about difficult questions.

Notes

1. Ken Fireman and William Douglas, "Rats' Nest for Bush," *Newsday*, September 13, 2000, p. A5.

2. Ibid.

3. See Clay Robinson, "Campaign 2000: Debate Mole Mystery Continues; Bush Aide Points to Gore Campaign," *Houston Chronicle*, September 27, 2000, p. A10.

4. Clifford, J. Levy, "The 2000 Campaign: The Ad Campaign; Making Breast Cancer a Political Issue against John McCain," *New York Times*, March 4, 2000, p. A10, late edition. See also any one of the following articles: Dan Fagin, "Campaign 2000, Barish on Politics: Cancer Activist under Fire for Campaigns, Ad for Bush," *Newsday*, March 6, 2000, p. A5.; Edward Walsh and Terry M. Neal, "Bush Begins N.Y. Swing Talking Breast Cancer," *Washington Post*, March 4, 2000, p. A6; Adam Nagourney and Frank Bruni, "Bush and McCain Battle for Support on Tuesday in High-Stakes Territory," *New York Times*, March 4, 2000, p. A10; Dick Polman, "McCain Raps Bush Tactics on Cancer Ad; He Wonders if Governor 'Is Ready for Prime Time,'" *Milwaukee Journal Sentinel*, March 6, 2000, p. 6A.

5. Whit Ayers, "Can Campaign Advertising Be on the Level?" *Campaigns & Elections* (October 2001), pp. 20–24.

6. Ruth Marcus, "Costliest Race Nears End; Bush, Gore Running Close; U.S. Campaigns Fuel $3 Billion in Spending," *Washington Post*, November 6, 2000, p. A1.

7. The scholarly evidence of money buying influence is mixed. For studies showing a limited nature of PAC influence, see John R. Wright, "PACs, Contributions, and Roll Calls: An Organizational Perspective," *American Political Science Review*, vol. 79, no. 2 (1985), pp. 400–14; Janet M. Grenzke, "PACs and the Congressional Supermarket: The Currency Is Complex," *American Journal of Political Science*, vol. 33, no. 1 (1989), pp. 1–24; John R. Wright, "PAC Contributions, Lobbying, and Representation," *Journal of Politics*, vol. 51, no. 3

(1989), pp. 713–29. For those studies showing more influence, see Thomas Romer and James M. Snyder Jr., "An Empirical Investigation of the Dynamics of PAC Contributions," *American Journal of Political Science*, vol. 38, no. 3 (1994), pp. 745–69; Theodore J. Eismeier and Phillip H. Pollock III, "Strategy and Choice in Congressional Elections: The Role of Political Action Committees," *American Journal of Political Science*, vol. 30, no. 1 (1986), pp. 197–213.

8. Mary J. Clark, "Campaign Contributions Don't Always Buy Influence" (editorial), *Columbus Dispatch*, May 29, 2001, p. 6A.

9. See, for example, Karen S. Johnson-Cartee and Gary A. Copeland, *Manipulation of the American Voter: Political Campaign Commercials* (Westport, Conn.: Praeger Press, 1997).

10. The claim that consultants are responsible for negative ads is questionable given the tone and tenor of many campaigns early in the American Republic. See Kathleen Hall Jamieson, *Dirty Politics: Deception, Distraction, and Democracy* (Oxford University Press, 1992) for a review of some harsh campaigns that included some advertisements and statements that would give any modern commercial a run for its money in terms of negativity.

11. See Robin Kolodny, *Pursuing Majorities: Congressional Campaign Committees in American Politics* (University of Oklahoma Press, 1998); David B. Magleby, ed., *Financing the 2000 Election* (Brookings, 2002); Mark Siegel's chapter 8 in this volume.

12. *Buckley* v. *Valeo*, 424 U.S. 1, 12–59 (1976).

13. As this book was going to print, the House and Senate passed the Bipartisan Campaign Reform Act of 2002 (known as McCain-Feingold in the Senate and Shays-Meehan in the House for the authors of the legislation, Senators John McCain and Russ Feingold, and Representatives Christopher Shays and Martin Meehan), and President Bush had just signed the legislation. The law prohibits federal candidates and national party committees from raising soft money but allows state party committees to do so in limited amounts. Whether this reform will take effect is uncertain at this point, given the legal challenges currently pending against it.

14. Bernard R. Berelson, Paul F. Lazarsfeld, and William N. McPhee, *Voting: A Study of Opinion in a Presidential Campaign.*(University of Chicago Press, 1954), p. 307.

15. Berelson, Lazarsfeld, and McPhee, *Voting*, p. 306.

16. See Greg Wersal, "See Why Minnesota Judiciary Could Use Campaign Reform," *Star Tribune* (Minneapolis), March 10, 2001, p. 21A; Mary Pasciak, "Campaign Letter Draws Criticism over Union Logo," *Buffalo News*, August 29, 2000, p. B3, central edition, for examples in local elections. See also Jim Brunner, "Nickels Campaign Avoids Payroll Taxes," *Seattle Times*, September 5, 2001, p. B1, for an example of other practices labeled as "unethical."

17. For more on the Gingrich ethics sanctions see, for example, William Douglas, Elaine S. Povich, and Susan Benkelman, "Passing Judgement: Ethics Committee, Gingrich Agree on Fine, Reprimand," *Newsday*, January 18, 1997, p. A5. On the Clinton book deal see, for example, "Hillary Clinton Gets OK for Book Deal" (June 18, 2001; *USA Today.com* [January 5, 2001]); "It Takes a Best Seller: Ethics Aside, Hillary Clinton's Book Is a Gamble," *Post-Gazette* (Pittsburgh), December 29, 2000, p. A22.

CHAPTER TWO

CAMPAIGN ETHICS

Civic Responsibility
or Self-Interest?

DALE E. MILLER
STEPHEN K. MEDVIC

Conventional wisdom suggests that, from an ethical perspective, the conduct of those involved in electoral campaigns in the United States has deteriorated in recent years. Whether this is, in fact, true—and how we might know it—is the subject matter of this book. The rest of the chapters herein offer answers to these questions. Judgments about the ethical standing of campaign conduct, however, must be made in reference to some ethical standard. The purpose of this chapter is threefold. First, we offer a characterization of ethical standards generally. Second, we develop a framework that explains in abstract terms the relations between potential standards of campaign conduct. Finally, we illustrate these standards by applying them to real-world and hypothetical campaign situations where questions of ethics are likely to arise.

The Meaning of *Ethics*

There is an important difference between two meanings of the word *ethics*. As philosophers understand the term, it refers to the subject matter of a very broad field of study. The fundamental question in ethics is the one that Socrates poses in Plato's *Gorgias*: "In what way should one lead one's life?"[1] It raises a number of subsidiary questions, such as: What ends should we pursue? What sorts of people should we be? What sorts of communities should we live in? What sort of state should we be ruled by? (As these last two questions suggest, the field of ethics subsumes most of social and political philosophy.)

Some of the most important questions that philosophers working in the field of ethics seek to answer have to do with morality. Morality is concerned with the evaluation of actions as right or wrong, and the central question of moral philosophy is what properties of actions make them right or wrong. Among our other moral concepts are those of obligation and blame: If it would be morally wrong for you not to do something, then you are obligated to do it, and if you have done something morally wrong, then there is at least prima facie reason to think that you are blameworthy.[2]

Outside of philosophy classes, *ethics* very often takes on a somewhat narrower meaning. Ethics is viewed as a part of morality, instead of the other way around. It is natural for us to say of both a used-car salesperson who rolls back odometers and a person who commits adultery that they are acting *immorally*. In contrast, it would be natural for us to say that the former only is acting *unethically*. Yet if the cheating spouse were a professor with a student for a lover, then we might well describe that aspect of the affair as unethical. The explanation for this pattern of usage seems to be that when we are not using *ethics* in the philosophical sense, we usually use it only in certain contexts. This is when we are talking about the specific moral rules that apply to agents—which means those (including individuals and also organizations such as companies, political parties, and so on) who act—because of special roles they occupy, especially when the normal reason for occupying such roles is to advance the agents' interests by getting money, power, and the like.[3] (The fact that we do not call a cheating spouse unethical seems to reflect our having a— perhaps unrealistically romantic—view of marriage, according to which one does not normally get married in order to promote one's interests.) This captures what most people understand by the term *business ethics,* for example: the special moral rules that apply to agents by virtue of the roles they occupy in the business world, which are certainly roles that agents normally enter into for the purpose of advancing their interests. Similarly, although some philosophers might consider this definition too narrow, most people would understand *campaign ethics* to be concerned with the special moral rules that apply to agents by virtue of the roles they occupy in political campaigns. And even most philosophers would probably admit that the most interesting and important problems of campaign ethics have to do with these rules.

This description of how *ethics* is commonly used is consonant with the formal "codes of ethics" that organizations draw up. These are almost invariably lists of moral rules that the organization takes to be binding on (at least) its members. For example—and this is meant merely as an illustration, although it will be referred to quite often in what follows—members of the American Association of Political Consultants (AAPC) are expected to obey the rules of the group's code of ethics.

It may not be immediately obvious that these requirements should be thought of as moral rules. Yet it does seem likely that the AAPC views these as things that political consultants would be blameworthy for not doing, so from the AAPC's standpoint these are things that political consultants ought to do, where "ought" has the force of the "moral ought": in other words, political consultants are morally obligated to fulfill these requirements.

As noted above, people commonly use the term *ethics* specifically, as opposed to *morality*, only when talking about the rules that apply to roles that agents normally enter into in order to advance their interests. A further qualification is that people usually use the term *ethics* only when what the rules of ordinary morality require from agents occupying the role in question is rather distinctive. What ordinary morality's rule against lying requires specifically from political consultants, at least according to the AAPC, is quite distinctive; for example, most people do not have to worry about how to deal with the media or how to handle public attacks on opponents or members of their family. Someone occupying the role of political consultant also presumably has a moral obligation not to murder a client, yet the AAPC does not feel compelled to make this restriction explicit in its code, and if a consultant does choose to murder a client it would be very peculiar for anyone to call this "unethical." Most people probably would not even say that it was unethical for a consultant to murder a client's opponent, and in fact the AAPC's code contains no rule that would forbid this. The moral rules that these acts would violate do not apply to political consultants in a distinctive enough manner to make violations of them a matter of ethics.

Moral Obligations

How did the drafters of the AAPC's code decide that consultants have these obligations? Their starting point, presumably, was our society's "ordinary morality." This might be vaguely described as our society's "common stock" of moral rules, rules that almost all members of our society

American Association of Political Consultants Code of Ethics

As a member of the American Association of Political Consultants, I believe there are certain standards of practice which I must maintain. I, therefore, pledge to adhere to the following Code of Professional Ethics:

—I will not indulge in any activity which would corrupt or degrade the practice of political consulting.

—I will treat my colleagues and clients with respect and never intentionally injure their professional or personal reputations.

—I will respect the confidence of my clients and not reveal confidential or privileged information obtained during our professional relationship.

—I will use no appeal to voters which is based on racism, sexism, religious intolerance or any form of unlawful discrimination and will condemn those who use such practices. In turn, I will work for equal voting rights and privileges for all citizens.

—I will refrain from false or misleading attacks on an opponent or member of his or her family and will do everything in my power to prevent others from using such tactics.

—I will document accurately and fully any criticism of an opponent or his or her record.

Source: American Association of Political Consultants (www.theaapc.org/ethics.html [August 17, 2001]).

embrace. Brad Hooker provides at least a partial inventory of our ordinary morality when he writes:

> Most of us confidently agree morality can require us to help others, even if we have no special connection to them. . . . Most of us also believe that we owe more altruism to certain people than to others. Other things being roughly equal, your allocation of resources should favour your own parent, or child, or friend, or those to whom you have a special debt of gratitude. . . . [But we also confidently agree that sometimes] other things aren't roughly equal. . . . For example, a nurse deciding whom to give the remaining medicine to is not morally . . . allowed to give her own friends or family special con-

sideration. . . . This sort of role-based obligation to ignore personal relationships comes from the fact that the agent in that role is allocating resources (money, services, whatever) that do not belong to her. We also share confident beliefs about the moral impermissibility of certain kinds of act. Morality prohibits physically attacking innocent people or their property. It also prohibits taking the property of others, lying, breaking one's promises, and so on. . . . We must acknowledge that there are disputes about which kinds of acts are morally prohibited or required. And there are disputes about what exception clauses are needed in moral norms. But these acknowledgments should not blind us to the fact that there is wide agreement that certain kinds of act are morally prohibited, at least in certain circumstances.[4]

The AAPC's code of ethics, like virtually every formal code of ethics, takes some general and universal rules of our ordinary morality and renders them more specific, so that they apply only to someone who occupies a certain role. For example, the code goes into considerable detail about what the duty not to lie requires from consultants in particular; they must "refrain from false or misleading attacks on an opponent or member of his or her family," "document accurately and fully any criticism of an opponent or his or her record," and "be honest . . . with the news media and candidly answer questions." It also requires them to "treat . . . colleagues and clients with respect and never intentionally injure their professional or personal reputations," and to use any funds received "from . . . clients, or on behalf of . . . clients, only for those purposes invoiced in writing"; these are more specific renderings of the general obligations not to attack others and not to steal their property.[5] The code of ethics for government service says that a government employee should "never discriminate unfairly by the dispensing of special favors or privileges to anyone, whether for remuneration or not; and never accept, for himself or his family, favors or benefits under circumstances which might be construed by reasonable persons as influencing the performance of his governmental duties";[6] here is an example of what Hooker calls a role-based obligation of impartiality, which derives from the fact that the public employee has control over public resources (and indeed the code concludes by admonishing the employee to be "ever conscious that public office is a public trust"). Universities often have codes of student conduct that include, inter alia, a requirement to "offer service to the University and to the community";[7] this is simply a "student-specific" formulation of the more general requirement to help others—especially those with whom you have a special connection—to which Hooker refers.

Despite all of these references to organizations' official codes of ethics, it is obvious that people do not always have a formal code in mind when they talk about ethics. Nevertheless, in most cases they are probably thinking in very much the same way it has been suggested that the drafters of formal codes tend to think; they have in mind some idea about what distinctive obligations the general and universal rules of morality impose upon agents who occupy some particular role.

Moral Disagreement

It should be clear that there is tremendous scope for reasonable disagreement over what ethical standards govern any given role. Most people—everyone, more or less, save perhaps a few philosophical theorists—base their judgments about what these standards require on their interpretation of our ordinary morality. But our ordinary morality might be wrong, in part or even (nearly, at least) as a whole.[8] Philosophers' moral theories often represent significant departures from our ordinary morality, because they typically seize on some subset of the properties of actions that ordinary morality says have moral relevance and say that *only* these properties are morally relevant. For example, ordinary morality says that sometimes we have an obligation to do something because it would bring about the best outcome, and consequentialist theories of morality say that this is our only obligation. Act utilitarianism, for example, which is probably the best-known consequentialist theory, says that in any situation the right thing to do is whatever will yield the greatest total amount of happiness possible (taking into account everyone whom one's actions could affect), and that to do anything else would be wrong. Ordinary morality also says that we are sometimes obligated to perform or to eschew certain kinds of actions regardless of their consequences; and deontological moral theories say that all of our obligations are like this. Immanuel Kant, for example, the most important deontological moral theorist, says that it is always morally wrong to make a promise that one knows one will break for a self-interested reason, even if the consequences of breaking it would be better in utilitarian terms.[9]

Even putting this worry about the status of ordinary morality (which perhaps only philosophers will take seriously) aside, however, the interpretation of the rules of our ordinary morality is still inherently controversial. Hooker's account of the rules of our ordinary morality is clearly only a summary, but it seems likely that if one tried to formulate these rules in much more detail, then the confident agreement of which he writes would start to break down. The abortion controversy illustrates this point. Most pro-choice and pro-life advocates base their arguments on what is the same basic set of moral rules. There are two main points at which most of their disagreements can be located, and both arise out of their different interpretations of these rules. The first is over whether the rule that prohibits the killing of innocents applies to the fetus. Some (though perhaps not many) "pro-choicers" might agree with the "pro-lifers" that it does, but then they will still disagree over a second issue, which is what we are to do when that rule comes into conflict with another that grants women control over what happens to their bodies. What this shows is that any list of moral rules that most members of our society could agree on would probably contain many that were stated very vaguely, and there would be little guidance regarding the conditions under which one rule takes precedence over another when they conflict. Reasonable people would start to disagree when they tried to compile more definite statements of moral rules.

One implication of all of this is that there is ample room for disagreement about what ethical obligations are associated with different roles. It is not to be taken for granted, for example, that the AAPC is right about the ethical obligations of consultants. It may be guilty of omitting obligations that should have been included and including some that should not have been. In particular, there is always a danger that an organization's account of the ethical obligations of its members will be biased in its own favor. The AAPC code requires consultants to protect the reputations not just of clients but also of other consultants. While this is hardly the most flagrant example of this type of danger, one can imagine scenarios in which this obligation might conflict with the public interest. In such cases, one might wonder whether a consultant would truly be morally obligated to look out for his or her colleagues.

There is even more room for disagreement about what a person should do when the moral obligations that attach to one of his or her special roles conflict with those attaching to another role or with universal moral obligations. It is the potential for conflicting obligations that gives rise to what Michael Walzer, in one of the most influential articles on political ethics, calls the "problem of dirty hands."[10] The dirty hands problem arises when a person is faced with "a situation where he must choose between two courses of action both of which it would be wrong for him to under-take" because either course involves violating some obligation.[11] Walzer suggests that situations like these are especially prone to arise in political contexts.[12] In one of his illustrations of this problem, he asks us to imag-ine a candidate faced with the following dilemma: "In order to win the election the candidate must make a deal with a dishonest ward boss, in-volving the granting of contracts for school construction over the next four years."[13] Let us assume that the candidate is a principled person who sincerely wants to solve pressing social problems by enacting good public policy. Assume further that the opponent is an unprincipled politician who is seeking office primarily for personal gain. Accepting the deal may mean that one's campaign is unethical, but it allows the candidate to win and do good once in office. After all, one may have an ethical obligation as a citizen to do what is in one's power to bring about the best outcomes for one's political community, or at least to prevent bad outcomes. Refusing the deal may be right from the perspective of campaign ethics, but the candidate will lose and not be able to do good in office. In reality, candi-dates often face this dilemma; in order to serve the public, they must first obtain (or retain) a position of power.

Civic Responsibility and Self-Interest

As indicated above, ethical standards (at least in the ordinary use of the term) apply to agents (including both individuals and organizations) who occupy special roles that are normally entered into in order to advance the agents' interests. The agents at work in campaigns and elections are easily identified—candidates, political parties, professional consultants, interest groups, the media, and voters. There are two different general ways of thinking about the ethical standards that apply to these agents: the civic responsibility model and the self-interest model.[14]

Whether contemporary campaigns in the United States are, in the main, conducted in a reasonably ethical manner is a fundamental question. Lev-els of trust in politicians and in our political institutions have recently been at all-time lows.[15] One commonly hears that the "person on the street" believes politicians will say—and do—almost anything to get elected. Is this low level of trust and high degree of cynicism justified? How bad are campaigns today? There have been few attempts to establish standards for judging the actions of the various agents involved in campaigns.[16] While it is not the purpose of this chapter to develop a set of such standards, we do hope to establish a framework through which readers can begin to think about the issues raised in this book.

Observation suggests that most of the agents involved in campaigns recognize few ethical constraints on the pursuit of their interests. Think for a moment about what each of the agents covered in this book is attempting to achieve though elections. Media outlets, as business entities, have to make money and they are in intense competition with other outlets. Thus their coverage is driven more by what will "sell" than by what is "good" for the audience. Voters are busy and are consumed with their own day-to-day lives. As a result, they are unwilling to put much effort into learning about candidates or issues and are not very involved in politics in even the most superficial way. Furthermore, at election time voters appear to ask one simple question—"What's in it for me?" Interest groups act on behalf of a limited set of citizens. They zealously protect the interests of their members and work to set the agenda of campaigns according to those interests. Rather than work to increase turnout across the board, they mobilize only "their" voters. Political parties have party goals in mind and are willing to sacrifice individual candidates for the sake of others. In addition, it often seems that a party's willingness to raise issues or bring legislation to a vote is based more on the electoral advantage that can be gained in so doing than on a sincere desire to solve pressing problems. Furthermore, the parties actively seek to reduce electoral competition by drawing district lines for the benefit of one party over the other and writing election law to effectively prohibit third-party challenges. Professional political consultants, as businesspeople, have to keep an eye on the bottom line. That could influence their financial dealings with clients and it may even determine the types of candidates for whom they will work (for example, incumbents or sure winners). Even their loyalty to candidates, which many say is their primary concern, can be said to be a business decision. And since future business depends, at least in part, on the consultant's won-lost record, victory is clearly the primary objective. Finally, candidates are single-mindedly concerned with winning. In our "candidate-centered" electoral system, office seekers routinely downplay their partisan and ideological identifications and make at least some promises they cannot possibly keep. Too often they create false distinctions between themselves and their opponents based on ambiguous criteria (for example, "values") while blurring distinctions on particularly popular, but complicated, issues (such as the "patients' bill of rights"). Rather than appealing to the concerns of all their constituents, they speak only to the desires of "likely voters."

Some may object to these characterizations, but there is considerable empirical evidence to support such claims. Assuming they are accurate accounts of the behavior of those campaign agents, the question becomes whether such behavior makes the agents ethically culpable. In other words, the answer to the fundamental question above—are contemporary campaigns conducted ethically?—depends on one's conception of what ethical constraints campaign agents in pursuit of their own interests should recognize. There are primarily two ways of thinking about this. The first is the civic responsibility conception. Campaigns play a vital role in our democratic system and the agents' commitment should be to democracy first and their own interests second. Campaigns are public debates over how society should operate. Thus agents have a duty to elevate the quality of dialogue in the campaign, and to this end their pursuit of their own interests should be more constrained. The second view is the self-interest conception. Campaign agents should be free to pursue their own interests subject to few ethical constraints beyond the universal moral rules that bind us all. Agents are expected to do whatever is necessary (without violating universal moral rules) to protect their interests, and they engage in the campaign process with only that goal in mind.

As Hooker observes, one strand of the ordinary morality that most of us share suggests that even though it is usually permissible for us to give preference to our own interests and to those of people to whom we have some close connection, agents who occupy certain social roles have a special obligation of impartiality. He notes that "this sort of role-based obligation to ignore personal relationships comes from the fact that the agent in that role is allocating resources (money, services, whatever) that do not belong to her."[17] Many people subscribe to the view that those who hold public office have a role-based obligation of impartiality that requires them to approach decisions by asking not what outcome would be best for themselves but rather what would best promote the public good.[18] In this view, public officials should be, in the words of Madison in *Federalist* 46, "impartial guardians of a common interest." Now of course the vague suggestion that officeholders bear this obligation to deliberate in terms of the public good can be interpreted in multiple ways. There are numerous conceptions of the public good, and even the makeup of "the public" is contentious (should a member of Congress, for example, be concerned about the interest of his or her constituency or the interest of the national public?—a question to which

Federalist 46 gives a rather subtle answer). Still, the notion of the public good stands in clear opposition to the idea that it is permissible to be self-serving while acting in the capacity of a public official.

Those who adhere to the civic responsibility conception of campaign ethics maintain that someone seeking office or otherwise taking part in a campaign has the same obligation to display a disinterested "public spirit" as someone who already occupies office. The public good will be better served if the agents involved in political campaigns recognize this obligation, because the democratic system will yield better results if they do. Certainly, campaigners should be allowed to make the case for their candidates, and certainly reporters and editors should care about selling newspapers. Yet in a democratic system, those involved in the campaign process also have a duty to create an informed electorate. Thus while campaigns cannot be expected to objectively highlight their own faults, they must act according to standards that encourage rational decision-making by voters.

Many of those arguing against raw self-interest on the part of campaigns adhere to a deliberative model of democracy and campaigning.[19] In one of the earliest and most detailed defenses of the civic responsibility model, Stanley Kelley Jr. addresses what he sees as a fundamental problem in our political system: "that the discussion found in campaigns tends to impair the judgement of the electorate and to upset the formulation of coherent policies," when instead it "should help voters make rational voting decisions."[20] Whether the function of elections is to guide public policy or to hold elected officials accountable, it cannot be performed effectively if voters are uninformed.

Kelley offers a set of "qualitative tests" for determining whether campaign communication assists voters in making rational decisions:

—Are voters exposed to the arguments of both sides?

—Does the discussion facilitate the identification of distortions and of false statements of fact?

—Are the candidates' statements of their views and intentions clear?

—Do candidates define their points of disagreement?

—Do campaigners offer evidence for their assertions and give reasons for favoring (or for having favored) particular policies?

—Are the sources of information clearly identified?[21]

To the extent that campaign discussions meet these criteria, the campaign has performed its "informing function." Theoretically, then, a campaign should be a debate.[22]

Recent advocates of deliberative campaigns draw similar conclusions about the regrettable state of contemporary campaign discourse.[23] All of these scholars draw on the classical democratic assumption that voters ought to be given full information about candidates and their campaigns. They recognize that campaigns have to draw distinctions between themselves; indeed, campaigns must do this if voters are to face a real choice. But those distinctions must be substantive, relevant, and should not appeal to voters' base instincts.

Very few people would admit frankly to holding the unconstrained self-interest perspective on campaign ethics. Still, it seems that a substantial number of people do subscribe to it. There are three main justifications to support this view. First, some people do not believe that an agent's involvement in a political campaign is sufficient reason to overturn the general presumption that it is permissible to act solely out of self-interest. Even someone who agrees that "public office is a public trust" might not think that candidates for public office have any particular obligation to deliberate in terms of the public good—let alone political consultants, journalists, or voters. Unless and until one is acting in the capacity of an officeholder, one is still a "private citizen" and only subject to ordinary private morality.

Second, a sort of political invisible-hand argument can be made whereby the public's interest is said to be best protected when campaigners act in their own self-interest. Defenders of contemporary campaigns often invoke the analogy of the American legal system. That system is adversarial, with attorneys making the best case for their clients rather than the most accurate one. Similarly, political campaigns pit adversaries against one another, and those with a stake in the outcome are expected to highlight their own strengths and raise doubts about the opponent.[24] In fact, from this perspective, negative campaigning plays a valuable role in democracy—without it, we would get only the sugarcoated exaggerations that campaigns put out about themselves.[25] Indeed, empirical evidence suggests that voters learn more from negative advertising (including both attack and comparative ads) than from purely positive ads because negative spots contain more policy content.[26] Thus the truth about candidates, far from being sacrificed in this process, emerges from the give-and-take of the campaign.

Finally, other proponents of this conception of campaign ethics take a different approach, which can be described as the political realist's argument. Realists say that when we employ the public good criterion in thinking about what kinds of constraints agents should recognize, we should limit ourselves to considering only constraints that we can realistically expect agents to impose on themselves—and that there are very few of these. We cannot, for example, reasonably expect candidates or parties to emphasize issue positions that may not be popular with the electorate. Nor can we expect them to provide *all* of the information that might be relevant to judging their opponents. Instead, it is perfectly acceptable for candidates and parties to point out the flaws in their opponents' records; it is up to the opponents to defend themselves by providing the other side of the story. From this perspective, a candidate can only be expected to put his or her "best foot forward," just as ordinary citizens seek to present themselves in the most favorable manner in their everyday lives. As Erving Goffman has noted, an individual is but a *"performer*, a harried fabricator of impressions involved in the all-too-human task of staging a performance."[27] Why should candidates (or parties or interest groups and so on) be any different?

It ought to be clear that there is no easy way to resolve the debate between these two conceptions of campaign ethics. It should also be clear that proponents of the civic responsibility conception may disagree with each other about precisely what obligations different agents bear in a campaign setting. This is one manifestation of a more general problem confronted by those who believe that political activity ought to be disinterested: Even if there is agreement on some abstract conception of the public good, which is by no means guaranteed, there is still abundant room for reasonable disagreement about what course of action will best promote the common weal; as Joseph Schumpeter writes: "even if a sufficiently definite common good . . . proved acceptable to all, this would not imply equally definite answers to individual issues."[28]

The upshot of this is that there is no agreed-upon standard that outside observers could apply to campaign activity and, even if an accepted standard existed, there is no mechanism in place to enforce it. Civic responsibility proponents argue that this is precisely the difference between the courtroom and the campaign trail. The legal system analogy "quickly breaks down," according to Hugh Heclo, "once we recall that the adversarial contest in court occurs under strict rules that are explicitly intended to maximize reasoned deliberation and to minimize 'irrelevant' information or appeals to emotion."[29] Rules of evidence determine what is admissible in court. They cover everything from the competence of witnesses and hearsay to when and how the character of a defendant is relevant.[30] Obviously, no such rules exist for determining what information candidates can and cannot interject into a campaign. Furthermore, there are no judges or juries in campaigns, at least not in the sense that judges and juries operate in the legal system. The media, which theoretically could act as a judge, are themselves agents in the campaign with their own aims and interests. Finally, unlike members of a jury, who are supposed to listen to the arguments on both sides objectively and come to a dispassionate verdict, voters view campaigns through various subjective lenses including partisanship, ideology, and issue positions. Thus from the civic responsibility perspective, it is an empty assurance to be told that campaigns, like courtroom trials, are held in check through an adversarial process. Without rules and judges to hold the actors accountable, we must ask campaigners to hold themselves to a higher ethical standard than self-interest would provide.

Those of the realist bent criticize the civic responsibility camp on nearly the same grounds. It is precisely because there is no set of rules and no judge that we cannot expect campaign actors to be held to some abstract standard. Indeed, the only protection that is needed—or even possible—against an "anything goes" campaign is the presence of other campaign actors.

The "Real World" of Campaign Dilemmas

The division between the two conceptions outlined here is far greater than might appear, because even where agreement seems likely, differences in interpretation become evident. For example, virtually everyone would agree that there is at least a prima facie obligation not to lie in the course of a campaign.[31] Yet deciding what constitutes a lie is notoriously complicated. It is very rare that a piece of campaign communication, like a television commercial, is entirely false. More often, there is at least a kernel of truth in what is said. In such a situation, the civic responsibility camp is likely to interpret campaign messages more rigidly than proponents of self-interest. That is, those committed to civic responsibility will emphasize those things that are "untrue," or at least "misleading," in an ad while those from the self-interest school will point to all that is true (even if only true in a technical sense).

A common form of such a disagreement centers on the use of roll call votes out of context. A legislator may, for example, vote against House Bill 123 because he or she believes it does not go far enough in addressing the problem at hand or because he or she opposes some tangential part of the bill. He or she could be on record as supporting legislation to solve the problem and may even have voted for an alternative bill. Nevertheless, an opponent charges that the legislator is "opposed" to solving the problem and cites as evidence the vote against HB 123. While the legislator's vote is reported truthfully in a technical sense, the implication drawn from the vote is false.

In the summer of 1991, a special election was held in Virginia's 4th congressional district to replace Representative Norman Sisisky (D). The Republican Party of Virginia ran an ad against Democrat Louise Lucas claiming that Lucas "didn't stand up for Virginia values" by voting to "oppose placing our flag in classrooms or requiring students to say the Pledge [of Allegiance]." The ad specified the bill number and date of Lucas's vote. While Lucas did oppose a version of the bill, it was a version that required suspension of students who refused to recite the pledge. Once mandatory suspension was removed from the bill, Lucas voted for it.[32]

Of course, many, if not most, campaign ads are misleading to some degree. In the same race, ads by the Democratic Party and by Lucas claimed that Republican Randy Forbes favored privatizing Social Security and that "experts say Forbes' plan would force deep cuts in monthly Social Security benefits. And take nearly a trillion dollars out of the Social Security trust fund." While Forbes supported allowing individuals to put some of their payroll taxes in the stock market, he did not support privatization of the entire system. Furthermore, experts never evaluated Forbes's plan; the comments the ads referred to were based on examinations of President Bush's proposal.[33] At what point does a misleading ad become "false"? And how damaging are misleading ads to democracy? If your standard is an informed electorate and a deliberative campaign, you will draw the line more quickly and you will take misleading ads more seriously than if your standard is winning an election.

It is not, of course, only advertising or other forms of political communication that create ethical dilemmas. Fund-raising presents numerous problems for candidates. For example, should a candidate accept contributions from interests on both sides of an issue or from someone who has given to both candidates in a race? While the money is given legally and would certainly be useful for the campaign, it also comes from sources who are less interested in vigorous debate than in influencing the political process after the election (if only by trying to gain access to whoever is eventually in office). The relatively new phenomenon of elected officials establishing political action committees (PACs) that allow them to raise money for other candidates also raises concerns, at least from the civic responsibility perspective. These "leadership PACs," as they are called, allow candidates to raise money in amounts larger than would be legal for their own reelection campaigns.[34] In addition, it allows them to circumvent the law prohibiting individual candidates from raising or spending "soft money" since, technically, it is the PAC that is fund-raising. Proponents of self-interest would note that very little of this money can be used directly by the elected official for his or her own reelection effort. The PAC simply allows an elected official to take a leadership role in helping the party's candidates get elected. But others would say that leadership PACs are a clever exploitation of a loophole in the law and that they give incumbents an additional arrow in their reelection quivers.[35] The result is a reduction in the chance that incumbents will face competitive challenges.

Candidates also face dilemmas when it comes to taking a position on popular "hot-button" issues. Specifically, when a candidate's issue position runs counter to majority opinion, he or she must decide whether to stick with the original position and possibly lose the election or change positions insincerely. In many districts in the South, for instance, opposition to the death penalty would virtually guarantee a candidate's defeat. Thus many otherwise liberal candidates can be found to support capital punishment. On the one hand, it makes little sense to throw one's hat in the ring if one has virtually no chance of winning from the outset. Especially when the issue may have less gravity or moral import—flag burning, for example—candidates may well concede the issue for the sake of remaining a viable candidate. Indeed, one could even argue that democracy requires a would-be representative to be responsive to majority opinion when the majority is overwhelming and the opinion is relatively informed and deeply held. Yet democracy also requires candidates and elected officials to maintain the trust of the citizens. In addition to one's duty to be true to oneself, therefore, there may be an obligation to take honest positions—that is, to take positions on issues that one sincerely believes. Furthermore, while it is unreasonable even from the civic responsibility perspective to expect that candidates can discuss all or even most of the issues that are currently debated in the political system, candidates may be expected to explain where they stand on the most pressing issues of the day. If, in fact, they are out of step with the majority on any of those issues, they may have a special duty to explain why they take the position they do. In so doing, they will not only inform the electorate about the specific stance, they will reveal something about their worldview or value system and will, in the process, contribute to a larger debate.

Candidates are not the only actors who face ethical choices in campaigns. Consultants, for example, must decide for whom they will work. Will they assist candidates of only one party or one ideological wing of one party? In an effort to improve their won-lost records, will they work only for certain winners (mostly incumbents)? Perhaps more importantly, will they run the campaign of a person they think will make a bad elected official? A survey of professional political consultants conducted in 1999 for the Improving Campaign Conduct project at the American University Center for Congressional and Presidential Studies revealed that half (51 percent) of all consultants have helped elect a candidate they were later sorry to see serve in office.[36] Working for candidates who are incompetent but who can nevertheless win may help keep the consultant's firm in business and will contribute to its list of victorious candidates, but it may well damage democracy. The tension, once again, is between protecting one's own interests and enhancing the public's interest.

The same can be said of horse-race media coverage of elections, targeted voter mobilization efforts (and particularly demobilization tactics) by parties and interest groups, apathetic and uninformed voters, and a host of other campaign circumstances. Thus the two conceptions of campaign ethics will continue to clash, and no satisfactory resolution to the debate is imminent. Worse, just as philosophers within a particular school of thought might come to divergent conclusions about the right course of action to take in a given situation, political observers who take the same perspective on campaign ethics may often disagree about which constraints are necessary to ensure ethical campaigns.

In the end, the question we posed earlier in this chapter—do contemporary American campaigns follow high ethical standards?—cannot be settled definitively because the answer depends on the standard to be employed. We believe the civic responsibility conception is the preferable standard because we maintain it better serves the public good. Unfortunately, it is beyond the scope of this chapter to explain exactly why that is the case—or why we think the public good ought to be the governing criterion for evaluating the two conceptions. We should note, however, that while we think those involved in campaigns have an obligation to enhance the democratic process, we also believe that politics necessarily entails conflict. As Bernard Crick writes in his classic *In Defense of Poli-*

tics, "Politics . . . is a way of ruling in divided societies without undue violence."[37] Citizens in a democracy must not be squeamish and they should insist that opposing viewpoints be attacked and defended vigorously. These two objectives—contentious politics and ethical politics—are not mutually exclusive. Ultimately, however, the key to both meaningful and decent campaigns is an active citizenry. Without that, campaigns are not likely to appeal to the "better angels of our nature."

Notes

1. Plato, *Gorgias,* trans. W. C. Helmbold (Indianapolis: Bobbs-Merrill, 1952.) Socrates observes that this is a question that "should engage the most serious attention of anyone who has a particle of intelligence" (73, 500c1).

2. If there is one movement in recent ethical theory that can be called fashionable it is the turn away from moral theory toward "virtue ethics." Several prominent philosophers have questioned whether the concept of morality is still coherent, if indeed it ever was; see, for example, the selections by Anscombe, Williams, and MacIntyre in Roger Crisp and Michael Slote, eds., *Virtue Ethics* (Oxford University Press, 1997). The positive counterpart to this criticism of morality is an effort to develop an ethics of virtue, which (in most cases) draws its inspiration from Aristotle. In an ethics of virtue the central question is how a person of good character would act, not how we are obligated to act.

3. Of course, there is no question of either the "philosophical" or the "ordinary" definition of *ethics* being better or worse than the other. The point is simply that *ethics* is ambiguous. Although note that some philosophical theories of ethics, especially act utilitarianism, might deny that any really distinctive moral obligations attach to particular roles.

4. Brad Hooker, *Ideal Code, Real World* (Oxford: Clarendon, 2000), pp. 16–19.

5. This analysis assumes that the AAPC takes the obligations spelled out in its code to be borne by everyone who engages in political consulting, even if they are not AAPC members. This would imply that the drafters of the code do not take any explicit or implicit promise to obey the code to be the only ground of obligation. Some formal codes of ethics might be thought by their drafters (or others) to apply only to those who have explicitly or implicitly promised to abide by them (perhaps as a condition of joining an organization).

6. See www.house.gov/ethics/appendices_gifts_and_travel.htm#_toc476623637 (August 17, 2001).

7. This specific wording comes from Old Dominion University's "Monarch Creed" (web.odu.edu/webroot/orgs/stu/stuserv.nsf/pages/creed [August 17, 2001]).

8. It is unlikely that our ordinary morality is entirely mistaken because a few of our ordinary moral rules seem to be so essential to social stability that a society in which most people did not act in conformity with them would soon collapse; think, for example, about the rules that protect our persons and personal property, that require parents to take care of children, and so on.

9. See, for example, Immanuel Kant, *The Groundwork of the Metaphysics of Morals*, trans. Mary Gregor (Cambridge University Press, 1997). There is, of course, a reason for this. Philosophers seek to account for *why* different properties of actions are morally relevant. Explanations for why one class of properties is morally relevant often tend to entail that this is true *only* of members of that class. The philosophical moral theory whose implications are closest to our ordinary morality is Ross's theory of "prima facie duties." That theory is notable for its abject failure to explain why any of certain properties of actions are morally relevant while others are not (W. D. Ross, *The Right and the Good* [Oxford: Clarendon, 1939]).

10. Michael Walzer, "Political Action: The Problem of Dirty Hands," *Philosophy and Public Affairs*, vol. 2 (1973), pp. 160–80.

11. Ibid., p. 160.

12. See C. A. J. Coady, "Politics and the Problem of Dirty Hands," in Peter Singer, ed., *A Companion to Ethics* (Cambridge, Mass.: Basil Blackwell, 1993); W. Kenneth Howard, "Must Public Hands Be Dirty?" *Journal of Value Inquiry,* vol. 11 (1977), pp. 29–40, for arguments that politics is not uniquely fraught with moral dilemmas. See Dennis F. Thompson, *Political Ethics and Public Office* (Harvard University Press, 1987), pp. 11–39, for an interesting treatment of the "democratic dirty hands problem."

13. Walzer, "Political Action," p. 165.

14. In this chapter we are interested only in the question of what ethical obligations attach to the special roles that agents occupy within the context of a campaign, and we will discuss this only in the most general of terms. To even begin to address questions about what agents ought morally to do when there are conflicts between the ethical obligations that attach to different roles or between the ethical obligations attaching to particular roles and universal moral obligations would carry us too far afield.

15. Joseph S. Nye Jr., Philip D. Zelikow, and David C. King, eds. *Why People Don't Trust Government* (Harvard University Press, 1997).

16. The Project on Campaign Conduct of the Institute for Global Ethics helps devise codes of conduct for candidates. These codes, which may vary from campaign to campaign, are statements of "guiding principles that act as a benchmark for behavior" (see www.campaignconduct.org/[August 21, 2001]). Fowler has also offered some "rules of thumb" for judging candidates (Linda L. Fowler, "Campaign Ethics and Political Trust," in James A. Thurber and Candice J. Nelson, eds., *Campaigns and Elections American Style* [Boulder, Colo.: Westview Press, 1995]). Other codes apply to political consultants (such as the AAPC's code of ethics), political parties—for example, the Code of Conduct for Political Parties from the International Institute for Democracy and Electoral Assistance (see www.idea.int/publications/conduct/ polparties.pdf [August 23, 2001])—and journalists—for example, the code of ethics of the Society of Professional Journalists (see csep.iit.edu/codes/coe/soc_of_prof_journ_code_ethics.html [August 23, 2001]).

17. Hooker, *Ideal Code, Real World*, p. 17.

18. In some instances officeholders are required to deliberate by following a procedure that is justified in terms of its promotion of the public good. Judges,

for example, should not normally ask themselves what decision would best promote the public good; they should interpret and apply the law. But their deliber-
ating in this way promotes the public good better than any other approach.

19. See John Gastil, *By Popular Demand: Revitalizing Representative Democracy through Deliberative Elections* (University of California Press, 2000).

20. Stanley Kelley Jr., *Political Campaigning: Problems in Creating an Informed
Electorate* (Brookings, 1960), p. 2.

21. Ibid., p. 16.

22. Ibid., pp. 19–21.

23. Although see Roderick P. Hart, *Campaign Talk: Why Elections Are Good
for Us* (Princeton University Press, 2000).

24. The legal analogy is occasionally used in a critical way. In the British context,
for example, S. E. Finer makes the analogy in order to condemn the "first-past-the-
post" electoral system ("Adversary Politics and Electoral Reform," in S. E. Finer, ed.,
Adversary Politics and Electoral Reform [London: Anthony Wigram, 1975]).

25. William G. Mayer, "In Defense of Negative Campaigning," *Political Science Quarterly,* vol. 111 (1996), pp. 437–55.

26. Kathleen Hall Jamieson, Paul Waldman, and Susan Sherr, "Eliminate the
Negative? Categories of Analysis for Political Advertisements," in James A.
Thurber, Candice J. Nelson, and David A. Dulio, eds., *Crowded Airwaves: Cam-
paign Advertising in Elections* (Brookings, 2000); Kim Fridkin Kahn and Patrick
J. Kenney, "How Negative Campaigning Enhances Knowledge of Senate Elec-
tions," in Thurber, Nelson, and Dulio, *Crowded Airwaves.*

27. Erving Goffman, *The Presentation of Self in Everyday Life* (Garden City,
N.Y.: Doubleday Anchor Books, 1959), p. 252.

28. Joseph Schumpeter, *Capitalism, Socialism, and Democracy*, 3rd ed. (Harper
& Row, 1949), pp. 251–52. For a discussion of the differences between two historically significant abstract conceptions of the public good—the common good
and the public interest—see Bruce Douglass, "The Common Good and the Public
Interest," *Political Theory,* vol. 8 (1980), pp. 103–15.

29. Hugh Heclo, "Campaigning and Governing: A Conspectus," in Norman
Ornstein and Thomas Mann, eds., *The Permanent Campaign and Its Future* (Washington: American Enterprise Institute and Brookings, 2000), p. 13.

30. See the federal rules of evidence at www.law.cornell.edu/rules/fre/ (September 3, 2001).

31. A prima facie obligation is one that can be outweighed by an even weightier
obligation. However, it is hard to conceive of instances where a candidate would
have an even weightier obligation to lie. Even in situations involving classified
national security information, an incumbent privy to that information is surely
more obligated to simply not divulge it than to lie about it. Still, instances of this
kind may be possible in principle.

32. Holly A. Heyser, "Ad Watch: 4th District Campaigns Intensify Their Claims:
Lucas, Forbes Decry Each Other's Pitches," *Virginian-Pilot,* June 14, 2001, p. B1.

33. Ibid.

34. Trevor Potter, "Where Are We Now? The Current State of Campaign Finance Law," in Anthony Corrado and others, eds., *Campaign Finance Reform: A*

Sourcebook (Brookings, 1997), pp. 7–8; for a recent example, see George Lardner Jr. "Hillary Clinton Starts PAC to Help Democrats," *Washington Post*, February 7, 2001, p. A17.

35. For example, money from leadership PACs is increasingly used by elected officials to cover travel and administrative costs.

36. See www.american.edu/academic.depts/spa/ccps/pdffiles/political_campaign_consultants.pdf (October 10, 2001).

37. Bernard Crick, *In Defense of Politics*, 2d ed. (University of Chicago Press, 1972), p. 146. Interestingly, Crick describes conflicts between interests as follows—"These conflicts, when personal, create the activity we call 'ethics' . . . and such conflicts, when public, create political activity" (25). "Political activity," then, "is a type of moral activity" (146).

CHAPTER THREE

CANDIDATES

Promises and Persuasion

L. SANDY MAISEL

The idealist would respond to the original subtitle of this chapter—The Twin Dilemmas of Campaign Ethics—simply: "At last someone is talking about ethics in campaigns. It's about time!" The cynic would respond: "*Candidate ethics* is an oxymoron. Campaigns are all about being unethical; everyone knows that!" The pragmatist would respond: "Here we go again. Candidate ethics are all well and good in theory, but they can never work in practice!" And readers of Dale Miller and Stephen Medvic's earlier chapter in this book undoubtedly recognize that *ethics* as applied to campaigns will be interpreted differently, depending on whether one is using a civic responsibility framework or one more based on self-interest of the candidate.

This chapter is written by a student of politics, one who has observed campaigns for more than three decades and one who has been involved in a number of different campaigns—as candidate, as campaign staffer, as political commentator. To be sure, I am a pragmatist, and I have my cynical side. But I am also an idealist. I think campaigns can be made better

I would like to thank the students in my seminar Ethics and Politics—particularly Mike Bates, Mark Cattrell, Cathy Flemming, Theresa Wagner, and Laura Walsh—whose ideas as we were debating some of the major ethical questions facing our polity today contributed significantly to my thinking on this topic. I would also like to thank David Shribman, Oliver Sabot, and Lydia Tomitova for their assistance.

from an ethical perspective, within either the civic responsibility or the self-interest conception of that term, but only after difficult questions are asked and answered. This chapter is an attempt to lay out some of those questions and to suggest some answers.

I start from one basic assumption: *Candidates for public office are generally ethical individuals.* They seek public office in order to advance policies that they believe will benefit the polity as a whole. To be sure, they have personal goals—to advance their own careers, to obtain benefits for their communities, to reset societal directions they feel those in office have imposed on our society in error—but generally they want to "do good." I do not deny that on occasion an individual enters or uses politics for personal gain, but those individuals are the rare exception, the rotten apples that in many ways do spoil the barrel. They sully the reputation of thousands of others from whose good efforts our country has benefited.

The argument in this chapter also depends on a second assumption: *Most candidates do not give a great deal of thought to ethical considerations before they enter a campaign, and many campaign decisions are made without explicit discussion of the ethical considerations involved.* Candidates want to win office; they believe that they are better suited for office than the individuals they oppose; they believe that their views of appropriate public policy will lead to a better future than the alternatives their opponents propose. And they run for office for those reasons. Their opponent is unqualified. The country will be better off if their party is in power. Their community will be better served if they and their party set the agenda for the city, state, or nation.

If the motives are not always totally pure, they are not badly tainted. Politics is about power. Ambition is needed to get ahead. Partisanship is central to the electoral process. But power, ambition, and partisanship are used primarily to forward a vision of the future. The campaign is an effort to convince the citizens that one individual's vision, one party's sense of direction, is preferable to those of another individual or another party.

Ethical Problems in Modern Campaigning

A corollary of these two assumptions is that ethical problems in campaigns sneak in unexamined. And the logical question to pursue is: What is the nature of the ethical problems about which we worry? Within the terms set by Miller and Medvic, what is it about campaigns and the roles of candidates that make certain kinds of actions unethical?[1]

The cynic's response to this chapter's original subtitle is instructive. One cannot use *ethics* and *campaigning* in the same phrase without an inherent contradiction. Our citizens expect the worst of our candidates. The assumption is that candidates will say anything and do anything in order to get elected. Every political observer can point to practices considered unethical—questionable advertisements, unsubstantiated accusations, misleading telephone calls, venomous personal attacks, unfulfilled promises. Examples are given that are really code words—the girl with the daisy; Willie Horton; Helms-Gantt; a secret plan to end the Vietnam War.

Let us look at each of these for a moment. In the 1964 presidential campaign, the Democrats ran an ad—just once, as is often pointed out—implying that the Republican candidate, Barry Goldwater, would use nuclear weapons without due care for the enormity of such an act. The advertisement—showing a little girl counting daisy petals as she picked them off a stem while a voice-over gave the countdown to a nuclear explosion—was deemed as having gone too far to make the point. The scare tactics were considered beyond some acknowledged but unspecified limit. Verdict: The Democrats had made an unethical use of advertising. Result: The Democratic campaign, the candidate for whom the ad was made, and the firm making the ad were widely criticized, and the ad was quickly withdrawn.

In the 1988 presidential campaign the Republicans attacked the gubernatorial record of Democratic candidate Michael Dukakis. As governor of Massachusetts, Dukakis had been responsible for a prisoner furlough program for those not eligible for parole. One of the black prisoners on furlough, Willie Horton, committed a murder. The ad used by the Republicans showed a revolving prison door with convicts leaving, seemingly at will.[2] The implication was that the program was a failure, that Dukakis was responsible for that failure, and that he would be equally inept as president of the United States. Verdict: There was no consensus on an ethical standard. Result: The ad ran its course, the Democrats cried foul and claimed that the ad sought to inspire racial fear, but the Republicans did not back down.

In 1990 North Carolina senator Jesse Helms, seeking reelection to a fourth term, was opposed by Harvey Gantt, the African American mayor of Charlotte. In what was at the time the most expensive Senate campaign in history, Helms, who trailed in early polls, viciously attacked Gantt, drawing out the racial and sexual prejudices of his constituents. In one such attack, Helms stated that Gantt was campaigning in out-of-state gay communities in order to raise campaign funds. In another he misrepresented Gantt's views of abortion. And in a particularly egregious example, he played on racial prejudice in an ad that showed a white pair of hands crumpling a job rejection letter. The voice-over said that "you" lost the job because of racial quotas that Harvey Gantt says are fair. The ad clearly implied that whites had to fear the election of a black senator. Verdict: Helms's tactics were roundly criticized as unethical. Result: Helms narrowly won the race, his campaign unethical but successful.

Finally, during the 1968 Republican primaries, former vice president Richard Nixon implied that he had a secret plan to bring about peace in Vietnam. While he never said explicitly that he had such a plan in place, Nixon implied as much by refusing to answer questions about it on the grounds he should not reveal in advance a bargaining position he would use if elected.[3] The secret plan never materialized; in fact, it had never existed. Verdict: The public should be aware of campaign promises; it might not be ethical to make promises one has no intention of keeping, but it certainly is a common practice of successful politicians. Result: Nixon won the election and the war dragged on, despite the American public's fervent wish for peace.

The ethical problem, then, involves what our campaigns have become and what we expect of those campaigns. The public expects exaggeration, innuendo, broken promises, whatever tactics are necessary to win. I do not believe that Lyndon Johnson or George H. W. Bush or Richard Nixon or even Jesse Helms went into a campaign thinking that they or their operatives would act unethically. I do not believe that they ever debated the ethics of the question. Evidence indicates that the Johnson campaign was surprised by the response to the daisy commercial; they withdrew the ad quickly in light of the negative response. Nixon made his statement on Vietnam to distinguish himself from his fellow Republican contestants for the party nomination and to demonstrate his criticism of the Democrats' war policy. George H. W. Bush thought that Dukakis was vulnerable on the crime issue and sought to exploit his differences with the Massachusetts governor on that spectrum of issues. Helms had a very different vision of America from Gantt's; I believe he genuinely (but wrongly) feared the consequences for North Carolina of a Gantt victory. Thus he fought by whatever means he could to whip up the enthusiasm of his followers. In my view—and I think in the eyes of most objective observers—serious ethical questions are legitimately raised in each of these situations. But they were not raised by the participants at the time.

The Democratic Principles behind the Electoral Process

Ethical questions are raised if an action violates accepted mores for action in a society; ethical principles should apply in virtually any context, including political campaigns. But Dennis Thompson notes that there are often conflicts between ethical behavior, which is inherently individual-based, and political behavior, when an individual is working with others and often acting on behalf of others.[4] Political ethics, according to Thompson, "joins ethics and politics without supposing that it can eliminate the conflict between them."[5] Much of Thompson's work on this topic relates to the actions of public officials in office, but by extension, the argument can be made to apply to candidates for office as well.

To demonstrate this point, let us return to the example of Richard Nixon's secret plan to end the war. And let us apply some assumptions that may or may not be true. First, let us assume that no secret plan in fact existed (an assumption that conforms with known facts). Second, let us assume that Nixon needed to distinguish himself from his Republican opponents and also from the Democrats in order to be elected (also conforming with known facts). Third, let us assume that Nixon believed that the Democrats had no plans for either winning or ending the Vietnam crisis and that the military had lost all faith in Democratic leadership (a hypothetical assumption with no basis in known facts). Fourth, let us assume that this country's most powerful enemies were poised to take advantage of significant vulnerabilities caused by our involvement in the Vietnam quagmire and that they were only waiting for a Democratic victory and the extension of the war that would follow to exploit our weaknesses (another hypothetical assumption without factual basis). Under those circumstances, Nixon decided that he had to lie to the American people in order to preserve the nation. He violated one ethical principle—that one should not lie—in order to prevent extreme harm to the country.

If those assumptions were accurate, should Nixon's unethical act be considered appropriate? Would he not have been more wrong to allow harmful consequences without taking any action? It is not difficult to pose similar hypothetical situations, but they are just that—hypothetical. And it is frequently easy to rationalize unethical behavior if one assumes the worst consequences of not taking that action. What is more difficult, but also necessary, is to set standards of political ethics against which to judge individual behavior.

To begin to propose these standards, we return to basic democratic theory, to the civic responsibility framework for considerations of ethics posed by Miller and Medvic. We hold elections in order to choose those who are to govern. We hold frequent elections in order to hold those whom we have elected accountable for their actions. We have campaigns so that citizens can judge the record of those in office against the prospects of what would be done by those seeking office.[6] The question of why we have campaigns is at the center of the discussion of what ethical standards should be applied to candidates for office. In the simplest terms, candidates should act in such a way that allows the electoral system to operate as it should within the framework of our polity. Further, they should be compelled to act in a manner that does no harm to the polity as a whole.

Our concern, therefore, is about actions that do not allow citizens to make informed judgments. Return to the Nixon example above. Under the hypothetical assumptions, Nixon's action would not be considered ethical unless he knew somehow that the citizenry would choose his solution with its consequences over the Democrats' course of action with the consequences that would follow from that. We assumed such dire consequences that one might also conclude that Nixon would know that, but situations in politics are rarely so black and white. And the difficulty is in the shades of gray.

Most of those running for office honestly believe that the country or state or city would be better off if they were in office than if their opponent won. Even most cynics would grant that assumption. But candidates cannot act to achieve that end if their actions deny the citizenry the information needed to reach that same conclusion. That is, the campaigns must be open and honest about what a candidate stands for and what the opponent stands for—and then the voters can decide. Candidates cannot act in such a way as to deny the voters information to make their decision without violating the very reason we have elections.

But that minimalist answer will not suffice. Campaigns and elections give legitimacy to our representative democracy. Candidates cannot act in such a manner as to undermine that legitimacy. If citizens do not believe in the sanctity of the electoral process, if they do not believe that their views are really determinative, if they believe that the entire process is corrupt, then that basic sense of legitimacy is lost and the critical connection between those who govern and the governed so necessary for a representative democracy is also lost. If the views of the cynic are prevalent, if most citizens believe that the process is basically corrupt, if the common view is that all politicians act unethically so why bother to vote, then our democracy is in jeopardy. And those politicians who have acted in a manner to encourage those views have violated the basic principles of political ethics.

Candidates for office thus must navigate along a narrow path. They want to win and feel that their victory is important. Thus they should campaign vigorously, make their best case, appeal to as many voters as possible, and demonstrate to those voters why electing them is preferable to electing their opponents. But they must do so in such a way that the process remains unscathed, that the citizens in fact can decide, and that the citizens understand their power so that they want to decide. In the remaining sections of this chapter we will look at two aspects of campaigns in which, whether they acknowledge it or not, candidates confront ethical dilemmas—the promises they make and the means they use to persuade voters to support them.

Promises: What Should Candidates Promise to Do if Elected?

If the purpose of a campaign is for the candidates to state to the citizenry what they will do if elected, so that voters can decide between alternative policy agendas, then the content of campaign promises is critical to the electoral process. Candidates realize this and work hard to propose policies that will appeal to the electorate. They want to put their best foot forward, to talk about those issues that will convince the electorate to support them. That is as it should be.

However, making campaign promises that appeal to the voters can be too easy. The ethical problem arises if candidates make proposals that are not possible or not genuine in order to win an election. Certainly, the first amendment to the Constitution, if it does nothing else, guarantees those involved in politics the right to say what they please. We are not talking about regulations of what can be said, what can be promised. But we are talking about what is ethical for a candidate to promise.

We should start with the easiest aspects of campaign promises. It is appropriate, beyond ethical question—and, in fact, necessary if campaigns are to serve the function they are designed to serve in a representative democracy—for candidates to state what they favor as policy alternatives and how they would implement those policies. "If I am elected, I will introduce legislation to outlaw practice X, and I will work as hard as I can to achieve passage of that legislation." The candidate's goal is clear; the candidate's actions if elected are clear. The candidate does not make promises that cannot be kept, and the voter can evaluate both the proposed policy and the candidate's likely chances for success.

Now take the next step. What if the candidate states his or her position on a policy and promises action. "If I am elected, I will introduce legislation to outlaw practice X, and I will see that that legislation is passed." The difference between these two promises might seem a small one, but it is important. In the second case, the candidate can guarantee the first part of what is promised but is powerless to achieve the second. How can an individual legislator—or even a president or governor—"see that legislation is passed"? No one official in our system of government has that power. Is it ethical to make that promise?

What is the ethical tenet that is violated? Put simply, the candidate lied. Lying is unethical; we could not successfully live in a society in which people routinely lied, and no one could accept the word of a fellow citizen as truthful. But "lying" is not a unidimensional concept. Some lies are clearly more serious than others. How seriously should we take candidate lies during a campaign? Do lies like the one in the second statement of campaign promises violate our society's sense of appropriate behavior?

A lie is a statement that conveys a false impression. But according to Sissela Bok, truth is not so important as truthfulness; that is, her concern about lying is with the intent of the person promulgating the lie, not with the absolute truth of the statement. In addition, she believes that a statement must also be viewed from the perspective of the person to whom that statement is directed.[7] A statement is deceptive and action is unethical if the person making the statement knows that statement to be false and intends for the listener to accept it as true.[8]

We can go further in differentiating among campaign promises that are not entirely truthful. Are there untruthful campaign promises that are the equivalent of "white lies," slight exaggerations of the truth that do no harm? I think that there are. A candidate for Congress says that she will come home to the district every weekend in order to stay in touch but knows that at times the House is in session on a weekend, such a trip will be impossible. Her statement was not truthful, but the point of the promise was to demonstrate that the candidate would not lose touch with the people who sent her to Washington. Those who heard the statement understood its intent. No harm, no foul.

Many candidates make promises during campaigns that they honestly believe to be true, but that are in fact not true. "If I am elected to the Senate, I will contribute to the Democratic majority, and we will prevent the president from fundamentally changing the ideological composition of the Supreme Court." The candidate might well have believed that his election would swing the Senate in his party's direction. But, lo and behold, it did not. The campaign statement was not true, but the candidate was not being deceptive. He was clear to the voters about his position (on Supreme Court nominations), his desired outcome (no change in the ideological composition of the Court), and his potential role in it (working with his party to halt undesirable presidential nominations). He was wrong about which party would control the Senate and thus about his ability to achieve his goal. In this case, no deception, no foul.

A third level of lying involves clear deception. The candidate knows that what he says is not true, and the reason he says it is to convince the voters to support him. Candidates cross the line of ethical behavior in two possible ways. First, if they make statements they do not really believe. If a candidate for the U.S. Senate says that he will not use a litmus test of an individual's position on abortion in weighing whether to confirm a nominee for a judicial post, and if that Senate candidate knows that he would never support a nominee who does not favor a woman's right to choose (or one who does), that candidate has intentionally deceived the voters with the goal of convincing them that he stands for or against a policy when he in fact feels the opposite. The candidate's action is clearly unethical.

But some actions are not that clear-cut. Candidates also cross into unethical territory if they try to convince voters to favor their candidacy with promises that they know or come to believe to be false. If a candidate questions the validity of her own statement, she should not make that statement or she should retract it. "If I am elected governor, I will improve the quality of education in our state's schools, from the elementary level to our state university." Fair enough—the candidate wants better education for citizens of the state. But then she meets with her advisers on educational matters and comes to understand the complexity of the problem facing the state's university. She wants a better university, but she is not willing to commit the time or money necessary to make significant changes in the short run. The candidate owes it to the people to discuss what she really can and cannot do. The problem here is not lack of good intentions, but rather exaggeration of what can be done. Like the guarantee that the candidate discussed above would "see to it that legislation is passed," this candidate undermines the electoral system by giving citizens reasons to be cynical.

Two decades ago Morris Fiorina wrote an eloquent defense of why rational citizens should vote retrospectively (based on a candidate's or a party's past performance) rather than prospectively (based on their promises of future action).[9] Essentially, he argued that voting prospectively is more costly and less rational—it is more difficult to evaluate the worth of promises than to judge past performance, and what evidence is there that candidates keep their promises in any case? One need not be a cynic to claim that politicians make promises that they cannot keep. We as a nation expect that most promises will not be kept.[10] To the extent that this is so, candidates act unethically by undermining the system that is at the theoretical heart of representative democracy.

Is there an ethical lesson to be learned from this discussion of various types of campaign promises and of various types of lies? Is there an ethical principle that candidates should seek to follow? I think there is. At the most obvious level, candidates should not speak falsely; they should not equivocate on key issues. They should be called to task by objective observers, not just by their opponents, if they are professing positions in a campaign that are popular with the voters but opposite of those they have taken earlier in their careers and are likely to take again if elected.

But more than that, candidates should be held accountable for their promises and for the ways in which they express those promises. We should praise candidates for the specificity of their promises and for making promises that they have the capability to fulfill if elected. We should criticize those who word promises vaguely, whose pledges lack specificity, who choose words carefully to cloud issues, not to clarify them.[11] The democratic process cannot function if citizens paying attention to a campaign still do not know what a candidate intends to do and will be capable of doing when elected. The responsibility lies with the candidates (and those who report on candidate campaigns) more than it does with the electorate, for the voters are only able to process what is given to them. In an important sense, candidates who do not live up to this responsibility are not acting ethically because they undermine the legitimacy of the representative system in which they seek to serve.

Persuasion: How Can Candidates Contrast Their Records with Their Opponents'?

Political campaigns are not softball. Candidates do not simply say, "I'm a good guy, so vote for me!" The whole point of campaigns is to convince the electorate that one candidate and policies are better than the other candidate and policies. One way to do that is through campaign platforms and campaign promises. The other way to do that is by campaigning *against* your opponent. While ethical considerations should be raised about promises made, most ethical concerns deal with what is said about the other candidate.

Negative Advertising: Comparisons or Attacks

Saying something about one's opponent is not necessarily a bad thing to do. Many candidates talk frequently about their opponents. Some even praise them for what they have done, for their distinguished service, for their dedication to the public. But then they have to give the voters a reason to reject this upstanding public servant in favor of someone else.

The generic term often applied to candidate efforts to make their case over their opponent's is *negative campaigning* or *negative advertising*. The latter is a misused and poorly conceived term. First of all, much of what is said about an opponent is not said in advertising. It is said on the stump, in debates, in media interviews. So the use of the word *advertising* overstates the importance of that one way of campaigning.[12] But it is more important to note that a difference exists between *comparative appeals* and *attacks*. Comparative appeals stress that one should favor one candidate over another because of differences that can be objectively observed—between their records, their experiences, their platforms, and so on. Attack appeals seek to undermine the opponent, to create a negative image about the individual or what consequences would follow from that person's election. Comparative appeals differ from attacks in tone and content; either can deal with policy differences between the candidates or with personal matters. I argue below that comparative appeals are appropriate and in fact central to the electoral process; on the contrary, attacks cross the line into unethical behavior.

Policy Differences

What could be more basic to the electoral process than one candidate comparing his stands on the issues to those of his opponent? That is the essence of comparative campaigning. That kind of comparison is how voters know what to expect when a candidate becomes an officeholder. That type of campaigning allows voters to hold officeholders accountable for prior actions. There is no ethical problem involved in straightforward comparisons of voting records or of policy differences as they have been expressed in campaign promises. In fact, as William Mayer has commented, this type of negative campaigning "provides voters with a lot of valuable information they definitely need to have when deciding how to cast their ballots."[13] One could even argue that a candidate has an obligation to make appropriate comparisons to give the voters the data they need to make informed choices.

However, differences that are presented as stark by one candidate may be seen as nuanced by another. Votes that one candidate says reflect certain ideological positions might be interpreted differently by his opponent. Campaigning is about politics, about gaining an advantage, not about civics lessons. Any campaign manager worth her pay will present comparisons that put her candidate in the most favorable light. The ways in which comparisons are made, in which policy differences are presented to the electorate, can in fact raise serious ethical questions. The questions raised are of two types: the accuracy not only of the information posed but also of the implications one intends the listener to draw from that information by the way it is presented (see the discussion of the "James Byrd" ad in chapter 1); and who is sponsoring an advertisement and what the responsibility of the candidate favored in an ad is, if the ad itself is questionable. We will deal with these separately.

In recent years various media outlets, in virtually every corner of the country, have begun airing or printing "ad watch" segments in which journalists assess the accuracy of the claims made in political advertisements. This development is clearly beneficial and has resulted in campaign after campaign literally footnoting claims made in their advertisements. If a candidate is involved in outright lying, he stands a good chance of exposure; most campaigns are careful on this point.

But political campaigns run against those with long voting records have a real advantage if they intend to "go negative." It is almost always possible to find an example of a vote cast by an officeholder that can be interpreted in a number of different ways. A congressman casts a vote against a large raise in the minimum wage because he knows that a bill with that number in it will fail while one with a slightly lower raise will pass. An opponent reports that the congressman cast a vote against raising the minimum wage to the higher level, implying that the vote was antilabor. Is that advertisement strictly accurate? Yes. Is it truthful? No. The opponent knew or should have known why the incumbent cast the vote that he did. Context is crucial in voting in any legislative body that relies on compromise and negotiation to reach results that approximate an optimal outcome. The opponent implied other motivations, knowing they were false. As with lying about campaign promises, the intent of the person making the claim is the relevant factor. One cannot legislate against such practices, but they are clearly unethical.

But this issue is even more complex. Political ads are all about tone and image as well as content. Let us look at two examples. First, when Leon Panetta (D) first ran for the U.S. House of Representatives in 1976, his opponent was the incumbent, Burt Talcott (R), who presented himself as a hardworking fourteen-year veteran. In point of fact, Talcott had missed about half the votes in his principal House committee. Panetta was certainly justified in pointing out that his opponent was less than honest in his claim, that he was in fact an absentee representative much of the time. But one of Panetta's own campaign workers wondered if they "were wrong to point that out in a spot with arresting music and dramatic close ups of an empty chair."[14] If the candidate or his staff raises these questions themselves, they are clearly meat for a discussion of ethical considerations.[15]

Mitch McConnell's (R) 1984 Senate campaign in Kentucky against incumbent Walter "Dee" Huddleston (D) featured one of the most effective (and funniest) ads in the history of modern television campaigning. McConnell's ad mentioned a series of votes in the Senate that Huddleston had missed, all accurately documented. The visual was a pack of bloodhounds roaming over the Capitol grounds in search of Huddleston, with the voice-over asking, "Where's Senator Huddleston?" The ad effectively portrayed Huddleston as a deadbeat who was not doing his job; the image stuck, and McConnell won. The ad was given a great deal of credit for that victory. The problem is that Huddleston had over a 90 percent voting participation record during his Senate career.[16] McConnell's staff surely knew that. McConnell has expressed no qualms about his tactics. Should he? Again, no one questions McConnell's right to have run this advertisement, nor were the specific claims in the advertisement inaccurate. But the implication was inaccurate—and the intent of the ad was to create the implication. It is difficult to imagine a definition of ethical behavior that would incorporate deliberate distortion of a record in order to deceive the voters.

The issue becomes somewhat murkier when it is not a candidate but rather a surrogate for a candidate who is sponsoring the offensive advertisement or carrying on a campaign that is ethically questionable. During the 1996 congressional elections, questionable negative campaigns run by surrogates dominated the political landscape. The AFL-CIO ran a $35 million advertising campaign directed against sixty-four Republican incumbents deemed to be vulnerable. The generic ads, which merely plugged in the incumbent's name and picture for a specific district, noted that the minimum wage had remained the same for five years while corporate profits and executive salaries had both increased dramatically. The ad stated that the viewer should send a message to Congressman X, never mentioning the name of the Democrat.[17]

In the same year the Republican National Committee and the National Republican Senatorial Committee joined together to produce and sponsor generic ads criticizing incumbent Democratic senators in five states. These ads dubbed the incumbents as liberals who favored increasing taxes on working families while they raised their own salaries and voted for wasteful programs. The Republican candidates in those races did not openly state that the incumbents were against "workfare" and in favor of wasteful programs, but they all referred to the implications in the ads as if they were factual.[18]

These examples are not unique. Surrogate campaigning has become one of the principal tools of election efforts in recent years. The two national party committees (the Democratic National Committee and the Republican National Committee) and their Hill committees (the Democratic Senatorial Campaign Committee, the National Republican Senatorial Committee, the Democratic Congressional Campaign Committee, and the National Republican Congressional Committee) (see Robin Kolodny's chapter 7 and Mark Siegel's chapter 8 for a broader discussion of political party ethics), labor and business groups, and single-issue advocacy groups of all kinds take on incumbents without coordinating their efforts with the candidate they support. They operate within the limits of the campaign finance laws as they are currently written and interpreted, but that does not absolve either these groups or the candidates they favor of acknowledging ethical considerations.

Distortion of a candidate's record or position on issues, campaigning by innuendo, and intentional deceit may all have proven to be successful in the campaign context, but that does not make them acceptable from an ethical point of view. It is difficult—if not impossible—to draw a line precisely. Again, the intent of the person making the appeal is the relevant variable. But a system that accepts unfettered actions deemed clearly detrimental to the process as a whole because legal language cannot be found to draw what are obviously fuzzy lines contains within it the seeds of its own destruction. And those who participate in such a system have an ethical obligation, within the framework of ethics concerned with civic responsibility, to observe self-restraint in order to preserve the democratic process.

Personal Attacks

If ethical questions are raised about questionable campaign appeals that deal with policy positions or a candidate's record of service, even more serious questions are raised about negative campaigning that involves personal attacks on a candidate. The basic ethical dilemma in this instance is whether politicians' private lives are relevant to their ability to represent the public and to exercise their official duties. According to Dennis Thompson, "The question of privacy arises for public officials when they decide what to disclose about themselves, and to whom to disclose it. The question also confronts public officials who have occasion to decide what to reveal about other officials, and to whom to disclose it."[19] If that is the case for all public officials, as Thompson asserts, it is perhaps even more true of elected public officials.

Intimate details of a candidate's life—or of the lives of his family—should under normal circumstances remain protected. The public does not necessarily have the right to know everything about an individual just because that individual seeks public office. However, the candidate does forfeit some degree of privacy. "The boundaries of what is intimate are neither precise nor absolute, and even the most intimate facts about public officials may not be protected if the facts are highly relevant to the performance of their duties."[20]

How can those boundaries be delineated? Richard Scher is among those who believe that truth is the only factor relevant in deciding whether to disclose private information about an opponent: "Calling a person a spouse abuser, if true, is not negative campaigning, as it reflects on the worthiness of the person to be given the public trust."[21] The argument is made that any personal misconduct is relevant, because the individual seeks to represent us all. If the public really needs to judge a candidate, they need to know everything about that candidate. If the public does not think previous misbehavior is relevant, they will ignore the charges and vote based on other considerations. Therefore, no holds are barred; everything is aboveboard.

That argument fails to meet standards for ethical behavior for two reasons. First, individuals do have a zone of privacy that demands respect. If an action represents a youthful indiscretion, if the behavior is that of a family member who is not seeking office (but will be hurt by its revelation), if the incident in question is a private matter that does not bear on official duties, that zone of privacy should be maintained, and those who violate it should be accountable for their actions. What is their motive? Is it truly to guard the public from representation by unfit individuals or is it to further their own careers?

Second, the argument that all should be revealed disregards the impact on the polity. If the nature of campaigning is merely to discredit the character of one's opponent, then the result will be representation by individuals who are in fact held in low regard by the public. Evidence exists that the public responds to negative personal attacks by thinking less of both the individual attacked and the individual making the attack. No one questions the strategic impact of personal attacks, but the overall result is increased public disapproval of politicians as a group and of the political process in general.[22] That result is detrimental to our system of government, and those whose actions lead to that result are acting unethically in undermining the very system they seek to serve.

If the "no holds barred" standard fails the ethical test, what standard should a candidate use in evaluating whether to use negative personal information about her opponent? The standard should be that of relevance. If her opponent is running a campaign based on "return to family values," then his aberrant sexual behavior or his lack of concern for his children would be relevant. If a candidate is running as "tough on crime," then efforts to help a misbehaving friend out of a legal jam would be relevant. But if a candidate is running on economic issues, then a five-year-old affair that he and his family have put behind them is not relevant.

Moral standards are highly personal. Candidates themselves must make the judgments about relevancy, and they must make judgments about their own motives. And it is in making these judgments that campaign ethics is involved. In the case of campaigning against an opponent based on his personal behavior in the past, candidates and their campaigns must be particularly aware of the consequences of their actions not only for their immediate campaign but for the process in which they participate. That is, not only their self-interest in winning an election is at stake; they have a responsibility to the system and the polity for the consequences of their campaign tactics as well. Candidates must ask the difficult ethical questions: Why am I doing this? Does the importance of this issue overweigh the costs I am inflicting on another person and her family? Does this issue really define the difference between me and my opponent on a criterion that the public should be using to judge us? The principle that candidates must consider involves looking beyond the campaign to ask whether they want to be the type of person who lowers the level of debate in this manner—and if they do, do they deserve to serve the public any more than their opponent? What will be the impact on the polity, on how citizens view all public officials? Rarely are candidates that introspective, and the polity suffers accordingly.

The Means of Campaigning

To this point we have discussed the messages that campaigns convey and the ethical implications of those messages. At least a word should be said about the means of campaigning. Most campaign tactics—leafleting, paid media advertising, speeches, debates, and so on—do not merit any comment; while they may be unethical under certain circumstances, normally they are not. But some techniques deserve special attention.

In recent years it has become quite common for campaigns to hire so-called "opposition research firms," political consultants charged with finding any information that might be in the public record regarding an opponent. The firms look at voting records of candidates who have previously held elective office, credit ratings, tax filings, divorce records, campaign finance reports, any and all information that can be made available to the public. Such efforts lower the level of campaigning; they are essentially looking for anything at all to exploit rather than assessing if some information on an opponent's personal life is relevant. The practice serves no positive purpose and, while certainly legal, is ethically inappropriate.

Second, and equally reprehensible, is the practice of push polling. Push polls are conducted by telephone and seek to implant doubt in the voter's mind about an opponent. "Would you be more likely to vote for or against Candidate X if you knew he had been accused of failure to pay child support?" The question does not say that the opponent has failed to pay child support, or even that he has been so accused. But the implication is there and the seed of doubt is planted. Push polls have appeared in various campaigns in recent years. Often the polling firm is an independent contractor from a different region of the country than the voters it is contacting. The organization sponsoring these polls is all but impossible to ascertain.[23] The practice is reprehensible and should be denounced in the strongest possible terms. Candidates willing to have push polls used in their campaigns fail to meet the most rudimentary tests of ethical behavior.

Conclusions

Is it possible to set standards for candidate ethics during a campaign? Perhaps before answering this question we should point to some difficulties. First, this problem is not a new one. Candidates since the beginning of the Republic have attacked their opponents on personal grounds, criteria unrelated to the duties of the office sought. When James G. Blaine ran for president against Grover Cleveland, his campaign slogan was "Ma, Ma, where's my Pa? He's in the White House, Ha! Ha! Ha!" And the response quickly came back, "Blaine, Blaine, James G. Blaine! Continental liar from the State of Maine!" It is difficult to think of a more disingenuous campaign slogan than Woodrow Wilson's claim in 1916: "He kept us out of war!" Not for long. The examples of personal attacks and half-truths in campaigns throughout the nation's history could fill books (and have).

Furthermore, we should point out that all things are not what they seem. Should a candidate be blamed for changing his mind on an issue because circumstances have changed? Many analysts claim that George H. W. Bush lost his reelection bid in 1992 because he went back on the promise made during his acceptance speech at the 1988 Republican National Convention, "The Congress will push me to raise taxes, and I'll say no, they'll push and I'll say no, and they'll push again. And all I can say to them is: Read my lips: no new taxes."[24] His words were clear; the context was specified; and the time between his promise and his reneging on the promise was short—eighteen months. Perhaps he deserved his fate, because he knew, or should have known, that he was making a pledge he could not keep and was courting voters based on that pledge.[25]

But was Bush's action really so different from that of Franklin Delano Roosevelt, who pledged in a speech in Pittsburgh in 1932 that he would balance the budget if he were elected president? Upon taking office, FDR was won over to the side of Keynesian economics and the desirability of deficit spending to combat the Great Depression. When FDR asked his aides how he could justify that action in light of his campaign promise in the Pittsburgh speech, Samuel I. Rosenman reports that he replied, "Mr. President, the only thing you can say about that 1932 speech is to deny categorically that you ever made it."[26] To be sure, there were differences. Roosevelt was spouting accepted doctrine in his Pittsburgh speech, not staking claim to a position that would distinguish him from his opponent. And evidence certainly points to the fact that he did not knowingly deceive the public; he believed what he said and had not engaged in extended debate over whether it was in fact true. But FDR did not keep his promise and was praised for his flexibility; George H. W. Bush reneged on his and was vilified. The lines are not easy to draw.[27]

Having said that, we as a society can do better. We can expect more of our candidates; we can demand more of our candidates. And candidates should expect more of themselves. Many candidates around the country have pledged to run clean campaigns and have been successful. Those who have shunned entreaties to go negative, even at difficult times in their campaigns, are especially deserving of praise.

A number of state bar associations, including those of Pennsylvania and Delaware, have proposed codes of ethics for judicial campaigns. In Maine, the Institute of Global Ethics, the Margaret Chase Smith Library, and the Margaret Chase Smith Institute for Public Policy at the University of Southern Maine proposed a code of election ethics that has been in place since 1996 and has been signed by all candidates for congressional and statewide office in the last three election cycles.

The Maine Code of Election Ethics is based on three assumptions—that negativism and attack advertising demean representative democracy; that negative campaigns contribute to citizen cynicism, alienation, and decreasing participation; and that candidates should be responsible for their own campaigns. The code specifies that campaigns will be based on four principles: (1) honesty and fairness, including not employing surrogates to use subtle deceptions or half-truths and denouncing those who do so without the candidate's knowledge; (2) respect for one's opponent, including no use or permitting of personal attacks, innuendo, or stereotyping; (3) acceptance of responsibility by the candidate for the actions of campaign staffers and for openness and publicity in discussing issues frankly and sincerely, including any criticism of the opponent; and (4) compassion for the opponent, including recognition that a candidate's behavior in a campaign affects the integrity of the society in which the election is held.[28]

Like most codes of ethics, this one carries no enforcement mechanisms (see chapters 2 and 9 for two other codes of ethics); however, citizens are encouraged to report violations to a toll-free number. While no one who has lived in Maine during the last three election cycles would rate them as flawless, the level of negativity has seemed to decrease and the extent to which the campaigns are issue-oriented has increased. These are clearly good signs. But not many states run elections on as high a level as those in Maine are run.

In the final analysis, there is little in the Maine Code of Election Ethics, nor in any other code of ethics, that one would not hope candidates would do on their own. That is, we expect our political candidates to act ethically, to act in a manner to bring credit to the process in which they participate and to the office they seek to hold, to work to better representative democracy. Not all candidates meet these expectations. One test of the success of a civil society such as ours is the extent to which we reject those who do not meet our expectations. To date, we have not passed that test. But the fact that we are asking the questions and discussing the issues is a hopeful sign.

Notes

1. I should note explicitly that I am *not* going to be discussing the ethical questions raised by our system of campaign financing. That topic has been dealt with more than adequately by many others.

2. I could equally well have drawn on an advertisement the Republicans also ran that attacked Dukakis's record on the environment and was also criticized for inaccuracies and misrepresentation.

3. Jules Witcover, *The Year the Dream Died: Revisiting 1968 in America* (Warner Books, 1997).

4. Dennis F. Thompson, *Political Ethics and Public Office* (Harvard University Press, 1987), pp. 1–6; Dennis F. Thompson, *Ethics in Congress: From Individual to Institutional Corruption* (Brookings, 1995).

5. Thompson, *Political Ethics and Public Office*, p. 1.

6. For the purpose of this chapter, I am not going to deal with the differences between those elections in which an incumbent is running and those in which there is no open seat. While evidence from those who study voting behavior is mixed, we will assume for the point of argument that candidates are judged by their past performance in other offices or by policies of their parties if they themselves have not held office.

7. Sissela Bok, *Lying* (Random House, 1979), chs. 1 and 2.

8. See also J. A. Barnes, *A Pack of Lies* (Cambridge University Press, 1994).

9. Morris P. Fiorina, *Retrospective Voting in American National Elections* (Yale University Press, 1981).

10. For a record of presidential campaign promises and performance, see Jeff Fishel, *Presidents and Promises* (CQ Press, 1985); see also Kelly Patterson, "Political Parties, Candidates, and Presidential Campaigns, 1952–1996," *Presidential Studies Quarterly,* vol. 29 (1999), p. 26.

11. Cynicism follows if a candidate makes a promise that cannot be measured. What did the hypothetical candidate cited above mean by "improve the quality of education"? Spend more money? Hire more teachers? Raise test scores? If a promise is so vague that a successful candidate can always find data to demonstrate that the promise has been fulfilled, the democratic values of an election have not been enhanced.

12. The term is most often used because some of the most egregious examples of unethical campaign practices of this sort are found in paid media advertising. Campaigns use this medium so that the candidate attacking his or her opponent is not deemed personally responsible for the attacks made; some anonymous announcer, not the candidate, makes the damning claims.

13. William G. Mayer, "In Defense of Negative Campaigning," *Political Science Quarterly*, vol. 111 (Fall 1996), p. 441.

14. John Franzen, "Common Sense on Going Negative," *Campaigns & Elections* (September 1995), p. 7.

15. It should go without saying, but cannot, that the time for such discussions is *before* the questionable act is taken, not after.

16. Ronald D. Elving, "'Accentuate the Negative': Contemporary Congressional Campaigns," *PS: Political Science and Politics,* vol. 29 (September 1999), pp. 440–47.

17. Ibid., p. 443.

18. Ibid., p. 443.

19. Thompson, *Political Ethics and Public Office*, p. 123.

20. Ibid., p. 132.

21. Richard K. Scher, *The Modern Political Campaign: Mudslinging, Bombast, and the Vitality of American Politics* (New York: M. E. Sharpe, 1997), p. 17.

22. See Stephen Ansolabehere and Shanto Iyengar, *Going Negative: How Political Advertisements Shrink and Polarize the Electorate* (Free Press, 1995); Karen S. Johnson-Cartee and Gary A. Copeland, *Negative Political Advertising* (Hillsdale, Calif.: Laurence Earlbaum, 1991); Darrell M. West, *Air Wars*, 2d ed. (CQ Press, 1997); but see also Richard R. Lau and others, "The Effects of Negative Political Advertisement," *American Political Science Review,* vol. 93, no. 4 (1999), pp. 851–75.

23. Elving, "'Accentuate the Negative,'" p. 440.

24. George H. W. Bush, "Our Work's Not Done, Our Force Is Not Spent," *Washington Post*, August 18, 1988, p. A28.

25. Stephen Skowronek, *The Politics Presidents Make* (Cambridge, Mass.: Belknap Press, 1993).

26. Samuel I. Rosenman, *Working with Roosevelt* (Harper & Brothers, 1952).

27. I am indebted to David Shribman for reminding me of the Roosevelt example.

28. The text of the Maine Code of Election Ethics is available online at www.campaignconduct.org/research/poster.html (March 21, 2002).

CHAPTER FOUR

CANDIDATES

Winning Ethically

L. DALE LAWTON

WILLIAM H. WOOD

When those of us at the Sorensen Institute for Political Leadership tell people that we run a program designed to teach campaign ethics and practical strategy to novice political candidates, they usually respond with an incredulous smile. We hear a lot of obvious jokes. "A class on campaign ethics? Must be a short course!" Put simply, many people are skeptical about the subject of campaign ethics. Contrast this popular sentiment with our actual experience working in Virginia with novice candidates. Since 1997 the Sorensen Institute's Project on Campaign Conduct[1] has been working to develop and test a unique candidate-training program designed to place high-quality instruction on the nuts and bolts of running a political campaign within a framework of campaign ethics and public responsibility.

This and other programs at the Sorensen Institute have allowed more than three hundred Virginians to take part in training programs and have given us an opportunity to learn a great deal from men and women who are considering a more active role in public life. We have found that the vast majority of participants in our programs who become candidates decide to put forth the tremendous effort required to run because they are convinced that their vision of the future is the best for their communities. They are ambitious and competitive, they have strong egos, and they want to win. But generally, they want to win because they want to serve. Of course, not every candidate participates in our program, so our experience may not be representative of all new candidates. And some candidates who do participate are clearly more interested in serving themselves than in serving the public. However, our knowledge of this group is reflective of our broader experience with a full range of candidates—they are most often driven by their commitment to public service.

Candidates' commitment to a vision of how the future should be, coupled with a desire to win, frequently brings them face-to-face with a very difficult set of ethical questions. In the course of a campaign, all candidates decide—consciously or unconsciously—just how far they will go to make sure that their vision carries the day. The decisions they make affect not only their own candidacy, family, and supporters but also the opponent and his or her family and friends and members of the public at large. While other participants (such as the media, the parties, and so on) may play a role in determining both the actual tone of a campaign and how the campaign will be perceived, the candidate must shoulder much of that responsibility alone.

Like Sandy Maisel in the preceding chapter, we begin with the assumption that most candidates take that responsibility seriously and want to be ethical. Most ethical problems in campaigns arise for one of two reasons: either candidates have never thought much about ethics in campaigning and are unprepared when faced with tough choices or, when it comes right down to it, they want to win more than they want to be ethical. Since there is little we can do about the minority of candidates who fall into the second group, we will focus our attention on the ethically unprepared candidates.

In this chapter we provide a blueprint for candidates who want to be ethically responsible as well as electorally competitive. Building on Maisel's chapter, we outline the basic elements of an ethical election campaign and examine the role that candidates should play in fostering such campaigns. Next, we discuss some evidence about how well candidates are currently fulfilling that role. Finally, we offer some suggestions to candidates and citizens aimed at helping them incorporate ethics into strategically sound campaigns.

Ethics in Political Campaigning

What is an ethical campaign? Perhaps we should take a step back: What do we mean by *ethics*?[2] Ethics can be defined as "obedience to the unenforceable."[3] An ethical person is someone who conforms to the unwritten rules of decency—the behaviors that people expect of one another—even if there is no formal sanction for failing to abide by these rules. While in most cases it would be unethical to violate the law, ethics goes beyond the written law and its penalties. Thus when we are talking about campaign ethics, we mean more than mere compliance with the few laws that govern campaign behavior. In fact, outside of the rules governing campaign finances, filing requirements, and a few other logistical elements of running for office, the law requires very little of political candidates. The vast majority of campaign activity falls outside the sphere of law, squarely into the more vague set of rules governing ethical behavior.

In the absence of law, can we provide some guidelines for what campaign ethics ought to be? In his chapter, Sandy Maisel suggests that the basis for such guidelines can be found by looking at why we have election campaigns in the first place, "so that citizens can judge the record of those in office against the prospects of what would be done by those seeking office." Based on this definition, he develops three standards for ethical campaigning: (1) a candidate should campaign vigorously to provide citizens with information about why he or she should be elected over the opponent; (2) a candidate should not act in ways that infringe on citizens' ability to make an informed choice among candidates; and (3) a candidate should not engage in behavior that undermines confidence in the electoral system.

The difficulty for candidates lies in the tension between the first two standards, which in a sense represent the primary goal of a candidate in a campaign (to win) versus the primary goal of a citizen (to make an informed choice). The candidate wants to win and, as the campaign progresses, will frequently begin to feel the *responsibility* to win. Supporters have spent time and money; they believe in the candidate and the things that he or she can accomplish in office. A political party or political action committee may also get involved, providing advice, organization, and cash. As these resources mount, the candidate may justifiably feel he or she has an obligation to these supporters and may feel ethically bound to fulfill that obligation by working to the utmost to win.

A key part of a winning campaign plan will include strategies for managing information about the candidate and the opponent. The winning candidate must provide enough of the right kinds of information to convince the voters that he or she deserves to be elected and that the opponent does not. The average citizen, however, wants primarily to gather enough information to make an informed choice. Since most voters are not personally invested in the election of one candidate over the other, they try to make their decisions based on which candidate will best serve their interests. While the media might provide some information about candidates, the public must rely to a large degree on information provided by the candidates themselves. To some extent, even the news media are dependent on the candidates and their surrogates for information beyond what is available in the public record.

Information is clearly the currency of the campaign world. Campaigns spend the vast majority of their resources providing information to the public. Voters spend most of the small amount of time they dedicate to campaigns to collecting information about the candidates. And what raises the ethical stakes in this flow of information is that most of the temptations for candidates to be unethical involve the choices they make about what and how they will present information—or misinformation.

What information should candidates use and how should they use it? Is it enough to be factual? These questions can be readily answered by Maisel's third standard or by referring to Stanley Kelley Jr.'s work, as Miller and Medvic do in chapter 2.[4] Providing details disguised as genuine information about the opponent that are false, misleading (even if factually true), or irrelevant[5] to the voters' decision should be considered unethical. Such tactics fail on two counts: they do not help citizens make informed choices, as Kelley's standards demand, and they violate Maisel's third standard by adding to the environment of public distrust that already surrounds candidates and campaigns.

The Role of Candidates in Fostering Ethical Campaigns

What is the candidate's role in fostering the kind of campaign we have just described? In a modern campaign, the candidate is only one participant among many, as the other chapters in this volume illustrate. The public is bombarded with campaign information from many different sources. In addition to the campaign ads, mailers, speeches, yard signs, bumper stickers, websites, and door-to-door visits that the candidates themselves make, both parties get in the mix with ads, mailers, telephone banks, and get-out-the-vote canvassing. Additionally, interest groups might weigh in with TV and radio ads or mailers. And finally, the news media cover the whole morass in print, radio, and TV reports.

Candidates frequently express frustration at the degree to which other people or groups have control over what happens in the course of "their" campaign. Former U.S. senator Chuck Robb (D-Va.), who lost his seat in the 2000 elections, recently told the authors that of the twenty-six ads aired in support of his candidacy, he had been directly involved in producing only two or three of them. While this example may not be representative of all candidacies, it serves to underscore the point: candidates cannot control everything that happens during an election campaign. With that said, however, candidates do play a major role in determining the ethical environment of their campaign. And equally important, the public expects candidates to be responsible for things that occur during a race.

While the candidate is only one player in the electoral game, he or she can, at a minimum, assume responsibility for the actions of his or her own campaign. As part of our candidate-training programs, participants draft a set of guidelines they will use to keep their campaign running well—both strategically and ethically. A recurring theme in these guidelines is personal responsibility. Virtually all of our candidates agree that they should take responsibility for the actions of their campaign, even actions taken without their direct knowledge.

Good candidates recognize this concept as strategically necessary as well as ethically sound. Consider, for example, the incident described in chapter 1, when U.S. senator John Warner's reelection campaign used a doctored photograph in a television commercial. Under pressure, the media consultant disclosed that he had digitally altered the picture to show Warner's opponent in a bad light. The important point here is that after some initial quibbling about who was responsible for the ad, which was paid for by the National Republican Senatorial Committee, *Warner* accepted full responsibility. In a press conference called the day after the allegations surfaced, Warner fired the media consultant, ordered that the ad be removed from the air, and apologized to his opponent and voters in Virginia: "Although I had nothing to do with it, knew nothing about it [beforehand], I accept the responsibility, and I extend an apology to all Virginia voters."[6]

Candidates foster ethical campaigns when they take their ultimate responsibility seriously, setting a standard of conduct for themselves and their campaign staff and sticking to it, even when victory seems tantalizingly close or in the face of inevitable defeat. When candidates fail to develop a standard of conduct for their campaign or do not follow through on their personal standard, it can be an ethical disaster waiting to happen.

A race we are familiar with provides a good illustration. A candidate we will call Gina Smith,[7] a challenger in a race for the state legislature, found herself within striking distance of her opponent in the final weeks of the campaign. Tracking polls showed her gaining ground but probably not quickly enough to close the gap before Election Day. Sensing possible victory, the state party had poured resources into the campaign: money, consultants, direct mail, and a campaign manager. Although Smith was a first-time candidate, she had managed to secure the endorsement of the local newspaper as well as financial backing from many prominent members of the community.

Approximately two weeks before Election Day, Smith's campaign manager proposed a direct mail piece on partial-birth abortion as a means of gathering support and feeding the get-out-the-vote effort. There was a catch—while Smith's staff thought they were familiar with the opponent's position on the issue, they were not completely certain. This triggered a bizarre sequence of events.

The consultants prepared the direct mail piece based on their assumptions about the opponent's position. Meanwhile, Smith's campaign manager called the opponent's campaign and asked what their candidate's position was on partial-birth abortion. The person who answered the call did not know but promised to find out and call back. But the wait proved too long for Smith's campaign. Time was running short and—after some intense discussion—the candidate reluctantly agreed to mail the piece before hearing back from the opponent's camp.

After the piece was mailed, the opponent called back—his position was clearly different from the one implied in the mailer. Soon thereafter, the press got the story and the newspaper took the unusual step of withdrawing its endorsement. Smith's poll numbers began to slip, and she lost handily at the ballot box.

After it was all over, Smith expressed frustration and shame for letting others convince her to do something that she felt all along was the wrong thing to do. She said she felt pressured by many factors: the narrowing gap in the polls, her own desire to win, and her supporters' efforts. Above all, Smith said that she felt pressure generated by the tremendous investment of time and resources that the party had made. Lacking personal political experience, she felt some obligation to listen to the party's consultants and campaign manager and rely on their experience. She allowed their arguments about the strategic value of the decision to overcome her uncertainty about the ethics of the advertisement. Failing to rely on her own sense of ethics and fair play may have cost Smith the election. It certainly exacted a terrible toll on her reputation; her supporters were embarrassed and surprised at her actions, and her own hopes for elected office were crushed. Had she simply lost a close fight, Smith could have immediately begun to prepare for another round. Instead, her postelection efforts were aimed at damage control and regaining a sense of trust.

This story illustrates another important point for candidates; contrary to popular belief, most consultants we know are generally ethical people. However, consultants are paid to give strategic advice on how to win elections, not ethical advice on how to choose among available tactics. The best thing to do strategically may not be the best thing to do ethically, and the candidate must make those choices.[8]

While frequently consultants get the blame for initiating unethical strategies, perhaps just as often they are used as scapegoats for unsound ideas that originated with the candidate. Regardless of the origin of a television ad or other campaign tactic, candidates' chief role in fostering ethical campaigns should be to filter out strategies that violate the minimum ethical standards outlined by Maisel or a personal standard developed by the candidates themselves.

Beyond this minimum standard, candidates can play a role in encouraging their opponents and other actors in the campaign drama to behave more ethically. Although candidates cannot control the actions of their opponents, they can publicize their own commitment to ethical campaigning and invite others to join them in pledging a clean and ethical campaign. As mentioned in the previous chapter, some candidates have worked with groups such as the Institute for Global Ethics, a nonprofit organization based in Maine that encourages ethical awareness, to develop a set of ethical standards that will govern their behavior during the campaign.

Many candidates are now faced with mounting campaign involvement from well-financed interest groups. This poses potential problems for at least two reasons. First, candidates have no control over what these groups say or how they say it. By law, candidates cannot coordinate their efforts with interest groups. Second, interest group advertising tends to be harder-hitting than most candidate-sponsored ads. Research by the Sorensen Institute on the 2000 race for the U.S. Senate in Virginia found that, on average, citizens perceive interest group ads as more negative, less fair, and less honest than ads developed by the candidates (see figure 4-1).[9] Voters may struggle to distinguish between candidate-sponsored ads and group-sponsored ads, leading to confusion about who is responsible.

While they do not have direct control, some candidates have denounced advertising produced by interest groups that they feel is misleading or

Figure 4-1. *Perceptions of Ads by Sponsor: 2000 U.S. Senate Race in Virginia*

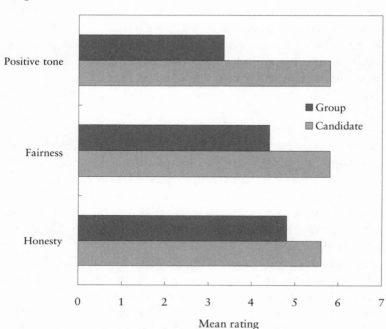

Mean rating

Source: Authors' calculations.

damaging to the electorate, even when the ads purportedly favor them. Others have asked interest groups not to advertise at all in their race. These kinds of actions may help sensitize voters to the problem and encourage them to make distinctions between candidate- and group-sponsored ads.

Candidates' Performance in Fostering Ethical Campaigns

How candidates are really doing at fostering ethical campaigns is only part of the question. The other, possibly more important, part of the question is one of perception: How does the public *think* that candidates are doing? Unfortunately, the public has a pretty low opinion of candidates and how they run campaigns. Public opinion polls, quotes in the newspaper, and conversations around the watercooler all tell the same story: Most Americans do not like political campaigns; they see them as a necessary evil or a legal blood sport. Few consider them the educational and motivational experiences of democratic lore.

A national survey conducted in 1999 illustrates the point. Nearly 60 percent of Americans strongly agreed that "negative, attack-oriented campaigning is damaging and undermining our democracy." Two-thirds (67 percent) strongly agreed that this type of campaigning is "wrong" and nearly as many (61 percent) strongly agreed that it is "unethical." A majority (53 percent) reported believing that in terms of ethics and values, campaigns have gotten at least somewhat worse over the past twenty years. Candidate behavior fuels the skepticism. Of those surveyed, 43 percent believed that most or all candidates deliberately make unfair attacks, while nearly as many (39 percent) believed that most or all candidates lie in the course of their campaigns.[10]

Public opinion data collected during the 2000 presidential race provides additional cause for concern about campaigns. According to a report for Harvard University's Shorenstein Center released just before that year's November election, nearly 70 percent of those surveyed said that "modern campaigns seem more like theater or entertainment than something to be taken seriously." And just over 70 percent agreed that "candidates are more concerned with fighting each other than with solving the nation's problems."[11]

At a minimum, political candidates face a tremendous public image problem; most people expect them to be dishonest, self-centered, and willing to do just about anything to get elected. Given this expectation, if one or two candidates have highly publicized ethical lapses each election cycle, public opinion is confirmed and people feel justified in their mass dismissal of candidates as bottom-feeders.

The nature of campaign news coverage only exacerbates the image problem. Scandal, like plane crashes, provokes news coverage. And just as news organizations rarely run stories headlined "Millions of Passengers Arrive Safely at Their Destinations Today," they are unlikely to devote much coverage to the fact that hundreds or thousands of candidates and consultants run clean and ethical campaigns each year.

Since each election cycle produces fresh instances of candidates meeting low public expectations, the public image problem will likely continue. Setting aside the problem of perception, though, how are candidates actually doing at fostering ethical campaigns? We have suggested that the primary things that candidates can do is to make sure that their own behavior and that of their campaign staff is ethical. Are candidates themselves behaving ethically? There has been very little systematic study of candidate behavior, and we are not aware of any research that attempts to study the ethical behavior of candidates. As we have noted above, it is easy to find examples in the news of candidates who are unethical. It is not even terribly difficult to find examples of candidates who have been applauded for conducting very ethical campaigns. But are candidates as a group running ethical campaigns, or is the public image of ethically challenged candidates justified?

One source of information on the subject is a survey of state legislative candidates conducted as part of a joint project of the University of Maryland and *Campaigns & Elections* magazine.[12] Men and women who had been candidates in the last four years were asked about several "practices that sometimes occur during a campaign." The results provide some evidence that, at least in the abstract, candidates hold views similar to those of the general public about what is right and wrong in a campaign context. For example, 65 percent felt that "focusing primarily on the negative personal characteristics of [the] opponent rather than on the issues" would be clearly unethical. Similarly, 64 percent of candidates said it would be unethical to make statements "that are factually true, but . . . taken out of context," while virtually all (99 percent) agreed that it would be unethical to make statements that "are factually untrue." Further, 70 percent indicated that it would be clearly unethical to "try to decrease voter turnout among certain groups" through the use of negative advertising.

These responses provide some evidence that, at least in response to a survey, a majority of state legislative candidates make ethical choices. Of course, the survey results also provide considerable support for the public's skepticism about candidates. Approximately one-third of the candidates surveyed were unwilling to say that it would be clearly unethical to make negative personal attacks, take facts out of context, or intentionally try to diminish turnout to gain electoral advantage. Each of these kinds of actions would clearly violate Maisel's proposed standards and, we suspect, would be considered unethical by a much larger majority of the general public.

Without more complete evidence, it is difficult to speak generally about how candidates are doing at fostering ethical campaigns. Based on our experience and the evidence at hand, we suspect that few candidates start out with limited or no ethical standards and a win-at-all-costs mentality. We also believe, however, that very few candidates have given the topic much thought. Follow-up conversations and focus groups conducted with participants in our candidate-training program provide evidence for this belief. Almost universally, candidates tell us that they had never thought much about the ethical dimension of running for office.

One of the first things that most candidates do is draft a campaign plan that includes details about message development, delivery, fundraising, and so on. Ideally, the plan lays out the steps that must be followed to take the candidate from the starting line to victory. In all this detailed planning, however, very few candidates give any consideration to elements other than tactics. This intense focus on garnering 50-percent-plus-one of the available votes can leave candidates unprepared for the ethical questions they are likely to face during the course of the campaign. The single-minded search for votes may cause even well-intentioned candidates to push all other concerns down to a lower priority. The first question becomes "Can it help me win?" followed distantly (if at all) by the question "Is this a good thing to do for me and my community?" Once a candidate becomes convinced that a particular tactic will help carry the day, it becomes that much easier to justify pushing forward even if the idea seems questionable.

When faced with a difficult choice, novice candidates frequently lack the political experience to understand the full repercussions of each decision. They are inclined to make difficult decisions on the fly, relying heavily on the advice of more experienced consultants and friends. In this kind of situation, candidates find it easy to believe that the ends justify the means. After all, they've been reminded a hundred times: You cannot govern if you do not win.

Improving Image and Performance

Candidates do play an important role in fostering ethical campaigns, and many do a good job at it. However, given the public's skepticism about office seekers and campaigns, candidates must be doubly cautious in their campaign behavior or risk deepening cynicism among the electorate. We believe that candidates can run campaigns that are clean and ethical, as well as being strategically sound, and that citizens can encourage ethical campaigning in their area.

Candidates

When candidates ask for votes they are, in essence, asking for public trust. The first step candidates must take toward solving the twin problems of public perception and campaign practice is to recognize this broader definition of political candidacy. The candidate's desire to win must be firmly placed in the context of the public good. Within this broader context,

candidates should consider the kind of campaign that they want to run—
not just strategically but also ethically. In our candidate-training programs,
we begin by asking new candidates to consider their core values. Inevitably, ideas like fairness, integrity, compassion, and responsibility emerge.
With these core values in mind, we work with candidates to develop a
personal code of campaign ethics that can serve as a guide for the candidate and staff during the campaign.

Only after candidates have considered their candidacies in this broader
sense and developed a draft code of ethics do we proceed to presentations
focused on the nuts and bolts of running for office. During three days of
intensive presentations, candidates alternate between classes with high-
quality political consultants and small-group discussions. The small-group
discussions give the candidates a chance to reconcile the tactical knowledge gained from the classes with their personal code of ethics to produce
a campaign plan that integrates both. Thus strategy is developed within
the framework of ethics rather than the other way around. Candidates
are then confronted with decisionmaking exercises based on actual campaign situations that allow them to test and refine their personal codes.

While few candidates have considered ethics before attending our work-
shop, postprogram evaluations confirm that the sessions on campaign ethics
consistently rate higher than any of our other sessions on strategy and
organization. Even the initially skeptical participants generally depart with
at least the idea that ethics can be useful strategically. One first-time candidate summed it up like this: "Good ethics is good politics."

We suggest this as a model for all candidates. Candidates should begin
by considering those values that form the core of their belief system. Based
on these core values, candidates should construct a personal code of campaign ethics that briefly describes the kind of candidate they want to be.
With this in place, aspiring candidates should begin to consider the kinds
of difficult decisions that they are likely to confront during their campaign, possibly consulting case studies of other campaigns to learn more
about the real pressures of campaigning. As they consider different situations and decisions, candidates can ask themselves: What would I do in
this case? What does my code of ethics suggest?

Having developed a personal code and considered what the future has
in store for them, candidates are better prepared both to act more ethically and to develop an image as an ethical candidate. This personal commitment by candidates will not only improve campaign conduct, but candidates who take this commitment seriously can reap the benefits of the
good publicity. And publicity about candidates making a serious effort to

raise the ethical bar might help rehabilitate the shattered image of political candidates. Provided, of course, that they follow through with actions.

We do not view ethical campaigning as a type of unilateral disarmament. An effective campaign must integrate both an ethical foundation and a sound campaign strategy. Candidates still must raise money, develop and deliver campaign messages, discuss the issues, and tell the voters why they should vote for them. We firmly believe that the strategic goals of the best-run campaign can be met within the framework of an ethical campaign. Will making difficult decisions sometimes lead to defeat at the ballot box? Probably. But we also believe that a victory gained through unethical tactics will ring hollow for the candidate and for American democracy.

Citizens

While candidates have the major role in fostering ethical campaign behavior, citizens share that responsibility, as Traugott's chapter 13 and Rourke's chapter 14 expand upon. Citizens have what candidates most want: resources and votes. Voters can use this leverage to get the attention of candidates and let them know that they expect candidates to run clean and ethical campaigns. Using the standards that Maisel has suggested (or standards that candidates might develop and adopt themselves), citizens can hold candidates responsible for their actions during a campaign. Concerned voters should tell candidates when they cross ethical lines by calling the campaign, writing letters to the editor of the local newspaper, and encouraging others to do the same. If candidates see that citizens are less likely to give their resources and votes to unethical candidates, they will be more likely to change their behavior.

Conclusion

In the past, candidate success has been judged almost entirely at the ballot box. In this chapter, we have argued that the definition ought to be expanded. Current levels of public discontent with campaigns strongly suggest that candidates should look for ways to both improve campaign behavior and rehabilitate the image of those who participate in politics. Careful ethical planning, as a companion to careful strategic planning, encourages candidates to consider their strategic decisions from a broader perspective. In a democracy where cynicism about politics continues to grow, *how* a candidate runs may be just as important as the final ballot count.

Notes

1. The Sorensen Institute's Project on Campaign Conduct is funded by a grant from The Pew Charitable Trusts.

2. See chapter 2 for a detailed discussion of the meaning of ethics.

3. Lord Moulton, a judge and member of the British Parliament in the early twentieth century, as cited in Rushworth M. Kidder, *How Good People Make Tough Choices: Resolving the Dilemmas of Ethical Living* (Simon & Schuster, 1995). The authors are indebted to Brad Rourke from the Institute for Global Ethics for this citation.

4. Stanley Kelley Jr., *Political Campaigning: Problems in Creating an Informed Electorate* (Brookings, 1960). Kelley argued that campaign discussion should be judged by whether it aids voters in making a rational voting choice. Miller and Medvic provide an overview of Kelley's thinking and a listing of his excellent qualitative tests for examining the quality of campaign discourse.

5. Of course the question of relevance is very subjective. Often a candidate can examine his or her motive for releasing the information. If the motive is to hurt the opponent, the candidate may also want to consider the damage it will do to an already skeptical public. Likewise if candidates are unwilling to release the information themselves for fear of repercussions, they may want to leak it to the press or pass it to a surrogate for release.

6. Spencer Hsu, "John Warner Fires Consultant Who Altered Challenger's Photo in Ad," *Washington Post,* October 11, 1996, p. B1, final edition.

7. Some details are withheld to protect the identities of those involved, including changing names where necessary.

8. On this dilemma with respect to consultants, see chapter 5 in this volume.

9. Mean perceptions were calculated from Internet evaluations of fifty-three of the fifty-four ads aired during the 2000 Virginia Senate race. In all, more than a thousand citizens participated in the evaluations, conducted between October 2000 and January 2001. Additional information about the study and the impact of perception on voting behavior can be found in: Dale Lawton and Paul Freedman, "Beyond Negativity: Advertising Effects in the 2000 Virginia Senate Race" (paper presented at the annual meeting of the Midwest Political Science Association, Chicago, April 19–22, 2001).

10. 1999 Civic Values Survey, sponsored by the Institute for Global Ethics' Project on Campaign Conduct. The report is available online at www.campaignconduct.org/polling/polling-top-page.html (March 19, 2002).

11. Shorenstein Center, "Americans Who Say They Will Vote on Tuesday Share Many of the Same Attitudes as Likely Non-Voters" (November 4, 2000; www.vanishingvoter.org/releases/11-04-00.shtml [March 19, 2002]).

12. The Campaign Assessment and Candidate Outreach project sponsored the survey. The complete survey results are available online at www.campaignline.com/survey.cfm (March 19, 2002).

CHAPTER FIVE

POLITICAL CONSULTANTS

Hired Guns or Gatekeepers of Democracy?

CANDICE J. NELSON

STEPHEN K. MEDVIC

DAVID A. DULIO

There has been a great deal of hand-wringing about the state of contemporary campaigns in the United States. While much of the criticism has come from journalists, academics have offered their share of complaints as well.[1] More often than not, political consultants are identified as a primary source of all that plagues our system of elections.[2] In fact, their deleterious effects are not just confined to U.S. elections; American consultants are also accused of "interference in the sovereign affairs of other nations."[3] So disgusted was the *Washington Post* with the behavior of consultants that it likened the obsession with their techniques to a disease—"consultantitis."[4]

This chapter examines the ethical responsibilities of political consultants and the ethical nature of the consulting industry. We begin by discussing frameworks that can be applied to the consultant's role in campaigns and identify some of the ways in which consultants can fall short of the ethical ideal. Next, we report on what consultants themselves think of the industry's ethical standards. Finally, we explore ways in which consultants might be held accountable for their actions.

Self-Interest versus Civic Responsibility

Whether one believes that consultants are harmful to the American electoral system probably depends on what one thinks the basic objective of a political campaign should be. Two standards that were described in detail in chapter 2—self-interest and civic responsibility—can be applied to the role of consultants. In essence, the question is: Should consultants serve their candidates only, or are they also responsible for the broader political process; are they merely campaign advocates or must they be defenders of the common good?

The advocacy perspective applies to political consultants more than most of the campaign actors described in this book, and they are often willing to acknowledge their adherence to it. In describing his work for President Clinton, Dick Morris, whose willingness to work for candidates in both parties is atypical, reflects the view of many consultants when he writes, "I had no agenda other than victory."[5] James Carville is equally blunt when he argues,

> I am a political professional. I am paid to win races. Without break-ing any laws, or lying, or appealing to people on the basis of bigotry, I have one agenda: to win. Let me say it again: The cause and pur-pose of a political campaign is to win the election. I will represent the interest of my campaign and my candidate as ferociously as I can, and I'll be equally aggressive in defending even the things I don't think are too good about him. The bottom line is, My guy is better than the other guy. If you're looking for somebody objective, don't talk to me.[6]

Occasionally, defenders of the industry make the case that consultants are actually *good* for democracy. Consultant Rob Allyn offers a list of the positive contributions consultants make to our political system, including making complicated issues easier to grasp for voters, serving as "gatekeepers for the republic" by weeding out ineffective candidates, telling "truths that the system hides," and keeping campaigns "on the high road."[7]

More often one hears consultants arguing that what they do is ethi-cally neutral. "To me," argued Joseph Napolitan, "a political consultant is *a specialist in political communication*. That's all there is to it, and I don't think it's anything very macabre or Machiavellian."[8] While not go-ing so far as to say that the presence of professional consultants in demo-cratic elections is automatically good or beneficial, many argue that they are no worse than the party operatives of a bygone era.[9] Indeed, an argu-ment can be made that by bringing rationality to what is a dynamic and complex process, consultants are in a position to help candidates, voters, and even political parties.[10] As such, consultants have at least the potential to actually enhance democracy. For example, consultants help candidates focus their campaign messages and communicate with voters in a very efficient manner and in a way that voters can easily remember. In turn, voters can benefit from consultants' use of communication techniques. While consultants are often criticized for bringing incivility into elections in the form of "negative" advertisements, such ads may be the most helpful to voters during the course of a campaign. Recent work by Kathleen Hall Jamieson shows that what many consider to be "negative" ads—what Jamieson and her colleagues call "attack" and "contrast" ads—contain more useful policy and issue content than do purely positive (or what they call "advocacy") ads.[11]

This is not to say that consultants have not crossed the line in advertising or other parts of a campaign. But while we often hear about the rogue consultant who appears to have no ethical standards, we rarely hear about the instances when the electorate was informed by a hard-hitting contrast ad that clearly laid out two candidates' positions on an important issue. From the self-interest perspective, such activity contributes to democracy even as it attempts to help one candidate over another. The point is that the self-interest perspective does not view the mere presence of consultants as something to lament and may view them as providing a necessary service.

In many ways, it has been easy to criticize consultants and their presence in campaigns because they have long operated in the shadows. However, as this changes, and as we learn more about what it is that consultants do, what they think, and where they come from, it may become clear that consultants have something to offer democracy.[12] Similarly, before a great deal of attention was paid to organized interest groups, it was easy to say that they were detrimental to the governing process. However, that view changed somewhat after greater study of their activity. The same may happen for consultants.

According to the self-interest perspective in its pure form, as long as their activities do not violate universal moral rules (they do not lie, cheat, steal, cause physical harm, and so on), the only ethical responsibility consultants have is to run the most effective campaign possible. Simply put, consultants are to politics what attorneys are to the legal system. In an adversarial system, both are duty-bound to be the best advocates they can be for their clients.

There are numerous hypothetical examples one could invoke to show how this perspective operates in practice. Assume a consultant determined that low turnout would benefit his or her client. Assume further that the consultant knew that running a particular negative ad or creating a generally negative tone in the entire campaign would drive turnout down.[13] The self-interest perspective suggests that the consultant should not hesitate to attack (as long as the attack is truthful).

Those who criticize consultants for that type of behavior—as well as for a litany of other alleged ills—usually come from a different perspective. This camp places the public good above all else and argues that campaigners should never do anything to harm the political process or, ultimately, democracy itself. Many consultants themselves claim to take this position. Gary Nordlinger, former chair of the American Association of Political Consultants' Ethics Committee, has written that consultants "have a responsibility to the political process. Appeals to prejudice and premeditated efforts to erode confidence in the political process or suppress voter turnout are unconscionable."[14] Acknowledging that there are instances "where consultants have consciously failed to act in the best interests of an informed electorate," pollster Frank Luntz suggests that "for the most part, the leading campaign consultants are reputable, hardworking people who care not only about winning elections but also about their impact on the democratic process."[15]

Most proponents of the civic responsibility view of campaigning, however, are skeptical that consultants are concerned about the political process. For instance, critic Nicholas O'Shaughnessy maintains, "Consultants are hired propagandists: their aim is not to enrich democracy, but to influence its processes so as to win."[16] Oddly enough, the self-interest and civic responsibility perspectives come to identical empirical conclusions about what actually motivates consultants—namely, the desire to win. Where they obviously part company is in the normative judgment as to whether or not that motivation is acceptable. Clearly, the civic responsibility camp believes it is not. As Larry Sabato argues, "The political consultant rarely sees his responsibilities as extending beyond those he has to his client. And yet the political professional, as a vital and powerful actor in democracy's greatest dramas, undeniably has broader responsibilities—to the public at large, to the political process, and to the electoral system."[17]

Underlying the civic responsibility perspective, as the discussion in chapter 2 explains, is an assumption that campaigns ought to be deliberative. Stanley Kelley Jr. was one of the first to explicitly make this point. His *Professional Public Relations and Political Power* held public relations specialists to an ideal level of campaign dialogue.[18] Sounding themes he would later develop in *Political Campaigning*, Kelley suggested that the town hall meeting is the democratic ideal to which we should aspire. But contemporary campaigns do not live up to the ideal, in part because their mode of discussion falls short of the kind of debate town meetings rely upon. Debate has been sacrificed, argued Kelley, "not because of any whim of the public relations man, but because what he conceives to be sound principles of strategy usually make it desirable for one side or the other to avoid it." Rather than the give-and-take of debate, "the public relations man presents his issues as simple alternatives."[19]

More recently, Peter Levine has argued that the consultant "approach to issues militates against careful, broad-based discussion of public concerns during an election campaign."[20] Instead of a dynamic exchange of ideas, according to Levine, we get the use of "wedge issues" that create a stagnant—and simplistic—division of the electorate into camps for and against the candidates. Indeed, consultants "are adept at using rhetorical formulas that discourage reflection and discussion, that freeze public opinion in place, and that polarize and inflame voters."

Consultants are thought to harm the electoral process, not to mention democracy itself, in other ways as well. Their techniques, it is said, reduce participation, their presence in campaigns undermines accountability, and their efforts lengthen campaigns while narrowing the focus, increasing the costs and homogenizing American politics.[21] Clearly, this criticism originates out of the civic responsibility perspective. To run ethical campaigns, these and other critics would maintain, it is not enough to be loyal to the candidate and follow universal moral rules. Consultants must also consider how their every decision may affect our democratic political system.

Interestingly enough, the American Association of Political Consultants' (AAPC) Code of Professional Ethics (see chapter 2 for the complete code) draws more heavily upon the civic responsibility perspective than the self-interest position. When they join, members of the AAPC are required to sign a pledge to uphold the code though, as we will discuss later, there is no enforcement mechanism.

In its current form, the code differs considerably from the original code adopted in 1975. Consultants were originally asked to pledge to "observe the letter *and the spirit* of the laws and regulations on campaign financing and spending."[22] In addition, consultants were to "appeal to the good and commendable ideals in the American voters and not to indulge in irrational appeals." They were also supposed to "urge our candidates to sign Fair Campaign Practice Codes and to abide by their provisions." The "false or misleading attacks" that consultants are now asked to refrain from making were originally "personal and scurrilous attacks."[23] Campaign professionals were not to "represent competing or conflicting interests without the express consent of those concerned." Whereas consultants were initially required to "repudiate" those who violate the AAPC code, today they must simply "not support" those individuals or groups. Finally, and perhaps most significantly, those who signed the original code pledged to report those who "willfully ignored or circumvented" it. Today the code is not as lofty, but it does theoretically hold consultants to a fairly high standard. At least six of the nine items are partly or entirely committed to a common good beyond the narrow concern of running an effective, if clean, campaign. The others essentially require ethical business practices.

The two schools of thought, then, provide frameworks through which to view consultant activity. Deciding whether a consultant has acted ethically is a matter of determining what the standard should be. A litany of practices that could be considered unethical if judged from the civic responsibility perspective would not be so according to the self-interest standard (see the discussion in chapter 2). Of course, there will occasionally be agreement on all sides that a campaign has crossed an ethical line. Yet even in the face of an egregious campaign act, the question remains, who is responsible? More importantly for our purposes, to what extent can we hold consultants accountable for what is said and done in campaigns?

We address this in more detail below, but it should be noted here that some campaign activities bear the mark of consultants more than others. To begin with, the most misleading aspect of campaign advertising may not be the content but the technological tricks that can be played with audiovisual material. According to Lynda Lee Kaid, these include (1) editing techniques; (2) special effects; (3) visual imagery/dramatizations; (4) computerized alteration techniques; and (5) subliminal techniques.[24] Though candidates or other campaign staffers may have a hand in writing an ad's script, only the media consultant applies the technology that produces the ad itself. Thus when ads employ these techniques in an unethical way, it is the consultants who must be held accountable.[25]

Other aspects of campaigns that are thought to be unethical and that are primarily technical rather than substantive place responsibility squarely on consultants. As also noted in chapter 3, so-called "push polling" is a practice of calling thousands upon thousands of potential voters and disseminating negative (and usually blatantly false) information about an opponent in the guise of a poll. The poll format is used to give the information credibility.[26] Push polls have been roundly criticized by consultants themselves and the organizations to which they belong. Yet the ethical clarity surrounding the issue of push polling is complicated by the fact that campaigns often use legitimate polling techniques to test negative messages. No one would criticize testing negative messages from the self-interest perspective; it is a necessary component of a well-planned campaign. But it raises red flags for those applying the civic responsibility standard. Sabato and Simpson, for instance, refer to negative message testing as "research-oriented push-polls" and find them "troubling" because "even balanced surveys yielding unbiased responses will disseminate negative information. This adversely affects the tenor and character of the campaign, and adds to the rampant negativism of modern politics."[27]

Consultants may be more directly responsible for the technical aspects of campaigns than for the substantive elements. Nevertheless, they have a great deal of influence not only over how campaigns communicate but what they say. Of course, it is usually next to impossible to identify the exact source of campaign mischief. Thus the conclusion at which so many observers arrive—that consultants are to blame for many of the ethical lapses in campaigns—is so far only theoretical. What follows is an empirical discussion of what consultants themselves see as the most pressing problems with their industry. As we show, the ethical concerns about consultant activity can be applied not only to their campaign practices but to their business practices as well.

Ethics in the Eyes of Consultants

The frequency with which unethical practices occur in campaigns and the campaigning industry depends largely on the standard one wishes to apply. Certainly, the civic responsibility perspective would find a greater amount of ethical transgressions than the self-interest perspective. As noted above, for the most part consultants themselves take the latter position. Thus it is not a surprise that when asked in a survey about how common unethical practices are in the consulting business, over a quarter of all consultants said they "rarely" occurred, and nearly half said that they "sometimes" occurred.[28] Only about 13 percent said that unethical practices occurred "fairly often."

Interestingly, consultants who are not members of the AAPC were more likely to report that ethical lapses occurred often; almost 30 percent of non-AAPC members said that unethical practices occurred either "very often" or "fairly often" in the business, compared to only 15 percent of AAPC members. Presumably, consultants join the AAPC at least in part because they are somewhat concerned about ethical issues. Otherwise, they might simply choose not to join the organization and avoid signing the code each year. Similarly, some non-AAPC members presumably do not join the AAPC because they do not want to be required to sign a code of ethics. However, while non-AAPC members' assessment of the number of ethical infractions is not any indication or judgment of importance of the issue, it may show that non-AAPC members are more attuned to ethics than originally thought.

In the survey, consultants were asked in two different ways what they considered to be unethical practices in the industry. The first measurement asked consultants to rate the ethical acceptability of different campaign tactics, to build some idea of how far consultants were willing to go in their work. The responses to these questions are found in table 5-1 and show there is a threshold that consultants will not cross. Consultants clearly find that lying is one act that is not an acceptable behavior in campaigns; taking statements out of context is also not widely supported but is not condemned, either. These results point to the attention that consultants pay to citing sources they use in many campaign communications. Whether it be a television or radio spot or a direct mail piece, any statement about a candidate's or opponent's record or stand on an issue is usually accompanied by a source for that information. This is likely because consultants know that any slipup with these kinds of statements will have serious consequences with the electorate and the media.

Even though consultants are evenly split across these questions, the number who reported that it is acceptable to use push polls and negative advertising to decrease voter turnout is troubling, especially for those who approach the question of ethics from the civic responsibility perspective. Clearly, these two practices—purposefully spreading false information in push polls and decreasing the number of individuals who take part in an election—do not enhance the democratic nature of elections.

One other aspect of the results in table 5-1 is striking. Consultants clearly believe that it is acceptable and appropriate to point out the differences between the candidate they are working for and the opponent. For

Table 5-1. *Consultants' Views of the Ethics of Campaign Tactics*
Percent

Campaign tactic	Acceptable	Questionable	Clearly unethical
Making statements that are factually untrue	0.8 (4)	5.0 (25)	94.2 (475)
Making statements that are factually true but are taken out of context	12.9 (65)	60.2 (302)	26.9 (135)
Using push polls	25.7 (121)	36.6 (172)	37.7 (177)
Using negative advertising to decrease voter turnout	38.0 (189)	33.6 (167)	28.4 (141)
Focusing primarily on the negative personal characteristics of an opponent rather than on issues	38.1 (189)	45.2 (224)	16.7 (83)
Contrasting your candidate's stands on issues with your opponent's	98.4 (494)	1.6 (8)	0.0 (0)

Source: "Are Political Consultants Hurting or Helping Democracy?" See www.american.edu/campaignconduct for more information.
Note: Numbers in parentheses are actual numbers of responses.

some critics of consultants, this practice is worrisome, as many call an effort to contrast a candidate's record with his or her opponent's an all-out attack. However, a campaign is next to useless to voters without strong comparisons between candidates. In addition, recent research has shown that television ads that are usually categorized as "negative" are often, in fact, contrast ads that contain more useful policy information than purely "positive" ads.[29]

Interestingly, with respect to two of the possible ethical transgressions (focusing primarily on negative personal aspects of a candidate and using factually true statements out of context), consultants who were members of the AAPC—and who thus have to sign the AAPC code of ethics every year as they renew their membership—were less likely than non-AAPC members to find them clearly unethical. However, with regard to the other two ethical questions that did not have unanimous or near-unanimous responses (the use of push polls and using negative advertising to decrease turnout), members of the AAPC were more than likely or just as likely as non-AAPC members to say the acts were clearly unethical.

Partisan differences emerged where there was disagreement among all consultants. On the questions of focusing primarily on negative personal characteristics and taking true statements out of context, more Republicans than Democrats reported that these were clearly unethical moves. The opposite trend was found on the questions of using negative advertising to decrease turnout and using push polls, where more Democrats than Republicans said these were clearly unethical practices.

Anecdotes from the Field

The second way in which consultants' views about the ethical nature of certain practices were measured was with an open-ended question that simply asked the respondents to discuss an example of what they regarded as a serious ethical problem in a recent political campaign.[30] We can make assumptions about the ethical decisions consultants make, but a more concrete understanding of consultants' practices will be based on what they themselves say about the situations they encounter in campaigns. From the consultants' open-ended responses we developed a typology of some of the most common ethical transgressions that consultants witness in contemporary campaigns. We believe that these responses have a high degree of validity and that they represent at least a baseline for identifying potential problems. If consultants are willing to point to certain questionable practices in the industry, those practices are likely to be problems that deserve our attention, since consultants cannot be expected to readily condemn the actions of their peers. One thing that the following typology should *not* convey is a judgment about the frequency with which the different transgressions or dilemmas occur; what follows is simply an aggregation of anecdotes about recent campaigns that consultants have experienced, witnessed, or heard about. We cannot draw conclusions about the recurring nature of these unethical practices with the data available—we can only conclude that the following are some of the difficulties faced by modern campaigners.

Six main categories of unethical practices emerged upon examination of the open-ended survey question: lying, push polling, using racist appeals, leaking information or sharing inside information, working for opposing candidates, and questionable financial dealings. However, as will be clear below, in many cases the lines between these practices can blur.

The "lying" category had by far the most responses and, in many ways, is the most nebulous category in the typology. Determining whether a statement is untrue can be very subjective; is a lie only something that is completely dreamed up about an opponent, or can it mean taking something out of context or something that is only partially untrue? Some consultants pointed to campaign advertising (and other communications) that was in some way misleading as being unethical. Instances like these normally consist of distorting an opponent's record, but it could also include a consultant misrepresenting his or her own client. Taking some part of an opponent's record out of context and using it to paint a picture that is not completely accurate also falls in this category. For example, as noted in chapter 1, in the 2000 presidential primary race between Governor George W. Bush and Senator John McCain, a pro-Bush issue ad told voters that McCain had voted against breast cancer research. While it is true that McCain did vote against one aspect of a bill that included funding for cancer research, the rest of his record indicated otherwise. Was this truthful? Technically, yes. But it was also misleading. Interestingly, when asked specifically about taking statements out of context, only about 13 percent of all consultants said that it was an "acceptable" practice. The number of consultants (over 60 percent) who said this was a "questionable" practice indicates that the industry finds these instances difficult to deal with. Most damaging are lies that come at the last minute in a campaign. Some consultants found this particularly troubling because the candidate or campaign that was the target of the lie had no time to respond or set the record straight. That the lie comes at the last minute does not make it any more unethical; it does, however, make the lie more damaging.

While defining what constitutes a lie is notoriously difficult, defining push polling is not. As noted above, push polling is a practice whereby a campaign (or its surrogates) makes phone calls under the guise of a poll designed for the purpose of gathering public opinion data, but instead asks a series of loaded or biased "questions" that include negative information about the opponent. These calls are not research calls at all but are designed to persuade members of the electorate. Consultants were not always clear about why push polling is unethical. Presumably, the information disseminated in a push poll is misleading or untrue, which makes the lie the problematic aspect and not the tactic. But one can make a case that the *technique* itself is unethical. By suggesting that the call is a poll, a consultant misleads the respondent about the purpose of the call. Rather than be "on guard" to evaluate the truthfulness or fairness of an attack against a candidate, the "respondents" are led to believe that their opinion is being solicited. This tactic also makes it more difficult for legitimate pollsters to do their work. Indeed, the tactic of push polling has been formally denounced by two major professional organizations of pollsters—the AAPC and the American Association of Public Opinion Research.[31]

A third general category of practices consultants said they had witnessed in recent campaigns was the use of racist appeals—either overt or symbolic—to play on the emotions of voters. Two commonly used examples of this tactic are the infamous "Willie Horton" ad in the 1988 Bush-Dukakis presidential race and the "White Hands" ad in the 1990 Helms-Gantt North Carolina Senate campaign. In 1988 a conservative political action committee ad tied Massachusetts governor Michael Dukakis to Horton, a convicted murderer "who had jumped furlough and gone on to rape a Maryland woman and assault her fiancé. The convict was black, the couple white."[32] In the 1990 Senate race, the Helms campaign concluded the race by running an ad that attacked Gantt's stand on affirmative action and claimed that it would result in racial quotas, meaning the loss of jobs for whites in North Carolina. The ad featured a visual of a white man's hand crumpling a job application, insinuating that the job went to an African American. The use of racist appeals is believed to be unethical because it violates a "norm of equality."[33]

Consultants also reported as unethical instances of "inside" information being leaked to organizations outside the campaign. Typically, the outside organization is the media, but it may also be another campaign. Of course, leaking positive poll results to the media is often a strategy consciously endorsed by the candidate. Occasionally, however, a consultant will leak polling information in an attempt to strengthen his or her own position (perhaps at the expense of the candidate). For instance, early results showing a candidate far behind might be leaked to insulate the consultant from later accusations that he or she was ineffective. In other circumstances, consultants use information that was paid for by one candidate to benefit another. For example, a statewide poll for a gubernatorial candidate might be shared with a candidate for attorney general. Even if the candidates are of the same party, some consultants found this troubling if the client who paid for the service was unaware of the activity.

The final two categories of consultants' observations of unethical practices in campaigns are more closely tied to business practices than campaign tactics, but that does not mean that they are any less problematic. First, consultants said that they knew of instances where a consultant worked for opposing candidates, a practice that can take a variety of forms. In the extreme, the consultant works simultaneously for opposing candidates. Alternatively, the consultant might work directly with one candidate while also assisting groups affiliated with the opponent (including that opponent's consulting firms). When this occurs, it is probably most likely to happen in a primary campaign where a consultant's firm may represent a candidate as well as a political action committee or interest group that wants to do an independent expenditure in that same primary. Finally, a consultant might go to work for the opponent of a former client. At least one consultant claimed knowledge of a case where a consultant was fired by a candidate and then immediately went to work for that candidate's opponent. Other cases involved consultants working against a former client in subsequent races. Nevertheless, the concern here is the potential for a consultant to use confidential information obtained in the campaign of a former client against that same candidate, regardless of how much time may have elapsed.

The existence of this practice is very surprising given the partisan nature of the business of professional political consultants. Campaign professionals who work for both parties, such as political consultant Dick Morris, are certainly the exception. Additionally, some consultants take steps to make sure that these kinds of charges cannot be leveled against them. For instance, one Republican consultant said that she divides up her business geographically: if she is doing an issue advocacy campaign in one area, she would not take any candidates in that same area. This step builds a fire wall between clients. Finally, we do not know what *types* of consultants the respondents to the survey were referencing. Clearly, a media consultant or pollster working for two sides in the same race is problematic and unethical. However, there are some "consultants" who do not provide strategic services but are vendors who provide campaigns with voter files and other direct mail lists or printing facilities. There is certainly a difference between the two, and it is less questionable if two campaigns get data that have no strategic value from the same vendor.[34] The voting history or demographics of a state or congressional district is not subjective.

The final category of responses consisted of questionable financial dealings of consultants, of which there are three main types: giving and receiving "kickbacks," double-billing or overcharging, and selling useless services. While kickbacks can occur in a variety of forms, a kickback is generally a payment by a consultant to another consulting firm or individual consultant in exchange for a contract to work for a client of that firm or individual. Initiation of the deal can come from either side of the exchange. As an example, suppose Consultant A is hired by Candidate X to run all aspects of her campaign. Consultant A, being a general consultant, will subcontract with a pollster, media consultant and direct mail specialist and possibly a fund-raiser or opposition researcher. If Consultant A knows a pollster, he may approach that pollster with an "offer" whereby the pollster can conduct survey research for Consultant A's candidate if that pollster is willing to pay Consultant A for lining up the contract. Conversely, the pollster might approach Consultant A with the offer.

The second two examples of questionable financial dealings can often run together and may be considered two sides of the same coin. Double-billing or overcharging is simply inflating the cost to a client of services performed. Many times, candidates and their treasurers (especially first-time candidates) are not well informed about what it costs to conduct a benchmark poll, create a thirty-second television spot, or place a spot on television for a week. The information asymmetry between consultants and their clients can lead to questionable billing. Whether a consultant is selling "unnecessary" services to clients can be a rather subjective determination. Unlike the "standard" rate for a service, which can be determined by an analysis of the consulting industry in a given market, what is essential to a campaign is a professional judgment. Is it unethical for a media consultant to recommend spending another $100,000 on television ads when the candidate is ten points down with two weeks to go? Is it unethical for the direct mail consultant to recommend that the campaign spend $50,000 on another direct mail piece in the same situation? These kinds of decisions can only be evaluated in the specific instance; it depends on how far behind or ahead the candidate is, what the costs and the context of the district or state are, and a host of other considerations. On the other hand, it would clearly be unethical for a consultant to recommend another poll or another television spot to a candidate who is twenty-five points down one week before Election Day. Nevertheless, these decisions are ultimately up to the candidate and depend on the situation at hand.

The Effectiveness of the AAPC Code of Ethics

The AAPC code of ethics discussed above is one of the only guiding forces, aside from consultants' own consciences, for professional campaigners. How many consultants actually know about it and how many follow it are questions that must be addressed if we are to understand the impact of this code among members of the industry. Very simply, a large number of consultants are familiar with the AAPC code, but few think it has made a great deal of difference in the way consultants behave and conduct their business.

When asked about the place of a code of ethics in the consulting industry, almost 80 percent of all consultants said they felt there should be a code of ethics for professionals who work on campaigns.[35] In addition, nearly three quarters of all consultants (72 percent) reported that they were aware of the existing AAPC code. However, over 40 percent of all consultants reported that the AAPC code had no effect at all on the behavior of campaign professionals. Additionally, only 61 percent of consultants said that a professional organization—in this case the AAPC— should be allowed to censure those individuals who violate a code of ethics.

Of course, the AAPC has only roughly 850 members, far fewer than the total number of active political consultants.[36] This poses a number of problems in practice if ethical standards are going to be imposed and enforced in the consulting industry. If more than half of all consultants are not members of the AAPC, and thus do not sign the code of ethics each year with the renewal of their membership, one might wonder how effective the code could be. If consultants' attitudes about the presence and enforceability of the code are evidence, this is a significant problem. As one would expect given the membership requirement of signing the code each year, nearly twice as many members of the AAPC report they are aware of the code than do non-AAPC consultants (92 percent compared to 57.5 percent). If the AAPC code is going to be the standard by which consultants' ethical nature is measured, the lack of awareness is problematic.

It should also come as no surprise that more non-AAPC members— nearly one quarter—believe there should not be any type of code of ethics for campaigners. However, what is startling and even more problematic for those who believe that political consultants should be guided by some type of code is the finding that over 14 percent of AAPC members said they felt there should not be a professional code of conduct. In addition, a significant number of AAPC members also believe that their professional organization (or any other for that matter) should *not* be able to censure violators of the code. As one would expect, many non-AAPC members reported that there should be no censure provision for a professional organization (36.6 percent), but nearly as many (27.4 percent) AAPC members agreed with that sentiment.

A final strike against the current AAPC code is that members and non-members alike also see it as having little effect on industry behavior. Only about 10 percent of non-AAPC members who were aware of the code said that they felt that the current code influenced consultants' behavior a "fair amount" or a "great deal," while about 20 percent of AAPC members said the same. AAPC members are more likely to see some impact, but this still leaves 80 percent and 90 percent of AAPC members and nonmembers, respectively, as seeing little or no impact from the code of conduct. These findings illustrate that the ethical standards of behavior for campaign professionals—whether one defines those from either the self-interest or civic responsibility perspective—are left almost totally to the personal beliefs, integrity, and principles of the individual.

Consultants with different partisan and ideological perspectives see differences in the need for, and effectiveness of, the AAPC code. More Democrats than Republicans said they were familiar with the AAPC code (77 percent to 69.5 percent), while more Republicans said that there should not be a code of ethics governing political consultants (24.5 percent to 18.5 percent). The largest partisan difference is found in Democrats' and Republicans' attitudes toward a censure for a code violation, where nearly two-thirds of all Democrats said that a censure was something they could support compared to only half of Republicans. However, with regard to the bottom line—whether the current code has any effect—Democrats and Republicans reported with roughly the same frequency that the code has little or no impact on the behavior of campaign professionals today. These results, then, beg the question: What can be done to enforce standards of practice on political consultants?

Enforcing Ethical Standards

Given that there is little agreement among consultants on what is acceptable ethical behavior, is it possible to hold consultants responsible for their actions? Who might do so? While it might at first seem that the professional association of political consultants, the AAPC, would be the likely choice to enforce ethical behavior, the preceding discussion suggests why such enforcement is unlikely. Less than half of all consultants are members of the AAPC, so even if the association had the ability to enforce a code of ethics, many political consultants would not be bound by the code. Moreover, a significant number of consultants believe that there should not be a censure mechanism for violators of the code of conduct.

If there is little support for official sanctions for unethical behavior by the AAPC, who *else* might enforce ethical behavior? We suggest there are five potential actors in the electoral process that could hold consultants accountable for their behavior: consultants themselves, candidates, the political parties, the media, and voters—the same group of actors addressed throughout this volume, save organized interest groups.

While consultants have little interest in an enforceable code of conduct, they do believe that the industry itself provides sanctions against clearly unethical behavior. As seen in the previous discussion, there is considerable variation in views as to what are considered acceptable campaign practices. Consultants themselves seem to fall much more in the self-interest camp than in the civic responsibility camp. However, consultants do believe that there is some behavior that is clearly unacceptable, and while they cannot necessarily define such conduct in the abstract, they, in the late Justice Potter Stewart's words, "know it when they see it." In a series of off-the-record discussions with the authors, consultants repeatedly said that a consultant who engaged in questionable behavior would see repercussions in terms of referrals by other consultants and the ability to attract clients.[37] Consultants believe that reputation is extremely important, and any activity that diminishes a consultant's reputation will hinder a successful career. Because consultants work with numerous other consultants on different races and in different election cycles—for example, a pollster may work with six or seven different media consultants in any given election cycle, and that mix may be entirely different in the next election cycle—consultants believe that they "know" who is doing what in campaigns and are able to self-police behavior. They believe that the risk of a diminished reputation is a far greater deterrent to unethical behavior than the threat of censure for going against a code of conduct.

A second group of actors that may enforce ethical practices are candidates. Candidate behavior in a campaign is carefully scrutinized, and questionable campaign tactics are likely to be questioned by the media, among others. For example, as noted in chapter 1, during the 2000 presidential general election, candidate George W. Bush spent several days answering questions as to why the word "RATS" appeared in a television ad. If a consultant engages in a tactic that the candidate finds questionable, the candidate may choose to fire the consultant. Also noted in chapter 1, in the 1996 Senate election in Virginia, the media consultant to Republican senator John Warner altered a photograph to discredit Warner's opponent as a "political insider."[38] Senator Warner claimed that he knew nothing about the doctored photograph, that the ad was entirely the work of his media consultant, whom he fired less than a month before the election.[39] While the consultant issued a written apology to Senator Warner, other consultants widely believe that his reputation, and subsequent ability to attract clients, was hurt by the ad.[40] It is not uncommon for a candidate, when interviewing prospective consultants, to ask for a list of prior clients and to talk to those clients. If former candidates are at all uncomfortable with some of the tactics used by a consultant, even if the tactics were successful in electing the candidate, the consultant's likelihood of being hired may be hurt. Again, even without formal censure procedures, informal norms of behavior may act to encourage ethical behavior.

Political parties are other actors in electoral politics that may enforce ethical behavior. Both the Democratic and Republican Party campaign committees keep lists of consultants to recommend to candidates.[41] While incumbent candidates have experience with consultants and know how to hire consultants, challengers and open seat candidates often turn to the party committees for help in deciding whom to hire. It is to a consultant's advantage to be on the list of consultants recommended by the party committees, and rumors of questionable campaign tactics may result in exclusion from the party's list of recommended consultants.

Furthermore, because parties spend so much money on consultants, they *could* be in a position to demand ethical behavior or take their business elsewhere. Political parties can spend money on political consultants in a number of different manners—from direct contributions to candidates that can be used to pay for consultant services, to soft money spending that today is often used for television advertising, to coordinated spending in which parties write checks on behalf of candidates. In 1998 political parties spent nearly $30 million in coordinated monies, of which over 90 percent went directly to political consultants.[42] In addition, parties hire consultants for their own needs. Thus parties are in the position to demand that the consultants they hire and that they pay on a candidate's behalf be of high ethical standards. Parties could make ethical behavior a condition of employment.

Perhaps the one group that has been the most successful in calling attention to questionable campaign tactics is the media. Through both ad watches and informal scrutiny of various forms of voter contact—television and radio commercials and direct mail pieces—the press calls attention to what it sees as questionable campaign advertising. This is what Paul Taylor calls the "watchdog" function in his chapter on the media. Ad watches evaluate the accuracy of political advertising. Typically presented in a box in a newspaper, an ad watch identifies the name of the ad, its text, its length, where it is being run, who produced it, and what organization purchased it, providing an analysis of the accuracy of the ad. Almost three quarters (72.5 percent) of the political consultants who responded to the survey discussed earlier reported that ad watches have made campaigns more careful about the content of their advertisements. Media and direct mail consultants reported the strongest influence on their behavior, with 77 percent of the former and 81 percent of the latter reporting that ad watches had made them more careful.

Ad watches are not the only way the media scrutinize political consultants. Political reporters pay attention to political advertising, and when a spot seems to overstep some loosely agreed upon boundaries, critical stories follow. As mentioned above, during the 2000 presidential general election the Republican National Committee ran an ad criticizing the then vice president and presidential candidate Al Gore's plan for prescription drugs for the elderly. When the line "The Gore Prescription Plan: Bureaucrats Decide" appeared, the word "RATS" flashed quickly on the television screen.[43] Major networks and cable stations, the *Washington Post*, and the *New York Times* all called attention to the ad, and the media consultant who made the ad was forced to defend it.

Finally, as political consultants' roles in elections become more prominent and more publicly recognized, consultants occasionally find their practices and their profession coming under media scrutiny. For example, in April 2000 the *Washington Post* ran a four-part series examining the business practices of political consultants and scrutinizing the tactics of some prominent political consultants.[44]

The final actors that have some ability to constrain the tactics of political consultants are citizens. While most citizens are probably unaware of the role of consultants in campaigns, or even that there is such a profession as political consulting, citizens are the recipients of many of the products of political consultants. To the extent that voters find advertising, direct mail, or fund-raising tactics distasteful, they could hold the candidates who put out those messages accountable, and candidates, in turn, may rein in the consultants who produce such material.

Conclusion

We began this chapter by discussing the responsibilities of consultants to their candidates and to the public interest. The data from the consultant survey suggest that consultants primarily view their role as advocates for their candidates. However, that is not to say that consultants will "do anything" to win. Consultants have in their minds a line that they will not cross, a line that defines unethical behavior. What is clearly unethical behavior may vary from consultant to consultant, but most consultants recognize that there is some behavior that is unethical. The question, of course, is whether this idiosyncratic approach to ethical standards is satisfactory.

While many consultants reject a code of conduct for the profession, and even more believe there should not be a formal means of censuring unethical behavior, there is reason to believe that sanctions are imposed on behavior deemed unacceptable. By their very recognition that some behavior is unethical, consultants constrain their own behavior. Political parties, by using reputation as one criterion for recommending consultants to candidates, also constrain consultants' tactics.

Both consultants and parties, because their primary motive is to elect candidates to office, use self-interest as a means to judge behavior. However, there is some evidence that the media and the electorate are also paying attention to the public interest. By searching for accuracy in political communications, both the press and citizens may hold consultants to a standard different from that to which consultants hold themselves. To the extent that self-interest falls short of civic responsibility and begins to harm the public interest, the media and the citizenry may call on candidates and political consultants to change the tactics they are using. It seems that even without a widely used code of conduct and without formal censure procedures, informal norms set standards of ethical behavior for consultants.

Notes

1. Kathleen Hall Jamieson, *Dirty Politics: Deception, Distraction, and Democracy* (Oxford University Press, 1992); Larry J. Sabato and Glenn R. Simpson, *Dirty Little Secrets: The Persistence of Corruption in American Politics* (Times Books, 1996).

2. Critics of consultants are too numerous to cite here. See Stephen K. Medvic, *Political Consultants in U.S. Congressional Elections* (Ohio State University Press, 2001), especially ch. 8, for a review of much of this work.

3. Larry J. Sabato, *The Rise of Political Consultants: New Ways of Winning Elections* (Basic Books, 1981).

4. "Consultantitis," *Washington Post*, November 26, 1993, p. A30.

5. Dick Morris, *Behind the Oval Office: Getting Reelected against All Odds* (Los Angeles: Renaissance Books, 1999).

6. Mary Matalin and James Carville, *All's Fair: Love, War, and Running for President* (Random House, 1994).

7. Rob Allyn, "The Good That Political Consultants Do," in David D. Perlmutter, ed., *The Manship School Guide to Political Communication* (Louisiana State University Press, 1999).

8. Joseph Napolitan, *The Election Game and How to Win It* (Garden City, N.Y.: Doubleday, 1972).

9. Indeed, one could argue that campaigns have always relied on individuals who specialize in communicating with the electorate. Furthermore, whether we like it or not, in an age of mass media–based campaigns and in a nation of 280 million people, consultants may well be a necessity for candidates.

10. See David A. Dulio, "For Better or Worse? How Political Consultants Are Changing Elections in the United States" (Ph.D. diss., American University, 2001).

11. Kathleen Hall Jamieson, Paul Waldman, and Susan Sherr, "Eliminate the Negative? Categories of Analysis for Political Advertisements," in James A. Thurber, Candice J. Nelson, and David A. Dulio, eds., *Crowded Airwaves: Campaign Advertising in Elections* (Brookings, 2000).

12. Much of this work comes from the "Improving Campaign Conduct" project. Examples are James A. Thurber and Candice J. Nelson, eds., *Campaign Warriors: Political Consultants in Elections* (Brookings, 2000); Dulio, "For Better or Worse?"

13. In reality, one could never be certain that this strategy would produce the intended consequence. Empirical research into this question has produced mixed results—many studies show that negative campaigns reduce turnout; others show no effect, or even a positive relationship between negativity and turnout; see Richard R. Lau and Lee Sigelman, "Effectiveness of Negative Political Advertising," in Thurber, Nelson, and Dulio, *Crowded Airwaves*, pp. 32–35.

14. Gary Nordlinger, "Ethical Responsibilities," *Campaigns & Elections* (April 1998), p. 63.

15. Frank I. Luntz, *Candidates, Consultants, and Campaigns: The Style and Substance of American Electioneering* (Basil Blackwell, 1988), p. 227. Readers may find this comment ironic given Luntz's misleading behavior with regard to the "Contract with America." Luntz had claimed support for the items in the contract that he never substantiated and later acknowledged had not properly tested (Frank Greve, "Pollster Admits Tilting Results for Contract with America," *Phoenix Gazette*, November 10, 1995, p. A26). The American Association of Public Opinion Research later concluded that Luntz had violated the organization's "Code of Professional Ethics and Practices" (see American Association of Public Opinion Research, "Major Opinion Research Association Finds Pollster Frank Luntz Violated Ethics Code," press release, April 23, 1997).

16. Nicholas J. O'Shaughnessy, *The Phenomenon of Political Marketing* (St. Martin's Press, 1990).

17. Sabato, *Rise of Political Consultants*, p. 336.

18. Stanley Kelley Jr., *Professional Public Relations and Political Power* (Johns Hopkins University Press, 1956).

19. Ibid., pp. 230, 231.

20. Peter Levine, "Consultants and American Political Culture," *Report from the Institute for Philosophy & Public Policy*, vol. 14, nos. 3–4 (1994), p. 3.

21. On reducing participation, see Mark P. Petracca, "Political Consultants and Democratic Governance," *PS: Political Science and Politics*, vol. 22 (1989), pp. 11–14; on undermining accountability, see David Lee Rosenbloom, *The Elec-*

tion Men: Professional Campaign Managers and American Democracy (New York: Quadrangle Books, 1973); on lengthening the campaign and narrowing the focus, see Sabato, *Rise of Political Consultants*.

22. See Sabato, *Rise of Political Consultants*, p. 306; emphasis added.

23. On the old code, see ibid. For the current code, see chapter 2.

24. Lynda Lee Kaid, "Ethical Dimensions of Political Advertising," in Robert E. Denton Jr., ed., *Ethical Dimensions of Political Communication* (Westport, Conn.: Praeger, 1991), p. 153. Note Kaid's use of the civic responsibility standard when she suggests, "Each [of the techniques] has the potential to interfere with the ability of an informed electorate to make rational choices" (p. 153). See also Lynda Lee Kaid, "Technology and Political Advertising: The Application of Ethical Standards to the 1992 Spots," *Communication Research Reports*, vol. 13 (1996), pp. 129–37.

25. See our discussion below of the infamous case from the 1996 Virginia Senate race.

26. Michael W. Traugott and Mee-Eun Kang, "Push Polls as Negative Persuasion Strategies," in Paul J. Lavrakas and Michael W. Traugott, eds., *Election Polls, the News Media, and Democracy* (New York: Chatham House/Seven Bridges Press, 2000), p. 283.

27. Sabato and Simpson, *Dirty Little Secrets*, pp. 246, 247.

28. The data reported below are taken from a survey of 505 professional political consultants conducted during March and April of 1999. The survey consisted of thirty-minute in-depth interviews with different types of consultants, including pollsters, media consultants, direct mail specialists, general consultants, fund-raising consultants, field or get-out-the-vote specialists, and opposition researchers. The survey was administered by Yankelovich Partners, Inc. for the Center for Congressional and Presidential Studies' "Improving Campaign Conduct" project, which is funded by a grant from The Pew Charitable Trusts. More information on the survey can be obtained from the authors or by visiting the center at www.american.edu/ccps.

29. Jamieson, Waldman, and Sherr, "Eliminate the Negative?"

30. To avoid placing the respondents on the spot or in an awkward position, they were not asked about a campaign on which they personally had worked.

31. The American Association of Public Opinion Researchers has formally issued a statement condemning push polling, saying: "Push polls violate the AAPOR Code of Ethics by intentionally lying to or misleading respondents. They corrupt the electoral process by disseminating false and misleading attacks on candidates. And because so-called 'push polls' can easily be confused with real polls, they damage the reputation of legitimate polling, thereby discouraging the public from participating in legitimate survey research. In order to reduce the impact of 'push polls,' it is important that the survey research community respond promptly when this technique is used. To do so, we need to know about 'push polls' when they happen." See the AAPOR website (www.aapor.org) for more information.

32. Jamieson, *Dirty Politics*.

33. Tali Mendelberg, *The Race Card: Campaign Strategy, Implicit Messages, and the Norm of Equality* (Princeton University Press, 2001).

34. For a further description of the different types of consultants and what they offer to campaigns, see Dennis W. Johnson, "The Business of Political Consulting," in Thurber and Nelson, *Campaign Warriors*; Dennis W. Johnson, *No Place for Amateurs* (London: Routledge Press, 2001).

35. Specifically, 72.2 percent of respondents said that there should be a code, while 7 percent volunteered that one already existed.

36. This figure is the total number of AAPC members, including nonconsultant members such as academics and students. The number of active political consultants depends, of course, on the estimate one uses of the total number of consultants who are active in electioneering. See Dulio, "For Better or Worse?" for a discussion of these different estimates. Only 41.2 percent of the respondents in the survey reported in this chapter were members of the AAPC.

37. Off-the-record discussions were held with groups of pollsters, media consultants, direct mail consultants, and fund-raisers between December 2000 and June 2001 as part of the "Improving Campaign Conduct" project of American University's Campaign Management Institute, funded by The Pew Charitable Trusts.

38. Mike Allen, "Warner Drops His Ad Team for Trick Photo," *New York Times*, October 11, 1996, p. A25.

39. Spencer Hsu and Ellen Nakashima, "Warner Gets Up Close, Personal," *Washington Post*, October 18, 1996, p. C1.

40. Off-the-record discussion with the authors, December 2000.

41. Paul S. Herrnson, *Party Campaigning in the 1980s* (Harvard University Press, 1988).

42. David A. Dulio and Robin Kolodny, "Political Parties and Political Consultants: Creating Alliances for Electoral Success" (paper presented at the annual meeting of the Western Political Science Association, Las Vegas, March 15–17, 2001); Robin Kolodny and David A. Dulio, "Where the Money Goes: Party Spending in Congressional Elections" (paper presented at the annual meeting of the Midwest Political Science Association, Chicago, April 15–17, 2001).

43. Edward Walsh, "A Vast Rat-Wing Conspiracy? Bush Campaign Beset by Questions on Medicare Ad," *Washington Post*, September 13, 2000, p. A26.

44. Susan B. Glasser, "Hired Guns Fuel Fundraising Race," *Washington Post*, April 30, 2000, p. A1.

CHAPTER SIX

POLITICAL CONSULTANTS

Wolves or Watchdogs?

CAROL WHITNEY

I like to con people. And I like to insult people. If you combine con and insult, you get "consult." I'm here to consult you.

—Dogbert, in Scott Adams's comic strip "Dilbert"

Calling oneself a *consultant* seems to be negative enough these days. But calling oneself a *political consultant* is, in the public's mind, the equivalent of staking out territory somewhere below lawyers, used-car salesmen, and con artists, and around the level of pond scum. It is no wonder political consultants are not taken seriously when we talk about setting an ethical tone for the campaign. Thanks to the power of television, movies, and the media, the simple fact of our involvement in a campaign sends the signal that the ethics of this venture must be questionable.

It can be argued that the consultant is on the front line in terms of setting ethical standards and should take responsibility for doing so. But how can this watchdog guard the flock if he looks like a wolf to the shepherd and the sheep? Is it worth the effort for political consultants to try to foster ethical standards for their campaigns if the public does not believe they are doing so? To answer that question, we have to take a look at the realities of modern political consulting.

Infinite Variety

Let us first dispel the notion that *political consultant* is a meaningful generic term. Politics is an unregulated industry, and any person interested in campaign politics can print business cards and introduce himself (or herself) as a "political consultant." A lot of people do just that; a young man or woman who has worked on one campaign and wants to continue in the business becomes a "consultant." A local expert (volunteer) who has worked informally with campaigns or the party for twenty years decides he or she knows as much as any of those so-called experts from Washington—and we have another "political consultant." The broad category of political consultant includes campaign operatives and experts in a wide variety of fields along with a lot of people who just plain like campaign politics and know a little more than the average citizen. So which consultants are we talking about when we worry about their negative influence on the political process?

Although it can be argued that political consulting has been around in some form since as far back as the 1930s, modern professional consulting followed the rise of television as an advertising medium. The first political television advertising campaign (Eisenhower in 1956) was minuscule by today's standards and was developed by an advertising firm. Other advertising firms joined in as campaign use of the medium grew. But as it became apparent that effective campaign advertising was very different from product advertising, some firms and individuals began specializing in political media.

The political pollsters, of course, are the senior members of the campaign consulting business. Presidential preference polls appeared as early as 1824,[1] and despite some notable embarrassments, such as the Dewey "victory" of 1948, by the late 1960s polling was considered a necessity for congressional races, and today's increasingly sophisticated polling techniques are invaluable to a campaign.

At the same time political campaigns were becoming more sophisticated, the influence of the two political parties over their candidates was waning. Party lines had blurred as ideology weakened and candidates ran on what they considered their own merits. The local political experts were not well equipped for the complexities of a modern congressional or statewide campaign, and certainly few state parties had the resources and experience to advise a major candidate. Candidates were averse to accepting direct guidance from the national parties because every candidate knows that "my state is different." As the parties became less able to assist their candidates in the most current techniques of campaigning, they lost the ability to control them. The traditional campaign role of the parties has been gradually—and almost totally—assumed by outside experts.

Media consultants began offering strategic advice and overall planning for their campaigns. Others with campaign experience began selling their knowledge of strategy and planning to campaigns. Now we had "general consultants," strategists and planners for the campaign who operated independently of—and on the Republican side, at least, in a position of authority over—the media consultants. The polling firms were already in place, providing their consulting services, and gradually were joined by other specialists, such as fund-raisers, opposition researchers, and direct mail specialists. Today, specialization is the rule. A campaign could conceivably hire a media consultant, a strategist, a direct mail consultant, a fund-raising consultant, a fund-raising mail consultant, an organizational consultant, a get-out-the-vote (GOTV) consultant, and more. So which of these is the "political consultant" the public considers so lacking in ethical standards?

It is important to understand where the public gets the image of the political consultant: that plotter in back rooms, devious manipulator of the electorate, creator of the candidate's false face. We can blame it on the movies and television, certainly, but the consultants themselves have had a hand in it. Although the political Svengali—inherently evil, incredibly wealthy, devious and parasitic—has never existed, that negative image has been reinforced by a few highly visible individual strategists whose own desire for public attention, coupled with questionable personal behavior and even more questionable campaign ethics, has fed the public's dislike for the profession.

Only the most naive believe that the media focus equally on the positives and the negatives of the political process. How often do we see articles about fair elections; about candidates who won through being genuinely good, qualified individuals; about ethical political consultants who set an example for their peers? To paraphrase the popular cliché, "good news is no news." Bad news is good news because it sells newspapers. Consequently, those political professionals who make outrageous statements, are caught in outrageous acts, engage in flagrantly unethical personal or campaign behavior, or are fired by their clients for unethical practices make the headlines. In the public eye, they become the model for all political professionals. These individuals will always exist. But the reality is that they are a minority in the business and do not present the true face of political consulting; most professional consultants do not operate in the headlines (and like it that way). In reality, the profession is incredibly diverse, and the professionals from both parties have demonstrated strong concern about the integrity of the process.

How Ethical Are We?

I have yet to meet a political consultant who admits to doing anything unethical. True, some rely on others to set the limits and are willing to go to any lengths to win, but the majority do have standards and try to live by them. Those standards differ from individual to individual. And the seriousness of ethical dilemmas as well as the pressure to violate ethical standards varies by specialization. Those who are closest to the candidates generally have the most influence over the ethical course of the campaign, but certain specific fields of political consulting offer more opportunity for getting away with unethical tactics than others.

The media consultant is a natural target of public scorn for developing those "negative ads" that are so harshly criticized. Yet in reality, the media consultant is probably more ethical—in behavior if not always belief—than the other specialists. Television advertising is more closely scrutinized than any other aspect of today's campaign. As Sandy Maisel points out in chapter 3, ad watches, news coverage, and general visibility make it almost impossible to use false or misleading information effectively in support of a candidate even if the consultant wanted to do so. The backlash makes such tactics counterproductive.

Also, despite the money involved and the suspicion there must be something wrong somewhere when a campaign raises and spends huge sums of money, the use of unethical practices by the fund-raising consultant is unusual since his or her activities are transparent at almost every level. Some question may arise in the case of fund-raising mail, since success in this type of fund-raising generally depends on how much fear and loathing can be generated. Such a ploy might include the language: "If you don't send $25.00 to my campaign today, the [big-spending liberal Democrats and the union bosses/right-wing Republican fat-cat big-business interests] will [waste all our hard-earned tax dollars on more big government/destroy our environment and starve our senior citizens]." Is this tactic unethical? Probably not. But it does give us pause when we realize how effective it is to remind people of their hidden—and not always rational—fears.

Recently, attention has been focused on so-called "push polling," in which questionable negative information is delivered in the guise of a telephone survey. Push polling is nothing more than organized rumormongering, and most professional political pollsters do not engage in this practice. The gray area comes when the media consultant or strategist asks the pollster to test the effectiveness of using some specific negative information that has been uncovered about the opponent. Then we have to consider whether (1) the information is true; and (2) whether it is relevant to the election. Certainly the pollster's professional ethics dictate that he or she needs to be certain the information is true. It is a stretch, however, to say that the pollster is responsible for deciding whether it is relevant.

Even with today's sophisticated techniques, it is certainly possible to "lie with statistics." But here we approach issues of competence more than ethics: Did the survey question bias the answer? Were the data interpreted correctly? Was the sample a true random sample, and was it sufficiently large for accuracy? It would be foolish for a pollster to purposely manipulate the results or simply give clients what they want to hear. In this business, Election Day tells the tale, and a pollster whose information has obviously been wildly inaccurate is not going to have a lot of repeat business. Bad polls are generally the product of bad (incompetent or inexperienced) pollsters.

There are temptations and difficult decisions for every type of political consultant. But today's most bothersome ethical questions arise in the field of political direct mail, which provides individual, highly targeted, "under-the-radar" contact with the voter. It is a perfect medium for distribution of inaccurate, misleading, or inflammatory messages. And it is not monitored by any entity other than the U.S. Postal Service, which is concerned only with specific violations of law. It is true that dissemination of certain types of false information through the mails violates federal law, but it is rare that political direct mail goes that far. Every direct mail consultant I have encountered considers himself or herself totally ethical. They all sleep well at night and face themselves in the mirror in the mornings. They are quite open and clear about their ethical standards. Some of us may disagree with those standards, but who has the right to judge?

Average voter mail specialists will tell you that they believe it is wrong to use information that is untrue and that as long as their messages are factual, they are ethical. What if the facts are misleading, create a false impression in the voter's mind, or are used to trigger irrational fears or prejudices? Their answer is that the sender of the message is not responsible for the way it is received.

The public judges only those forms of campaign activity that are most visible, so public and media attention focuses on television advertising and campaign finance. It would be well for them to refocus some of their efforts on political mail.

Money, Morality, and the Political Professional

Money may not be inherently evil, but the need for money plays a powerful role in setting and complying with ethical standards. Political consultants are *professionals*; this is not a game for them but the way they earn their living. The necessity of earning that living creates strong pressure to conform to "generally accepted practices" rather than to one's own moral code. A media consultant, for example, may have half a dozen major campaigns during the course of one election cycle. The profit from producing and airing the radio and television for these campaigns must cover the expenses of staffing and running a business in addition to the direct costs and time involved in the project. If he or she loses or resigns from two of these campaigns, that can mean the loss of one-third of the year's revenue base. It's simple accounting. If the candidate turns out to be less than ethical, it's easier not to notice than to assume the financial loss.

Consultants of every type deal with the pressure of cash flow, but the pressure is greater for major media consultants and general strategists. A media consultant can bring in $1 million plus in placement commissions from one major campaign.[2] How easy would it be to give up $1 million because you question the ethics of the candidate? Most media consultants would continue to work with the candidate as long as their own products (television and radio spots) are honest and ethical. For the general consultant/strategist that line is harder to define, since he or she is advising on the overall conduct of the campaign. If a consultant has proof that the candidate has lied, has done something illegal, or is pressuring campaign staff or consultants to do something illegal or unethical, then the consultant faces a serious ethical dilemma.

We may be asking too much. After all, no other profession expects you to make certain every one of your clients is an honorable human being. On the other hand, we cannot help but think about the consequences:

possibly one more unethical individual elevated to a position of responsibility in our government. So, uncomfortably, we try to balance our responsibility to society against the need to earn a living. It is a tough choice,
particularly when we know there are many other consultants out there
who truly believe that it is not their job to assess the candidate's worthiness. And they are probably right. It really is not fair to ask the consultant
to judge the ethics of the candidate. But a lot of us do it for our own peace
of mind.

The Need to Win

The pressure to win is tied to the question of money, but it goes further
than the spoils of victory (in political consulting, the "spoils of victory"
sometimes just means getting paid; when a candidate loses we may be left
with a stack of never-to-be-paid invoices). A good list of winners is a plus
in signing up future candidates, and a solid stable of incumbents has a
real impact on a consultant's earning ability. Some notable victories, a
nice list of reelection campaigns each year, and the fees can add up nicely.

But there is more to it than that. The majority of political professionals, contrary to popular opinion, are not just hired guns who will work
for anyone who pays. Most of them truly care about the process; they
invest as much of themselves in the campaign as anyone involved, and the
losses feel very personal.[3] Not only are they are dedicated Republicans or
Democrats, but some work only with candidates of their own particular
ideology, such as conservative Republicans, liberal Democrats, pro-choice,
pro-life—wherever their own beliefs happen to lie on the ideological spectrum.

When victory for the candidates matters personally as well as profes-
sionally, it becomes even harder to maintain high ethical standards. When
a consultant sincerely believes that it is vital to the country's future that
the right person (his or her candidate) is elected, cutting a few corners or
exaggerating a bit does not seem so serious. Think about this: If you are
convinced that the opponent is dishonest, unworthy, and would do terrible harm if elected, is it so wrong to do everything possible to ensure
that it does not happen? It's the classic dilemma: Is it still evil if it is done
in the service of good?

Political consulting is not perceived as a noble profession or one that
demonstrates high moral standards. But most of us think about ethics a
lot, even if we avoid discussing it because it is so difficult a concept to

apply to the political arena. All of us who have worked in politics face serious ethical dilemmas on a regular basis, and the question for us remains: Who sets the standards?

The Question of Loyalty

When a political consultant signs a contract with a client, the client assumes that the consultant will be loyal. It is similar to an attorney-client relationship, in which communication between the two is privileged. Good consultants honor client confidentiality and maintain that confidentiality even after the election.

But the tough decisions come when another candidate decides to run against good old Joe, the man you worked with in 1998 but are not working with this year. Maybe you do not think Joe is doing a great job; maybe Joe has decided he prefers another consultant this time. What happens when Sam comes along and asks you to do the media (and strategy) for his campaign against Joe? Joe is no longer a client, but you know a lot about him—and it is not all good. Is it an ethical violation to work with Sam? How long do you have to wait before opposing good old Joe? Does this client confidentiality mean that you can never work for anyone running against a candidate you worked with in the past?

These are tough questions. There is no one right answer. It depends on how long it has been since you worked with Joe and whether the campaign is still for the same office. A consultant frequently works repeatedly in the same states, and it is not unheard of that two members of Congress, both clients of the same consultant, would choose to run against each other in a senatorial or gubernatorial primary. Now what? It is another tough call and a personal, rather than an ethical, decision. It is generally considered unethical for a consultant to work with Joe in one election and against him in the next election using the information he or she learned while working with him.

Political professionals may be faced with another loyalty issue: What if you discover your candidate is hiding something, or lying about something, that reflects on his or her honesty or integrity? What if it is something that would have kept you from taking the campaign if you had known about it? Now you have a contract, and it is a month or six weeks before the election. Is it ethical to stay with the campaign and keep quiet? Is it ethical to simply quit and open the candidate to questions about why the consultant suddenly refuses to work with the campaign? Does the consultant owe his or her first responsibility to the client or to the public?

The dilemma is a real one. Our actions in this situation can make the difference between winning and losing for the candidate. It is an awesome amount of power and responsibility. So who has the authority to set rules to help us resolve these dilemmas? The answer for the consultant is, as usual, "you're on your own." I contend once again that the average political consultant is far more aware of ethical considerations than the average citizen and is faced with ethics-based decisionmaking far more often.

Political consultants have no choice but to be their own watchdogs.

The Consultant as Effective Watchdog

Academics want consultants to take responsibility for providing the public with the information that will enable them to make "rational decisions" on Election Day. Unfortunately, one person's definition of "rational" may be another's definition of "insane." In addition, voting decisions are not made on the basis of pure logic. Voters assimilate the information provided, add it to their store of facts and opinions (their interpretation of reality), and vote on the basis of their *feelings*. People vote because they *care* about the election results and have emotional attachments to their political beliefs, not because pure reason tells them that one candidate will do a better job than the other.

With that understood, we will agree up front to provide the voters information that *we* believe will allow them to make an informed decision; and in that process, we can indeed play a role in improving ethical conduct. Laying aside the fact that no two consultants will have exactly the same perception of the ethical line that should not be crossed and agreeing that there is no universally accepted authority to set standards for the business, there remain some very clear ways in which the consultant can foster ethical election campaigns. I would suggest to consultants the following five practices as a good start:

Have a clear, up-front discussion with the candidate regarding ethical boundaries. I am not suggesting a lecture about what is or is not ethical, but a mutual exploration of ethical boundaries. I suspect this is rarely done, but having such an open discussion early can forestall later problems. For example, many of us have encountered the candidate who sees the consultant as the scapegoat, or the candidate who says, "I don't believe in things like that, but he made me do it." It is not that the candidate plans this from the beginning, but when the race gets tight and temptation arises, having someone else to blame certainly salves the conscience. Talk about this tactfully at the beginning of the campaign relationship. The consultant must take responsibility for his or her own actions, but not for those of the candidate.

At the same time, the candidate can bring up questions such as, "How far are you willing to go if this race gets tight? Will I be able to maintain final control over what goes on in the campaign?" In the heat of the contest the boundaries may still blur, but establishing an understanding in the beginning can make a huge difference.

Ask the candidate to sign a code of ethics, and sign one yourself. This is the candidate's campaign, and his or her own code of ethics should serve as the standard for the campaign. The code can be very simple; the following statements should suffice:

—"I pledge to provide the voters with accurate information regarding myself and my opponent in order that they may make informed choices on Election Day."

—"I accept responsibility for the information delivered by my campaign and the way in which that information is presented."

—"I will maintain vigilance over my campaign to ensure that campaign personnel do not misrepresent the facts or mislead the voters, and I will make it clear to them that I demand the highest level of integrity from those who represent my campaign."

It may appear the height of arrogance to ask the candidate to sign an "agreement to be ethical," but this is not the point of the exercise. The candidate code establishes *for everyone involved* in the campaign just what the candidate's expectations are, demonstrates the candidate's control over the conduct of the campaign, and draws a line for the consultant(s). This is the candidate's campaign, and it is his or her right to establish the ethical standards for its implementation. The candidate's initial response may be that a code is not necessary, that his or her high ethical standards are not in doubt. Unfortunately, in politics nothing can be taken for granted— including the assumption that the campaign staff and consultants all have a clear understanding of what is ethical and what is not.

There are a number of model codes for political professionals, including one developed by the American Association of Political Consultants (see chapter 2). Almost any of them, or one's own personal ethical statement, is sufficient to demonstrate your own commitment to ethical campaigning. The point is to establish that the consultant is aware of the importance of maintaining ethical standards, and that he or she is committed to those standards.

Remember that this is the candidate's campaign. It is time we returned to the old rule of consultant invisibility: that the candidate should be the focus of attention, and the campaign is not an opportunity for the consultant to gain media attention. Also, while it is the consultant's job to advise the candidate to the best of his or her ability on what has to be done to win the race, it is the candidate's right to say no. The consultant is obligated to make the consequences of particular decisions totally clear, but all critical decisions are the candidate's province because, in the end, he or she will have to live with them.

If the consultant and the candidate have a disagreement about the conduct of the campaign, and the consultant makes the decision to leave, he or she must do so with discretion, understanding that the departure—if handled badly— may have a negative impact on the campaign.

Set an example. The next generation of consultants is always the generation we have to worry about. Young people are drawn to the excitement of political campaigns, to the high-energy, urgent, sometimes seat-of-the-pants decisionmaking of the campaign process. For them, the romance of the campaign is enhanced by secretiveness, by action behind the scenes and plotting in back rooms. They are generally fascinated with the idea of "dirty tricks" and clever ploys to damage the opponent's campaign. It is the young staffers who tear down yard signs, go through the opposing campaign's trash, suggest volunteering for the opposition in order to spy on them, disrupt the opposition's rallies or press conferences, and the like. The mature consultant does not have to be a spoilsport. But share the wisdom you have gained through experience; let campaign staffers know what kind of trouble they can cause themselves and the campaign through "dirty tricks." The consultants have been there, and almost every one of us can tell at least one story about some young political staffer we knew who ended up in deep trouble over a clever trick that turned out to be illegal or caused the campaign serious embarrassment.

We all know that some of the campaign staff antics are simply good clean fun, and we've done them ourselves. (I have fond memories of sneaking out during the night and putting one of our bumper strips on the governor's car.) But we also took some risks we know now were foolish. Today's young people may not listen to us, but we owe them a warning about the consequences.

Remember, today's opponent may be tomorrow's client. Unless you have so many clients that you will never need to market your services, sheer practicality says that you do not cheat and you do not viciously gut the opposition—particularly in a primary. Experienced consultants know the danger of being perceived as the expert at below-the-belt politics. Most candidates do not want a consultant they are afraid to turn their backs on. A lot of prospective candidates observed your last campaign. As a consultant, you want some of them to call you for their own races. It is better to have a reputation for being "very tough, but fair and a great strategist" than someone who would do anything to win.

As consultants, we face more ethical questions than answers. Most political consultants are more than willing to play a role in fostering ethical campaigns. But we need the help of the public and the media if we are to succeed. We need an honest look at what goes on in the campaign, not just what is most visible (see Robert Denton's chapter 11 and Paul Taylor's chapter 12 for more on the media). We need an understanding on the part of the media that we are, for the most part, highly ethical people in a difficult business, not backroom schemers with no personal standards. We need the public to get the message that we play a vital role in the political process, and that modern campaigns cannot function without us. Most of all, however, to paraphrase comedian Rodney Dangerfield, we need a little respect.

Notes

1. The *Harrisburg Pennsylvanian* published the results of a straw ballot between Andrew Jackson and John Quincy Adams. Jackson won the straw ballot handily. Adams won the election. See Richard Jensen, "Democracy by the Numbers," *Public Opinion*, vol. 3, no. 1A (February–March 1980), pp. 53–59.

2. Media consultants typically receive the bulk of their revenue from a commission on the purchase of television time for campaign commercials. The commission is usually 15 percent of the total ad buy, but that figure is becoming negotiable.

3. For empirical evidence of this, see James A. Thurber, Candice J. Nelson, and David A. Dulio, "Portrait of Campaign Consultants," in James A. Thurber and Candice J. Nelson, eds., *Campaign Warriors: Political Consultants in Elections* (Brookings, 2000).

CHAPTER SEVEN

POLITICAL PARTIES

It's the System, Stupid!

ROBIN KOLODNY

Perhaps the most quixotic actors in the ethical dimensions of election campaigns are political parties. In this chapter, I argue that political parties do behave ethically in election campaigns, but that the structure of electoral competition the parties have created is itself unethical because it denies access to anyone outside the two major American political parties. These parties ensure the maintenance of the political system that favors them by manipulating laws and customs of the democratic process at the expense of the participation of other possible competitors. However, most observers of American election campaigns would not come to this conclusion because the role of political parties in elections seems confusing. We have no consensus on whom the parties truly represent in the system, and the debate about that distracts us from the system's underlying unfairness.

In chapter 2, Miller and Medvic explain that ethical norms, as opposed to morals, are meant to judge and constrain the behavior of agents on behalf of their principals. In the case of political consultants (the example they use), it is clear that the client (for example, a candidate, interest group, or political party) is the principal and the consultant is the agent. But when we talk about the ethical dimensions of political party activity, precisely what principal-agent relationship do we mean?

Principal-agent theories have normally been applied to the legislative or bureaucratic arenas of American politics because the givers of power (principals) to the leaders or agencies who exercise it (agents) are readily identifiable.[1] While we know that political parties act as agents in the electoral process, a classic problem in political party research is agreeing on the proper specification for the principal. Is the party an agent for the voters who identify with a party, for the activists who carry out its work (by volunteering or working as paid employees for a party organization at any level of government), or for the candidates (both incumbents and challengers)? Clearly, one of the biggest problems in assessing the ethics of political parties is determining who their principal is. If we cannot make this determination, then proceeding with our discussion is problematic, for to say that the party is an agent for all these principals is to concede that parties cannot engage in consistently ethical behavior at all (or achieve meaningful results, for that matter) because the demands of the principals compete.[2]

It is the confusion over principal-agent relationships that leads many political scientists and political pundits to claim that parties are less relevant now than they once were in elections. This argument conjures up images of the "golden age" of parties, a time before the Progressive Era when political parties had tight control over their nominees and issue positions, making them an agent for only the electorate. Candidates were thought to be the agents for the parties, not the other way around. Many scholars argue that around the 1960s, the entire electoral process became centered around candidates, not parties, making the parties agents for candidates as well as for voters.[3]

Contrary to this school of thought, I agree with Katz and Mair that political parties are in fact agents for the state, and in this role they determine the background for how elections are waged in the United States.[4] Katz and Mair's theory of the "cartel party" describes a system wherein political parties no longer have a role as straight intermediaries between civil society and the state but are in fact embedded in the state. They make some stark claims about the implications of the cartel party for democratic thought:

> Democracy ceases to be seen as a process by which limitations or controls are imposed on the state by civil society, becoming instead a service provided by the state for civil society. . . . Feedback is necessary if rulers are to provide government that is broadly acceptable, and contested elections, which signal public pleasure (or displeasure) with policy and outcomes, provide that feedback. Thus,

the state provides contested elections. And since democratically contested elections, at least as currently understood, require political parties, the state also provides (or guarantees the provision of) political parties. In the end, of course, it is the parties in power that are the state and that provide this service, and it is thus their own existence that they are guaranteeing.[5]

When put in this way, the question of the campaign ethics of political parties cannot be asked solely in the context of tactics employed in particular elections. Instead, we must ask if the entire system of electoral competition created by the political parties as agents of the state is consistent with our conception of democracy, and if it is not, whether the two parties' domination of electoral politics in the United States is itself ethical.

The central problem in making this case is that most Americans would not acknowledge either the central role of parties in elections or the existence of a cartel between the two major parties. Because party identification has low salience for voters, and because voters claim they vote for the candidate, not the party, we attribute ethics in campaigns to individual candidates and their "handlers," political consultants.[6] However, it is difficult to deny that elected officials of the two major parties are the ones who determine how nominations are made, how campaigns are financed, how ballots are created and administered, and how electoral disputes are settled—all clear foundations for how the "state" operates.

Leon Epstein argued that the fifty states view the role of political parties in elections as they would public utilities in other aspects of public policy. Party functions became regulated by the states in the same way that the electric and gas companies were.[7] One of the distinguishing characteristics of all public utilities is that they are monopolies. Thus, although some might argue that American political parties, like many public utilities today, are really private associations subject to governmental regulation, I would argue that political parties do not qualify as private organizations. Unlike water, gas, and electricity, which must be provided centrally in order for the public to be safe, and therefore must be provided by a state-run entity or a private entity tightly controlled by the state, democracy in America can exist without a duopolistic party system. The idea that only Democrats and Republicans can maintain control of any elected body in the United States (at the national, state, and the vast majority of local levels) and the fact that regulatory bodies for elections exist in every one of the fifty states and perform virtually identical functions should show that the broad concept of the "state" in the United States has become intertwined with the two major parties.

American political parties form a cartel and they act as an agent for the "state." Political parties are questioned for their ethics in elections not because parties are doing anything extraordinarily corrupt, but because the consumers of party goods (the various principals) have conflicting expectations of them and fundamentally, they all fail to see that the state is the true principal. For this reason, it is difficult to indict political parties as acting under the "self-interested" school of ethics rather than the "civic responsibility" school outlined by Miller and Medvic in chapter 2. Though Miller and Medvic acknowledge that defining the public good makes the "civic responsibility" school difficult to achieve, we can say that if the parties are agents for the "state" and if preserving democracy/civic responsibility/the public good are all dimensions of the responsibility of the "state," then the parties have an enormous role in determining the acceptable limits of campaign activity. The recognition that the state, rather than the voters, activists, or candidates, is the true principal of political parties should lead to the understanding that in order to change the behavior of the political parties in elections, one would have to change the very structure of the political system itself. In other words, in the current system, parties are acting as ethically as they must, and their actions are constrained only by the context in which they are operating—which they themselves define.

Political Party Paradoxes

Borrowing from a device Thomas Cronin used to explain contradictory expectations Americans have of the presidency, I have developed a series of paradoxes to examine the degree of ethical behavior shown by political parties in elections.[8] These paradoxes identify some familiar charges against the ethics of political parties (such as in the area of campaign finance) and some less familiar (as in the restriction of multiparty competition). In each paradox, the puzzle for assessing political party ethics lies in the confusion over which principal the party serves. The paradoxes demonstrate that political party behavior that appears to favor one principal is deemed unethical or improper by the others. That no true solution is found for these paradoxes is further evidence that the true principal for American political parties is the state.

Paradox 1

In the United States, it is generally agreed that we should have a free and open political system where anyone should be able to run for election to public office. However, candidates should have a good chance of winning, and so the number of candidates on the ballot must be small so voters are not confused and the system is "orderly."

It is a well-established "fact" that anyone can run for public office in the United States as long as he or she meets the legal requirements of citizenship, residency, and age. It is equally well established that candidates who expect to get elected run for public office as either a Democrat or a Republican. As Herrnson and Green and Lowi and Romance show, the two-party system in the United States has many supports.[9] While some are assuredly cultural (the belief that two parties are "natural" in a democracy), some are legal or institutional barriers to minor-party access.[10] For example, each state regulates how parties obtain and retain ballot position. The two major parties have privileged access to the ballot, meaning that as long as their candidate for a flagship office (usually governor) receives a relatively high percentage of the vote (20 percent) in the previous general election, they do not have to reapply for status as a political party, while newly formed political parties face considerable obstacles from state election bureaucracies and state and federal courts in their efforts to obtain and retain ballot access.[11] Therefore, serious contenders for public office will run in the primaries of the two major parties. This ensures the dominance of Democrats and Republicans in American elections.

As Katz and Mair have argued, the perpetual opposition party (also a cartel party) is acceptable to the party in power.[12] What is not acceptable is the idea that an upstart party such as the Reform Party or the Green Party could gain access to office and succeed in changing the rules of the established game or that such a party's success would force a major party to change its rules and leave the cartel. The result of two-party dominance is a homogenization of candidate types, issue stances, and campaign appeals. Consequently, qualified candidates for office who decide not to call themselves Democrats or Republicans must first get over the "sideshow" factor of their candidacies before the electorate will even consider them.

So, while Representative Bernard Sanders (I-Vt.), a socialist, has worked hard *not* to be called a Democrat in the U.S. House of Representatives, his efforts have been treated dismissively. He is officially referred to as an

Independent in the House, and his struggles with former Speaker Tom Foley (D-Wash.) to retain his committee assignments without pledging allegiance to the Democratic Party in the early 1990s have taken on legendary status. Additionally, Ralph Nader's pursuit of 5 percent of the popular vote in the 2000 presidential election was ridiculed as much for his audacity at pointing out that the two major party candidates were essentially similar on issues of great importance as for his "spoiling" the election for Al Gore.[13]

The important point is that political parties have not done anything illegal in terms of violating the existing laws regulating party competition; instead, the parties—through their elected officials—have written laws designed to constrain competition that are *inherently* unethical with respect to the general principles of democracy. If the state favors stability, democratic principles (a small "d"), capitalism, and predictability, then creating supports for the Democratic and Republican Parties makes a great deal of sense. Creating a system that discourages new parties and encourages increased primary competition forces candidates with a good chance of winning to essentially accept the "legitimate" aura of a major party nomination, which in itself constrains them. In essence, the parties have defined party competition and fair electoral practices to mean that whatever the Democrats and Republicans have traditionally done is ethical, and anything outside the mainstream is not. Thus while Democrats and Republicans have nearly identical systems for nominating presidential candidates, the presidential nominating practices of the Greens and the Reform Party are ridiculed. Neutral monitors of election practices (the Federal Election Commission, the Federal Communications Commission, the Commission on Presidential Debates) are hailed for their nonpartisan status, while in fact the individuals who run the commissions are affiliated with one of the two major parties (though the evenness in their division is meant to convince us that one party is not favored over the other—but the point is that the two-party system is favored in all instances).[14] These organizations may be bipartisan, but they certainly are not nonpartisan.

The two major parties do seem to referee each other in the arena of campaign finance, where one often finds one party suing the other. However, in cases where the states try to change major party practices, as in the recent challenge to California's blanket primary, the Democrats and Republicans filed a brief *together* against the state action.[15] Democrats and Republicans frequently decry the other's tactics, only to be found later engaging in similar behavior themselves (the Democrats' recent increase

in soft money fund-raising is only one of a number of examples). Under
the guise of pragmatism, neither party unilaterally ceases practices of ethical
uncertainty, a point made by Siegel in chapter 8. The two major parties
are constantly expanding the definition of ethical practices in campaigns
to include most activities one or the other engages in and to exclude many
of those engaged in by potential rivals.

Why do voters put up with this? Our single member plurality (SMP)
system allows only one winner in a district, and the desire of the voting
public to be behind a winner leads them to choose between major-party
candidates (the state's agents) rather than from among all parties on the
ballot.[16] Thus the paradox stated above forces us to reconcile the idea
that our system cannot both promote representation of all individuals'
views and encourage only "serious" candidates at the same time. So while
some can claim that the exclusion of Ralph Nader from the presidential
ticket in some states and from the televised presidential debates is undemocratic, others can claim that voters who ultimately cast their ballots
for Nader are responsible for the "illegitimate" election of George W. Bush
and are undermining our democracy by casting votes for a candidate who
best represents them.

Paradox 2

*Political parties are supposed to run coordinated campaigns up and down
the ticket and across states based on common themes or ideologies, but at
the same time do the best they can to help competitive candidates win
elections.*

This paradox finds the candidates and voters squarely at odds with
their agent, the parties. Voters say they want political parties to present
candidates of consistent ideologies, so that the "brand name" appeal of
party affiliation has some meaning for them.[17] Candidates for office include incumbents, competitive candidates, and noncompetitive candidates.
The incumbents and competitive candidates see the parties as their agents
for getting elected to office and expect a disproportionate amount of resources to be given to them, *without regard* to their ideologies as long as
they are members of the party. This paradox pits voters against candidates. Since the winning candidates become part of the state, the pragmatism of ignoring ideological inconsistencies wins. Since virtually all eligible voters choose either to legitimize the actions of the parties by voting
for one of the major parties or not voting at all (as opposed to, say, a civil

uprising or supporting a minor party), the unethical behavior of political parties is accepted.

In *Pursuing Majorities* I detail the operations of the congressional campaign committees (CCCs) since the late nineteenth century.[18] I argue that the collective benefits of campaigning on the basis of party affiliation, and not just on personal characteristics, have real rewards, an argument that has been specified by others in other dimensions of political life.[19] Simply put, candidates for office have a logical preference ordering of ambitions. First, they want to be elected. Second, they want to be a member of the majority party. To exercise power, a candidate must win office. To exercise maximal power, the officeholder must be in the majority party that controls the agenda, personnel, committees (in the legislature), and other aspects of power in governments. Senior elected officials have the most to gain by serving in the majority party and are normally the ones for whom the first goal (their own election and reelection) has become relatively easy to secure.[20] These senior members are the ones responsible for the proliferation of political party organizations at the national and state levels (for example, CCCs and legislative campaign committees— LCCs) and for the explosion in political action committees formed by congressional leaders (leadership PACs).[21]

The problem with this strategy is that it promotes winning (the goal of the candidates) at the cost of everything else. This is a problem not only in the United States but in most places where majority control of the government is sought. In multiparty systems where coalition governments are assumed, the imperative behind pursuing majorities is less urgent. It is more likely, then, that parties stress their issue positions and policy agenda (responding to voters and activists) when their goal is only to be elected to office rather than to control the government, where their positions are normally moderated to please the maximum number of people.

Therefore, in the American party system, we rightly debate whether the two major parties actually differ from each other or whether they are in fact simply vehicles to enable ambitious politicians to achieve their goals. While I will not debate the merits of the considerable literature that argues this point, the real imperative of majority status (especially in recent elections where the control of so many legislative bodies is determined by such a few seats) means that political party leaders simply cannot afford to create hard and fast rules to determine who will wear their party label. One recent example is Vermont senator Jim Jeffords's switch in May 2001 from the Republican Party to an Independent aligned with the Democrats, giving Democrats control of the U.S. Senate chamber.

If the party believes its candidate has a chance to win the seat, then it will feel morally bound to create viable campaign strategies for a pro-choice Republican or pro-business Democrat, even if that is at odds with its activists' or voters' dominant ideology. But is it ethical for the party to abandon its platform, issues, and strongest supporters for pragmatic reasons? The answer to this question depends again on the principal. Some would say (Mark Siegel, for example, in chapter 8 of this volume) that the American political system demands pragmatic responses, and that for the American parties to do anything else would be political suicide. Others would say that putting pragmatism over substance makes American political parties simple electoral machines, not genuine political parties. Indeed, Katz and I have termed American parties "empty vessels" to describe this reality.[22] Ultimately, if the state is the true principal of the American party system, then the triumph of pragmatism over ideology is inevitable, for pragmatism promotes stability and that is what the state values most.

Paradox 3

Parties are supposed to recruit candidates but not endorse them, as this would violate the spirit of primaries.

One of the defining characteristics of political parties is their ability to "run" candidates for office. The consumers of political party products (voters, activists, and the media) expect parties to find good candidates to run for office under their party label. If a weak candidate (one who is inexperienced, inarticulate, or holds views contrary to the party's central principles) receives the party nomination, the party's supporters chastise the party for not having recruited candidates well. If parties are agents for candidates and elected officials (that is, the ones who want to serve in the majority), then they should indeed take a proactive approach to candidate recruitment. Indeed, the political party organizations have committees of individuals who dedicate their energies to this task. When the parties engage in recruitment, they try to demonstrate to prospective candidates that their organizations can offer significant resources if they win the party nomination.[23] However, in most circumstances, parties cannot promise a direct endorsement of a recruited candidate, which leads us to the present paradox.

Political parties have a policy that they usually do not endorse candidates before the primary election or other nominating process (such as a convention or a caucus) is concluded. The argument is that the voters or party activists who participate in nomination events (the principals in this case) are the best judges of which candidates will do best in a general election contest. For the most part, parties actually abide by this policy of nonendorsement. The openness of the candidate selection process, one of the prized achievements of the Progressive Movement, stops parties from clearly identifying their best candidates early in the election cycle. In this way, any individual who wishes to identify with a major party can put his or her hat in the ring as a prospective nominee. A major study of congressional candidates is aptly titled the "Candidate Emergence Study," rather than the "candidate recruitment study" because the best way to describe how candidates are selected is that they emerge at the behest of a variety of catalysts (not the least of which is their own personal ambition).[24]

Still, there are cases where political parties do not simply stand by and let candidates "emerge." This leads to an important question: When the parties violate their own norms, has an ethical transgression occurred? There are certain conditions under which the parties offer preprimary endorsements. When one candidate is highly objectionable to the party's mainstream (such as former Ku Klux Klansman David Duke, who ran for various elective offices in Louisiana), or a member is under indictment (such as former congressman Joe McDade [R-Pa.] who, though identified as a Republican, regularly ran with both parties' nominations), or when there is a special election or a runoff (because of a tight time horizon—as in the Republican Party primary for the special election in CA-22 in 1998), the party will typically take a side. Ironically, when parties endorse, their strategy tends to backfire.[25] Perhaps it is because the objectionable candidate has such fame (or infamy) that a party's endorsement does not appear to mean much in the arena of public opinion.

Short of offering an official endorsement, parties do much to encourage certain candidates' chances over others, clearly crossing an ethical line if they are the agents for candidates. One of the most effective ways to do this is a "whispering" campaign in Washington or in state capitols about which candidates are polling well in possible general election matchups and which are not. This sends important cues to PACs, political consultants, and the media about the consensus candidacy. Why do parties engage in informal favoritism? The answer is that although they are discouraged and sometimes prohibited by state law from endorsing candidates in the primary, they are expected to promote candidates with the best chance of winning. Because the resources (see below) that candidates need are scarce, the parties do tend to direct resources in a way that will do the most electoral good and will mollify their activist base. This explains why sometimes the parties will shy away from potentially winnable races with candidates who only marginally appeal to their activist core.[26] If parties are agents of the state, then encouraging mainstream candidates by any means is acceptable.

Paradox 4

Parties are supposed to be national and provide services to all candidates, but also be sensitive to individual candidates' needs, especially regarding locales and personalities.

Following on the previous paradox, American political parties are expected to service all candidates fully, which promotes the ideas of party responsibility and unified campaign themes, and at the same time be cognizant of the local needs of candidates, which is important for winning offices. When the parties endeavor to treat all candidates the same, they invariably receive great criticism from all fronts: The advice is generic and therefore useless; it wastes valuable time for little in return. However, doing the converse stretches the party's institutional capacity: There are simply too many variables in each district for a relatively small party staff in Washington or the state capitols to service adequately. The limited utility of party support is another factor that frequently leads to charges that we have a "candidate-centered" system.

Pragmatism has again produced an interesting solution for the parties: They provide broad, generic advice and resources directly and provide specialized services indirectly through the hiring of professional political consultants. The money the CCCs are legally allowed to spend on behalf of their candidates is mostly paid to professional political consultants who take only a few clients at a time.[27] The political parties seem to have solved this immediate paradox by subcontracting resource provision to other vendors, but this activity has exposed the parties to other criticisms, especially that the political consultants they hire have replaced parties.[28]

Earlier, I quoted Katz and Mair stating that the state recognizes the need to stage competitive elections. Because the state has managed to create a system that has mostly uncompetitive elections, the parties, media, and voters shower lavish attention and resources on the very few seats that are in contention.[29] Since each major party desires majority status and since true competition is confined to a handful of seats, the parties find ways to give competitive candidates the maximum amount of resources while providing all their candidates with some minimal support. By asking other party agents (such as political consultants, staff members of incumbent officeholders who are technically governmental employees, and interest groups affiliated with the party) to do whatever is needed to win competitive races, parties create a campaign environment that clearly shows that the ends justify the means. Therefore, campaign activities that might be personally unethical for candidates (such as making misleading or false statements or ignoring or ridiculing third-party candidates) are considered marginally ethical for parties because of the importance of majority status and a stable two-party cartel.

Paradox 5

Parties are supposed to raise money for their operations from the private sector but not in excessive amounts. However, the idea of state-financed elections seems inconsistent with American democratic principles.

Campaign finance is certainly the first topic that comes to mind when people put *political parties* and *ethics* in the same sentence. Yet conflicting imperatives again make judgments about unethical behavior difficult. The money paradox stated above finds that we generally agree that too much money spent to elect candidates means wealthy contributors have too much influence over those same elected officials, and that there must be a quid pro quo involved. We want to regulate the campaign finance system tightly, but moving to a state-financed system, which would eliminate private money altogether, is never seriously discussed. Why is this the case? Because, we are told, the political parties in Congress cannot come to agreement over minor reforms, much less a wholesale change in the character of the political system.[30] That is exactly the point—a state-funded campaign finance system would change the nature of American electoral competition.

Aside from the conventional institutional barriers that keep new parties out of the system (such as ballot access), privately based campaign finance keeps new parties from becoming effective participants in the electoral process because they will never be able to raise the money they need to be competitive. As agents of the state, the Democratic and Republican Parties do not seriously advocate public funding. One could say that a true cartel should be able to institutionalize public funding for the two major parties. This cannot happen for two reasons. First, the cartel is founded on a general American notion that the state must be as small as possible and that any expansion is for "nonpolitical" reasons only (such as the creation of Medicare or the nationalization of airport security personnel after September 11, 2001). Thus while it was permissible to expand the number of professional staff for elected officeholders even if these staff members performed some political work,[31] it would not be acceptable to do this for direct party purposes (as some western European states do). Second, the U.S. Supreme Court consistently finds in favor of First Amendment rights to use money in campaigns as guaranteed free speech, making it likely that a new cartel could emerge among interests opposed to the idea of public funding.

If, then, we find that public financing of elections is not possible, why is better regulation of campaigns not possible? Aside from the above argument that the current system sustains both parties, the suppliers of the funds (despite their faint objections) are willing to continue to invest in the current system. Thomas Ferguson argues: "the fundamental market for political parties usually is not voters . . . the real market for political parties is defined by major investors, who generally have good and clear reasons for investing to control the state."[32] Ferguson also says that major investors (specifically those who represent corporate America) are willing to donate to either or both political parties to prevent any substantive tinkering with the nature of the state-supported capitalist system. This explains why every time the parties discover loopholes in campaign finance laws, the "moneyed interests" respond with the requested funds. This has escalated the reasonable cost of competitive campaigns dramatically, guaranteeing that most would-be minor-party participants are deterred from participating. The only exception we have witnessed to the major-party money advantage in elections is H. Ross Perot's failed attempts at a successful candidacy and new party. The individualistic nature of Perot's "billionaire populist" appeals made him a relatively easy target for ridicule by mainstream politicians, contributing to his political demise. Perot's momentary success also helped enforce the myth that the party system is open to challenges, thus discouraging criticism of the party system (including from Perot himself).[33]

Today's campaign finance debates center around the appropriateness of "soft money" and the use of issue advocacy campaigns by both parties and interest groups. Soft money refers to funds raised for party-building purposes instead of direct electioneering costs.[34] Starting with the 1996 elections, political parties began to spend soft money in ways that barely conformed to the spirit of the law. By not using the "magic words" of direct electioneering ("vote for," "vote against," "elect," or "defeat") in advocating for a particular candidate, parties could claim they were informing the public about issues, not candidates. This allowed them, in their view, to use soft money to help pay for these communications. As Siegel points out in the next chapter, a unilateral refusal to engage in unethical behavior would be political suicide, so both parties sponsored soft money–funded issue ads at virtually the same time. Indeed, the loose interpretations of how money may be raised and spent in elections have been pushed by both parties almost equally.[35] But in contrast to Siegel's view, I believe that political party soft money spending does not seem unethical in a system where parties are agents for their candidates—they are bound to do what they must to elect them to office. It does not seem unethical in terms of the voters, as these "issue ads" provide more, not less, issue content than is normally witnessed in campaigns.[36] It does seem problematic in terms of disproportionate influence by monied groups over nonmonied groups (more about that below), but fundamentally, soft money just reinforces Ferguson's argument about investors. If the two major political parties can continue to raise huge sums from wealthy donors,[37] it is the nature of the political system that allows a handful of elites rather than the masses to control the boundaries of political debate that has serious ethical problems, not the political parties that this system produces.

Paradox 6

Parties should be responsive to group concerns but should not court their financial support.

Interest groups also engage in issue advocacy campaigns with funds that do not have to be disclosed to the Federal Election Commission. They can do this because they have successfully argued that it is their First Amendment right to do so.[38] Likewise, interest groups have donated unlimited amounts to political parties in the form of soft money, a concept many in the media find both unethical and objectionable. However, the interest group–political party tension is another paradox. Our parties are supposed to be "big tents," collections of myriad interest groups that reflect the variety of concerns in society at large. Thus political parties are encouraged to be inclusive and in many important ways are described by their constituent groups (for example, Democrats are synonymous with organized labor; Republicans have affinity with corporate America). Political parties are applauded for their affirmative action measures to be race- and gender-inclusive with delegates to the national conventions, and President George W. Bush's "compassionate conservatism" is the latest effort to reach out to all groups. If parties are agents for voters, and voters are aligned in groups, then it makes sense for parties to court the favor of groups. Indeed, much of American democratic theory (including the founders' own thinking) is expressed in terms of the importance of group participation. However, issue appeals seem to be one thing: donations of soft money quite another.

Once again, a political system that sanctions the idea that those with more money are entitled to more speech should be blamed for the ethical lapse here, not the parties. *Buckley* v. *Valeo* put the Constitution on the side of unlimited money in politics.[39] The parties have taken this to be another tool in their arsenal designed to win elections. It seems impossible for parties to embrace groups' ideas and followers without embracing their donations as well.

Closing Thoughts

Political parties appear to behave ethically within an unethical system. They have a clear goal: winning elections. They have a variety of strategies to accomplish this, many of which often seem contradictory. They appear to encourage democratic discourse while in fact stifling it in fundamental ways. If the barriers to real party competition were removed (such as the single member plurality system; restrictive state-run ballot access laws; airwave access run by cost, not fairness), the current practices of the Democratic and Republican Parties would change almost instantly. Since they are the parties in power, and their officeholders *are* the state, then the rules of the game that favor two parties, such as issue-free campaigns, election funding by wealthy interests, and suppressed competition, will remain in force.

In sum, parties have a number of ethical responsibilities and obligations during elections, but what these are depends on who the principal is in the principal-agent relationship. They have different and competing duties if the principal is the state, candidates, or citizens. Therefore, parties both are and are *not* acting ethically today. When they are not, it is the result of an electoral system that constricts competition. Finally, other electoral actors have a major effect on parties' ethical actions. Unlike any other actor discussed in this book, parties face competing demands from candidates, citizens, and the state. Additionally, and possibly most importantly, the system in which parties operate goes a long way to create these competing demands on political parties.

Notes

1. A straightforward discussion of how principal-agent theory works in legislative and bureaucratic contexts can be found in Kenneth A. Shepsle and Mark S. Bonchek, *Analyzing Politics: Rationality, Behavior, and Institutions* (W.W. Norton, 1997), pp. 358–404. Chapter 2 of Barbara Sinclair's *Legislators, Leaders, and Lawmaking: The U.S. House of Representatives in the Postreform Era* (Johns Hopkins University Press, 1995) gives a detailed case for the roles of various agents in the U.S. House.

2. For how this works with committees in Congress, see Forrest Maltzman, *Competing Principals: Committees, Parties, and the Organization of Congress* (University of Michigan Press, 1997).

3. David Menefee-Libey, *The Triumph of Campaign-Centered Politics* (New York: Chatham House, 2000); John Aldrich, *Why Parties? The Origin and Transformation of Political Parties in America* (University of Chicago Press, 1995); Paul S. Herrnson, *Party Campaigning in the 1980s* (Harvard University Press, 1988).

4. Richard S. Katz and Peter Mair, "Changing Models of Party Organization and Party Democracy: The Emergence of the Cartel Party," *Party Politics*, vol. 1 (1995), pp. 5–28.

5. Ibid., p. 22.

6. However, as Traugott points out in chapter 13 of this volume, party identification is still the best predictor of individuals' vote choice.

7. See Leon Epstein, "Parties as Public Utilities," in *Political Parties in the American Mold* (University of Wisconsin Press, 1985).

8. See Thomas Cronin, *The State of the Presidency* (Boston: Little, Brown, 1980).

9. Paul S. Herrnson and John Green, *Multiparty Politics in America* (Lanham, Md.: Rowman & Littlefield, 1997); Theodore J. Lowi and Joseph Romance, *A Republic of Parties? Debating the Two-Party System* (Lanham, Md.: Rowman & Littlefield, 1998).

10. For a discussion of the legal and institutional barriers to minor-party access, see Herrnson and Green, *Multiparty Politics in America*; David A. Dulio and James A. Thurber, "America's Two-Party System: Friend or Foe?" *Administrative Law Review*, vol. 52 (2000), pp. 769–92.

11. Herrnson and Green, *Multiparty Politics in America*.

12. Katz and Mair, "Changing Models of Party Organization and Party Democracy."

13. The contention that Nader was a "spoiler" has been variously argued but is impossible to prove. The assumption that Nader voters would have voted for Gore if Nader were not on the ballot is the same argument made for the importance of Perot's candidacy for George Bush in 1992.

14. For example, Federal Election Commission commissioners are political appointees who are nominated by the president and confirmed by the Senate: "by law, no more than three Commissioners can be members of the same political party" (see Anthony Corrado and others, *Campaign Finance Reform: A Sourcebook* [Brookings, 1997], pp. 277–80).

15. *California Democratic Party et al.* v. *Jones, Secretary of State of California et al.,* 530 U.S. 567 (2000).

16. For a summary of arguments about how the electoral rules in the United States (the SMP rules) foster a two-party system, see Dulio and Thurber, "America's Two-Party System."

17. Aldrich, *Why Parties?*

18. Robin Kolodny, *Pursuing Majorities: Congressional Campaign Committees in American Politics* (University of Oklahoma Press, 1998).

19. See also Gary W. Cox and Mathew D. McCubbins, *Legislative Leviathan: Party Government in the House* (University of California Press, 1993); Aldrich, *Why Parties?*

20. Richard Fenno, *Home Style: House Members and Their Districts* (Boston: Little, Brown, 1978).

21. On leadership PACs, see Kathryn Pearson, "Congressional Leadership PACs: Who Benefits?" (paper presented at the annual national meeting of the Midwest Political Science Association, Palmer House Hilton, Chicago, April 19–22, 2001).

22. Richard S. Katz and Robin Kolodny, "Party Organization as an Empty Vessel: Parties in American Politics," in Richard S. Katz and Peter Mair, eds., *How Parties Organize: Change and Adaptation in Party Organizations in Western Democracies* (London: Sage Publications, 1994).

23. Paul S. Herrnson, *Congressional Elections: Campaigning at Home and in Washington* (Washington: CQ Press, 2000), p. 68.

24. See L. Sandy Maisel, Walter J. Stone, and Cherie D. Maestas, "Quality Challengers to Congressional Incumbents: Can Better Candidates Be Found?" in Paul S. Herrnson, ed., *Playing Hardball: Campaigning for the U.S. Congress* (Upper Saddle River, N.J.: Prentice-Hall, 2000).

25. The 1998 special election in California's 22d district is a case in point. The Republican Party's support of moderate Brooks Firestone allowed eventual nominee Tom Bordanaro to make the claim that "Gingrich was interfering in local political processes" (Jeff Gill, "One Year and Four Elections: The 1998 Capps Campaign for California's Twenty-Second District," in James A. Thurber, ed., *The Battle for Congress: Consultants, Candidates, and Voters* [Brookings, 2001]).

26. One case is the 2000 Pennsylvania Senate race where Democrat Ron Klink was unenthusiastically supported by his party even though his opponent, incumbent Senator Rick Santorum, was considered one of the most vulnerable members running for reelection. Klink's pro-gun and pro-life views made him unattractive to Democratic Party fund-raisers even though his economic issue stances were considered quite progressive.

27. Robin Kolodny and David A. Dulio, "Where the Money Goes: Party Spending in Congressional Elections" (paper presented at the annual national meeting

of the Midwest Political Science Association, Palmer House Hilton, Chicago, April 19–22, 2001).

28. For a discussion of the argument that consultants have replaced parties, see David A. Dulio, "For Better or Worse? How Political Consultants Are Changing Elections in the United States" (Ph.D. diss., American University, 2001); Robin Kolodny, "Electoral Partnerships: Political Consultants and Political Parties," in James A. Thurber and Candice J. Nelson, eds., *Campaign Warriors: Political Consultants in Elections* (Brookings, 2000).

29. On uncompetitive elections, see James E. Campbell, *Cheap Seats: The Democratic Party's Advantage in U.S. House Elections* (Ohio State University Press, 1996).

30. Diana Dwyre and Victoria A. Farrar-Myers, *Legislative Labyrinth: Congress and Campaign Finance Reform* (Washington: CQ Press, 2001).

31. J. P. Monroe, *The Political Party Matrix: The Persistence of Organization* (State University of New York Press, 2001), details the evolution of district staff at the national, state, and local levels and argues that the state is in effect subsidizing political party work that was previously funded by party organizations in the "golden age."

32. Thomas Ferguson, *Golden Rule: The Investment Theory of Party Competition and the Logic of Money-Driven Political Systems* (University of Chicago Press, 1995), p. 22.

33. Theodore Lowi's "conversation" with a Perot representative is something everyone should read to understand this point (Lowi and Romance, *A Republic of Parties?* pp. 22–30).

34. Diana Dwyre and Robin Kolodny, "Throwing out the Rulebook: Political Parties in the 2000 Election," in David B. Magleby, ed., *Financing the 2000 Election* (Brookings, 2002).

35. For detailed examples, see Darrell M. West, *Checkbook Democracy: How Money Corrupts Political Campaigns* (Northeastern University Press, 2000).

36. James A. Thurber, Candice J. Nelson, and David A. Dulio, eds., *Crowded Airwaves: Campaign Advertising in Elections* (Brookings, 2000).

37. On March 27, 2002, President George W. Bush signed the Bipartisan Campaign Finance Reform Act into law. The new law forbids national political parties from raising soft money effective after the November 2002 elections. Court challenges regarding the constitutionality of this law were filed immediately.

38. See Thurber in chapter 9 of this volume for more on this point.

39. *Buckley v. Valeo*, 424 U.S. 1, 12–59 (1976).

CHAPTER EIGHT

POLITICAL PARTIES

Conduct, Codes,
and Common Sense

MARK A. SIEGEL

O ver the last political generation, and certainly in the post-Watergate era, the public's perception of politicians—and political parties— has deteriorated.[1] This is manifest in public opinion polls and survey research as well as political behavior, most specifically in voting patterns and party identification. Since the classic study *The American Voter*, the percentage of Americans identifying with political parties has decreased dramatically.[2] The consequences of an increasingly tripartite electorate— composed of one-third Democrats, one-third Republicans, and one-third Independents—emerged most clearly in the summer of 1992 in support levels for Independent candidate H. Ross Perot, even though his idiosyncratic candidacy lost much of that support by Election Day.

Recognizing that a problem exists is the first step in correcting it. If one is committed to strengthening the relationship between the governing and the governed and to reinvigorating the concept of representation in the American political culture, it is critical that the polity's concerns with its political system be addressed. The perception of political parties today among the American people is a good place to start.

Both major political parties do a reasonably good job of maintaining their political bases in presidential elections and, in fact, in most federal elections. Exit polls from the 2000 election show that almost 90 percent of Democrats actually voted Democratic while over 90 percent of Republicans voted Republican. This is partly attributable to the fact that both

128

parties are reasonably successful when it comes to mobilizing their supporters (though the Democrats' get-out-the-vote (GOTV) effort held a slight edge in 1998 and 2000). Even so, the battleground of American politics is found not in either party's political base, but rather at the political margins. Independents, weak-identifiers, ticket-splitters, and ticket-switchers now determine the course of American politics. And it is in this critically important and expanding electoral segment that contempt for political parties is the strongest.

This development is somewhat surprising given the fact that American parties have become more cohesive, more programmatic, and more clearly distinguishable from each other over the course of the last generation. The familiar refrain that "there isn't a dime's worth of difference between the Democrats and the Republicans" certainly is not consistent with the kinds of candidates the respective parties nominate, the specific party platforms and issues they endorse, and the legislation each congressional party supports in the House and Senate. Despite former president Clinton's "third way" or George W. Bush's "compassionate conservatism," it is becoming easier to distinguish between parties on questions of ideology and policy.

What, then, explains the perception, especially among Independent voters, that the Democratic and Republican Parties are virtually identical? The explanation, I believe, is that nonaffiliated voters find the two major parties indistinguishable where political ethics, or the lack thereof, is concerned. It is not that the parties' programs and ideologies have failed the system, but rather that the parties' ethical conduct has delegitimized the political culture.

Beyond the continuing resonance of corruption as a perception of politics in the post-Watergate era, the deceptions of Iran-Contra, or the personal conduct of former president Clinton, has been the extraordinary pattern of activity of independent political committees. These groups have been transparently undertaking efforts that appear to be very much coordinated with various campaigns and candidates. One example from the 2000 campaign, also discussed in chapter 1, is the group that falsely and maliciously suggested that Senator John McCain (R-Ariz.) opposed breast cancer research. As noted in chapter 1, Senator McCain has traditionally supported research for breast cancer, aside from the few votes discussed by this particular group. Another equally abhorrent example, this time from the 1998 elections, was the contention that the Republican Party condones racial lynching. The recent perception of the ethical corruption of politics quite possibly reflects the rapidly increasing sums of money

invested in the political system and the obvious benefits to those who
fund winning candidates. It may involve the recent revelation that Republican Party operatives uniformly challenged improper absentee ballots from
registered Democrats while simultaneously demanding that the irregular
ballots of registered Republicans be counted during the Election 2000 recounts in Florida.

Very likely a combination of these factors and more has compounded a
public perception of the moral corruption of American politics. The American people increasingly have come to believe that politics has become de-
void of ethics and moral content and that politicians and their parties will
do whatever it takes to win, including violating both the letter and spirit
of the law. By undermining the faith of the governed in those who govern,
this perception erodes the legitimacy of our political system and may ultimately lead to destabilization if future mobilization of public policy support is mooted at times of national crisis.

This chapter reviews the ethical pressures—implicit and explicit—in
contemporary party politics and examines how the Democratic and Republican Parties have attempted to resolve them, including the development and exploitation of the "soft money" loophole for financing political activities; attempts to constrain intraparty noncompliance with national
party rules; attempts to constrain negative, misleading, or distorting campaigning in both primary and general elections; and how Democratic and
Republican Parties have attempted to deal with ethical ambiguities in this
new political era. It concludes with concrete recommendations as to how
to strengthen both the perception and actual behavior of political parties
in America and how to restore to them their critical function as legitimate
intermediaries between the polity and the government.

The "Winograd Loophole": Soft Money and Ethics

The massive infusion of soft money into the political system, especially
during the 1996 and 2000 presidential election cycles, fundamentally re-
cast American politics. In 1974 the Federal Election Campaign Act (FECA)
had limited the amount of money individuals could contribute to federal
campaigns. It also had prohibited the use of corporate and union treasury
"soft money" funds to influence federal elections. But amendments to the
FECA subsequently allowed individuals, corporations, and unions to contribute unlimited sums of money for "generic party building activities."

Since that time, both the Democratic and Republican Parties deliberately and repeatedly have sought to circumvent the spirit and letter of the law by characterizing expenditures made on behalf of their respective presidential candidates as "party building" or "issue advocacy."

Since 1991 alone, a staggering $1.1 billion in soft money has been contributed to the two major parties, with more than $437 million going to the Democrats (47 percent of total 2000 cycle receipts) and more than $622 million to the Republicans (35 percent of total 2000 cycle receipts).[3] Many would argue that such huge sums of corporate and union treasury funds—and the public outrage at their scope and the methods by which they were raised—have accelerated the erosion of the trust and confidence Americans have in their political system. The ethical debate over the quantity and sources of these funds and the manner in which parties and candidates have coordinated their expenditure with that of regulated funds ("hard money") in federal campaigns was crystallized in the then president Bill Clinton's "Lincoln Bedroom" fund-raising scandal and Vice President Al Gore's Buddhist Monk controversy. These became key elements in the 2000 presidential campaign. Additionally, the use of unregulated soft money by so-called independent committees against Senator McCain in his unsuccessful bid for the Republican presidential nomination against George W. Bush transformed McCain into a quixotic, high-profile, "victimized" champion of campaign finance reform.

It is nothing less than extraordinary that the history of the specific Federal Election Commission (FEC) exemption permitting the use of soft money in American political campaigns—a seminal political event—never has been reported.[4] As a result, the exemption has remained shrouded in mystery and distorted by inaccurate perceptions for more than twenty years.

The soft money exemption arises from an interpretation of the legislative history of the FECA that could be called the "Winograd loophole." Morley Winograd is a Democratic Party Rules impresario, former state chairman of the Democratic Party of Michigan, former president of the Association of State Democratic Chairs, and director of the National Performance Review ("Reinventing Government") led by former vice president Gore during the Clinton administration. Winograd's efforts to strengthen American political parties—and specifically to expand party-building activities at the state level—resulted in a provision of the law allowing so-called soft money to circuitously wind its way back into American national elections. Winograd discussed the objectives and expectations driving the enactment of this provision in the course of an extensive dialogue with this writer in July 2000.

In the wake of the 1976 presidential election, it became clear that state parties that had previously played significant roles in presidential campaigns were extremely concerned about the restrictions imposed on them by the FECA in 1974. While drafting the law in the wake of Watergate, Congress indirectly had singled out state parties by limiting their ability to participate in campaigns through independent expenditures. While truly "independent" committees were allowed to make independent expenditures, the law correctly assumed that Democratic and Republican state parties were not independent of their respective presidential nominees. As a result, all independent expenditures by state parties were counted against the overall limitation on campaign expenditures imposed by the new system of public financing for presidential campaigns.

Interpretations of the FECA all but excluded direct participation by state parties in the 1976 presidential campaign. The state parties, in turn, sought remedies to this exclusion following the election so they might once again engage in traditional party-building activities. In 1976 there was a de facto prohibition on such previously commonplace activities as printing bumper stickers with the candidate's name on them or manufacturing the campaign buttons that had been signature fixtures of American political campaigns since the nineteenth century. The state parties found they were not allowed to produce such items without first obtaining permission to expend the funds required from their respective national campaigns. The national campaigns, in turn, quite rightly placed the cost of bumper stickers and buttons so far down among their priorities that these state expenditures never would be approved. Consequently, all active members of the Association of State Democratic Chairs (ASDC) called for an amendment to the FECA that would allow state parties to function effectively in future presidential elections. Winograd noted that the state parties strong enough to have felt the new limits imposed on activities previously permitted were most likely to participate in the ASDC and its policy deliberations. The critical issue facing state political parties was how to amend the law to permit commonsense party-building functions that were not geared specifically to influencing the outcome of federal elections. Suggestions as to how to fix the problem circulated among members of the ASDC throughout 1977 and 1978.

This particular issue obviously was not the principal concern of the then members of Congress, who were far more worried about the rise of political action committees (PACs), the ability of single-issue committees to raise vast amounts of money, and the incongruities of a system providing public funding for presidential elections but not for congressional campaigns. The first resolution considered in the U.S. House of Representatives in 1979 (H.R. 1) was the focal point of campaign finance reform efforts during the 96th Congress in 1979–80 and would have established a system of public financing for all congressional campaigns, using the same framework as 1974's FECA did for presidential campaigns. Under the proposal, the role of state parties would have been further diminished, if not eliminated entirely.

After Winograd was elected president of the ASDC in 1979, he decided to make addressing the problems of campaign finance laws as they related to state parties the association's number one priority. In a series of internal meetings beginning in early 1979, Winograd won his members' approval for an active lobbying campaign in Congress to reestablish the traditional roles of state political parties in grassroots campaign activities.

The ASDC's main thrust was that political parties alone could aggregate all the competing claims for financial support and in turn allocate funds to the most effective registration and GOTV efforts of a given campaign cycle. By focusing the expenditures on these more candidate-neutral activities, the party would help preclude the possibility that an individual candidate's vote or policy position would be unduly influenced by large contributions from either PACs or individuals.

The first attempt to incorporate this policy idea in campaign reform legislation came during the debate on H.R. 1, the bill proposing public funding of congressional campaigns. Curiously, objections came from members of Congress representing the states having the strongest state parties (with the exception of Michigan, where Winograd obviously had "wired" the votes). These members were reluctant to cede to competing political entities any more money than they already had with which to influence their campaigns' expenditures.

The House Administration Committee took up H.R. 5010 (also during 1979) in a raucous session. The committee's senior staff member, Bob Moss, had previously met with the ASDC following the failure of its amendments to H.R. 1 and had agreed to include among the chairman's amendments a proposal to permit unlimited, and predominantly unreported, expenditures of funds by state parties for volunteer activities—including registration and GOTV campaigns—during presidential campaign years.

Such activities simply were removed from the scope of the FECA so that state laws alone could restrict which sources of funds (corporate contributions, union dues, and so on) could be used, how much of each could be raised, and what kinds of expenditures would be permissible. Winograd quite specifically asserts that the amendment did not contemplate expenditures of any of this money on advertising of any kind, especially on behalf of individual candidates. Advertising was considered to fall clearly within FECA limits involving the coordination of independent expenditures. H.R. 5010 was voted out of the House Administration Committee before the 1979 summer recess and was adopted by the full House later that year.

Senate adoption of H.R. 5010 proved far more uncertain and politically difficult. While the Senate Democratic leadership was persuaded by party-building arguments, it remained concerned about the impact party building would have on statewide races. Southern Democrats, in particular, were unenthusiastic about voter registration and turnout efforts that might enfranchise new voters. However, House Democrats proved persuasive of their need for such activities to maintain their majority.

The Carter White House posed a second major obstacle, having finally recognized the amendment's potential consequences. The White House asked the Senate to block the proposed amendment because it would limit the ability of the presidential staff to totally control presidential campaigns. By this point, however, the Carter administration's influence over Democratic members of Congress had so diminished that supporters of the amendment successfully portrayed White House concerns as typical, provincial southern Democratic paranoia inconsistent with the interests of the national Democratic Party and its congressional and senatorial caucuses.

Winograd specifically recalled what he believed was the turning point in the consideration of his amendment. As key Democratic Senate staffers working on the ASDC proposal met with members of President Carter's staff to debate the issue, Winograd felt defensive concerning its implications. Carter staffers pointedly asked Winograd, "Don't you think the Republicans will use this provision to raise a ton of money and send it through their state party structures in 1980?" Winograd answered, "They might. But if we can't match them on raising this kind of money for parties, then shame on us."[5]

One can argue that in the long run, Winograd's provision did in fact work, at least in part, as anticipated. The Republicans' advantage in the use of soft money during 1980 spurred the national Democratic Party to use the same mechanism in 1984 and thereafter. The revolutionary institution of the "coordinated campaign" among the Democratic National Committee (DNC), presidential campaign, state parties, and federal candidates across the states arose because this new source of money could not be spent on media advertising. This forced the party to coordinate a massive and multifaceted field organization.

While the courts later abolished this restriction, Winograd believes the FEC's interpretation of the FECA's provisions was very different from what its supporters envisioned. As a result, state parties, especially those in control of their expenditure decisions, became much more interesting—and appealing—to elected officials. The political parties emerged as far more important elements in the political process. Subsequent efforts to increase registration and turnout initially were ineffective, but this critical goal of the amendment gained momentum from presidential cycle to presidential cycle.

But by the 2000 election cycle, it had become obvious that coordinated field organizations and carefully targeted turnout campaigns eventually did impact voter participation and election results, encouraging, in particular, a historic Election Day turnout by African Americans nationwide. Unfortunately, in a consequence altogether unforeseen by the amendment's drafters, state parties' roles increasingly had been relegated to "funding pass-throughs" for their respective national parties. Thus while the soft money provision proved totally inadequate to the task of resuscitating national and state political parties, it actually did help to partially achieve the primary goal of party building from the start: increased voter participation in the political process. The soft money that passes through state parties for the purposes of minority (in particular African American) registration and GOTV has been effective. While general turnout has gone down between 1960 and 2000, minority turnout has increased.

The FEC has catalogued myriad uses of soft money:

> Soft money is used to pay a portion of the overhead expenses of party organizations, as well as other shared expenses that benefit both federal and non-federal elections. In addition, it is used for issue advocacy, as well as generic party advertising. It may also be transferred from national committees to state and local party committees as well as being used to support construction and maintenance of party headquarters.[6]

Winograd found the recent debate in the Senate over McCain-Feingold (named for Senators McCain and Russell Feingold [D-Wis.]) and in the

House over Shays-Meehan (named after Christopher Shays [R-Conn.] and Martin Meehan [D-Mass.]) banning soft money to cover essentially the same philosophical grounds and legislative pattern as the 1979 action. The House would not pass the Senate's ban on soft money unless the use of soft money for voter turnout and party registration campaigns was exempted. And Democrats from urban constituencies having smaller wealthy donor bases found common ground with Republicans seeking to preserve what the amendments to the 1974 law allowed by way of party activities. The Congressional Black Caucus has been reluctant to cosponsor the Shays-Meehan bill because soft money has helped African American participation.

The perversion of the clear intent of the ASDC proposal to allow soft money expenditures for genuine party-building activities was not conceptual but interpretative. The soft money exemption for genuine party-building activities did not cause the money scandals of the 1996 and 2000 cycles. Rather, it was the hundreds of millions of dollars that the national campaigns passed through state parties to fund so-called "issue advertising" that circumvented the spirit, if not the letter, of federal campaign finance legislation. Winograd maintains that the thrust of his original amendment (before its interpretative expansion allowed it to include issue advertising) was to allow individuals, corporations, and unions to strengthen political parties and increase political participation in America. Winograd argues that that core principle has stood the test of time and should remain a permanent part of the American political landscape.[7]

The Criminalization of American Political Parties?

Others, however, disagree with Winograd, disputing not the intent of the loophole exempting the use of soft money for party-building activities, but rather the consequences of the loophole's ultimate exploitation. For example, some argue, "Though soft money can only go to the political parties, the parties have found ways to spend it to help individual candidates. The distinction between hard and soft money has become a fiction."[8] Only a small portion of the soft money raised by the Democratic and Republican Parties has been used to implement the amendment's original and express intent: to support systematic party building, voter registration, and GOTV. Republicans transferred 51 percent of the $252.8 million in soft money raised in 2000 to state parties, primarily for issue

advocacy advertisements. The Democrats transferred a staggering 61 percent. The national committees directly spent hundreds of millions of dollars more on so-called issue advocacy. These combined funds were spent
on deliberate, organized, and directed activities that circumvented the spirit,
if not the letter, of the FECA with respect to limits on political contributions by individuals, corporations, and unions in federal elections.

Those having the slightest doubt as to the intent of the Democratic and
Republican Parties' 2000 cycle soft money "party-building" expenditures
need only review the principal recipients of these funds as superimposed
on a map of Electoral College marginality. Allocations were not made by
population size or by the number of state elections being contested; they
were decided based exclusively on how competitive the parties' presidential candidates were in each state. Both parties selected the identical ten
states as principal recipients of their nonfederal "party-building" or "generic" funds: Pennsylvania, Michigan, Florida, Ohio, Missouri, Washington, Oregon, Wisconsin, California, and Illinois.[9] While there were vari-
ances in the two parties' internal rank ordering and total dollar amounts
transferred, the presidential campaigns certainly directed the flow of funds
to these "battleground states." In other words, nonfederal soft money
funds were assigned on the basis of targeting for campaigns for federal
office.

A law born of an attempt to eliminate the corrupting influence of big
money in national politics—and most specifically the campaign fund-raising
abuse manifest in the 1972 Committee for the Reelection of the President—had come full circle. A law aimed at preventing actions of individuals such as Bebe Rebozo (who pumped hundreds of thousands of unreported dollars into President Nixon's reelection campaign) had by the
1996 and 2000 election cycles quite openly encouraged both parties to
solicit, receive, and expend even larger contributions from individuals,
corporations, and labor unions in support of their respective presidential
campaigns. As journalist Elizabeth Drew notes:

> As of the 1996 election, the post-Watergate reforms—enacted to end
> the ability of the very rich to buy access, ambassadorships and
> policy—had been rendered null and void. The overall limit of $25,000
> on individual contributions in one year, or $50,000 per election cycle,
> became meaningless. The idea that there were any limits on raising
> and spending private money for presidential candidates who accepted
> public financing was rendered obsolete.[10]

Winograd stated in an interview with the author that drafters of the 1979 Winograd loophole did not foresee that soft money raised to build stronger political parties would be used to produce issue ads. The loophole had been intended to maintain the vitality of grassroots politics in the states, not to allow presidential campaign managers to direct state political parties to use consultants selected by the national campaign to produce and buy media disseminating specific themes and messages of the national campaign.

Some would argue—as Winograd did to me—that state parties were indeed strengthened by the loophole because it forced the coordination of state and national campaigns and generated registration and grassroots GOTV in presidential marginal states. The Gore-Lieberman ticket pursued the party-building and coordinated strategy course in seventeen states during their 2000 campaign. What is extraordinary is that thirty-three noncompetitive states and the District of Columbia were *excluded* from such targeted efforts in 2000 despite the fact that their state parties—and candidates for the U.S. Senate, U.S. House, and statewide and municipal offices—had clear and pressing electoral interests beyond the presidential race.

Massachusetts, Rhode Island, Connecticut, Vermont, and Washington, D.C., did not receive a single dollar in "party-building" soft money from DNC in 2000. The DNC was by no means alone in its selective concern for party building: The Republican National Committee (RNC) refused to invest a single dollar of soft money for "party-building" efforts in Senator Joe Lieberman's (D) Connecticut, even as it spent $9 million on "party building" in the critical battleground state of Florida.

In nontargeted presidential states, incumbents and challengers alike among House and Senate candidates—like the Republicans in Connecticut—were denied all soft money "party-building" benefits by their own national committees. It mattered not at all how tight their races were or how likely they were to achieve an upset victory. State legislative candidates, who would implement the redistricting mandates of the 2000 Census, likewise were excluded from soft money party-building assistance in nontargeted states.

Normatively and systemically, the practice of denying soft money support to "noncompetitive" states is both wrong and dysfunctional, for it assumes that a national party's sole function during a presidential election year is to elect a president. The problem can be addressed in a manner that honors the original intent of the Winograd loophole while eliminating massive abuses arising from its circumvention. But in a political climate that considers all soft money to be corrupting—even the minuscule amounts actually used for party building itself—the positive elements of the Winograd loophole may be beyond saving. The McCain-Feingold and Shays-Meehan legislation both ban all uses of soft money in what very likely is a classic case of throwing the baby out with the bath water. The Winograd loophole's positive intent is the baby, but the practices that loophole encouraged in the raising and spending of more than $1 billion in soft money in the last decade alone constitute very dirty bath water indeed. Today, reformers would prevent individuals, corporations, and unions from spending any money whatsoever for voter registration efforts and other initiatives to increase rates of political participation, which have hovered embarrassingly close to 50 percent in each of the past two presidential election cycles.

Money Machines for Political Candidates

Our political parties' traditional functions have gradually eroded over the past century. As Robin Kolodny noted in the previous chapter, the Progressive Era of the early twentieth century reflected antiparty sentiments that took the political parties' most critical function—selecting party leaders—out of the hands of party elites, diffusing that responsibility to party rank-and-file members in that uniquely American contribution to comparative politics: the primary. Progressives and reformers continued their assault on the power of political parties by attacking the "machines" that had grown strong in most urban areas and, for the most part, eliminating the patronage that had given the machines their power.

During the 1970s the Democratic Party's reform movement continued the Progressive agenda by removing the role of party leaders in candidate selection, further diffusing responsibilities for candidate selection to the parties' grassroots. The Democrats replaced the elite caucus delegate and candidate selection systems with various forms of primaries, including the notorious "open primaries," which render all but meaningless the concept of party membership.

The consequences of a century of systematic assaults on American political parties continue to ripple throughout our political system. From the elimination of party-strengthening caucuses to the institution of structural separations of congressional (both House and Senate) parties and national parties, the unintended consequences of reform appear to have had more impact on our political system than those that were intended. The same very likely is true as regards campaign finance reform.

The soft money infestation of our political system during the 1990s clearly was neither intended nor anticipated in the original 1974 FECA or its subsequent amendments. Nor was it the intent of court decisions limiting political contributions and activities to violate constitutional freedoms of speech and association. Nevertheless, starting in 1996 and peaking in 2000, our national political parties for the most part have redirected their energies to focus all but exclusively on raising and spending money at the expense of their traditional roles in education and training, registration and issue development.

Few would disagree that both Democratic and Republican National Committee chairs view fund-raising as their most important responsibility. "I really have the sense that the sole reason for people at the national committee getting up each morning is to raise money," stated former Democratic national chairman and Presidential Debates Commission cochairman Paul Kirk.[11] Their fund-raising operations have become the largest, most important, and best-supported divisions of both national committees.

During presidential campaigns, our national and state parties engage in a soft money shell game. On behalf of presidential candidates, the national parties solicit huge soft money contributions from individuals, corporations, and unions that sometimes go straight to their own coffers but frequently are solicited directly to their sister state parties in targeted "competitive" Electoral College states. On the same day that state parties receive soft money checks, they are explicitly instructed by the national parties how to spend those funds to enhance the national parties' prospects in the presidential campaign—a clear violation of the spirit, if not the letter, of the FECA. In 2000 the Democratic national party transferred $150 million in soft money; its Republican counterpart transferred $130 million. The national parties' instructions routinely are so explicit that they identify the issues that are to receive the most media advertising, how much airtime should be purchased, where messages should air, and who should produce them.

In short, the national parties, twisting the intent of campaign reforms until it bears no resemblance whatsoever to the underlying legislation, have transformed themselves into bank pass-through windows laundering funds generated ostensibly for one purpose to functions altogether different in a transparent circumvention of the law. No less important, the national parties have abdicated their once-critical core functions—education and training, party building, and more—to do so. Money has become "the mother's milk" of politics and the raison d'être of our national political parties.

Conduct, Codes, and Common Sense

While one American national political party has adopted a rather rigid written code of ethical conduct and the other has not, we should beware the urge to judge the former as "ethical" and the latter less so. For the record, the Democratic National Committee, which in 1986 adopted an impressive "Code of Fair Campaign Practices for Democratic Candidates for Elective Public Office," was, by 2001, altogether unaware that any such code existed and had been incorporated into the DNC charter until this writer insisted (as a former DNC member who had voted for the code's adoption) that it did and it had.[12] When a party, its leaders, and candidates are unaware of the very existence of a standard of conduct, its enforcement is problematic at best. The Democrats' code nevertheless constitutes an interesting case study as the sole effort by an American political party to codify political ethics.

The genesis of the Democratic Party's ethics code was Chairman Paul Kirk's initiative to apply lessons learned in 1984 to the future conduct of Democratic presidential campaigns.[13] Foremost among these was an effort to ensure that Democratic presidential candidates avoid "going negative" in a manner that would hobble the eventual nominee. Kirk subsequently sought to address the issue of ethics in party politics by creating an intraparty code, an agreement among the national chair and all the state chairs to abolish straw polls before delegate selection, to have state parties comply with national party rules, and to have all parties commit to "no negative campaigning" guidelines. The prohibition on straw polls was a meaningful attempt to enforce party rules that no part of the delegate selection process commence before the presidential election year. Finally, Kirk addressed political ethics in the development and adoption of the Code of Fair Campaign Practices, which is now part of the DNC charter. The code, adopted simultaneously with the rules for the 1988 Democratic National Convention, was part of Kirk's effort to expedite major reforms that would best serve the party's interests in 1988.

The Democratic Party's Code of Fair Campaign Practices is an extraordinarily broad set of principles intent upon *reethicizing* American politics.

It commits to "civility, honesty and decency" in American political campaigns, instructing all Democratic candidates to defend the rights of all Americans to full and equal participation in the electoral process. In this respect, it addressed issues manifest in some Florida counties during the disputed 2000 presidential campaign recounts and the findings of the Civil Rights Commission on voter intimidation and purging of voter lists. The code specifically prohibits negative campaigning (defined as "the use of personal vilification, character defamation, whispering campaigns, libel, slander, negative innuendo, or scurrilous attacks"); and it prohibits Democratic candidates from misrepresenting, distorting, or falsifying facts to mislead an electorate concerning the record of opponents as well as "dishonest or unethical" practices that corrupt the will of the voters.

The Democratic code also appears to prohibit assistance from 527-type committees when it states that "Democratic candidates shall . . . repudiate support deriving from any individual or group which resorts, on behalf of their candidacies or in opposition to that of their opponents, to [unethical] methods, practices and tactics."[14] It concludes with a highly problematic requirement that all Democratic candidates abide by the "letter and spirit of all relevant statutes and regulations" in conducting and funding Democratic campaigns. But who can reconcile the DNC's massive soft money issue advertising program in targeted Electoral College states with the "spirit" of the FECA?

Codes are viewed by many in politics as naive. None exists in the RNC bylaws and some Republicans have in fact dismissed codes as unworkable gimmicks.[15] Some Republican strategists suggest that only self-enforced standards are meaningful, adding that the consequences to a campaign or reputation of public exposure of unethical activity are the best way to limit it.

The DNC position, despite its soaring rhetoric, seems far more symbolic than substantial. While recognizing and rhetorically addressing the problem, the DNC has yet to undertake a systematic effort to inform Democratic parties and candidates what the party charter demands of them. And unilateral adoption of fair campaign standards is as appealing as unilateral disarmament was at the height of the cold war. Written codes can sensitize participants to ethical issues but of themselves cannot solve the problem.

Neither party has the organizational clout or public standing to unilaterally foster ethical political campaigns. However, parties can do a number of things to move in the right direction, including jawbone candidates, attempt to resolve primary campaign complaints over tactics, and work across party lines to establish broad guidelines for general election behavior. But none of these efforts will withstand the onslaught of candidates determined to win by any means and at any cost.

With our political parties appearing increasingly anachronistic (or worse) to significant elements of our electorate, there is little they can do to sanction candidates who violate whatever guidelines are established. In the end, the outcome rests on the shifting sands of a candidate's good will and position in the polls. As former DNC chairman Kirk observes, "We have to do a lot about ethics. But the first and most important element is to rely on gut common sense on what is right and what is wrong, and how the image of the party is presented."[16] Kirk's sense of ethical pragmatism informs the ethics curriculum currently taught by the DNC.

Teaching and Sensitizing Candidates to Ethics

Can political ethics be taught? The DNC believes so, and thinks it knows how. Incorporated within the educational programs of the Brown-Tulley Institute (the DNC's training vehicle at national, state, and local levels) is a significant ethical training component.[17] The intent is to improve ethical behavior in campaigns without moralizing about what should or should not be done in specific situations. The curriculum seeks to link personal and community-based concepts of right and wrong to campaign decisionmaking, increase awareness of ethical dilemmas, illuminating where, why, and how they occur, and address a range of solutions accepted as ethical by the broadest possible audience. The Democratic ethics curriculum appears to be modeled along the lines of other forms of interpersonal sensitivity training. It is not designed to stop the desperate or premeditated unethical actions of persons intent upon committing them. Rather, it tries to heighten candidates' and staffers' awareness of problems and their causes and consequences, aiming to prevent unintended slips and mitigate the creation of a campaign culture that ignores unethical decisionmaking.

The pragmatism of the Democratic approach is its most salient feature. It stresses the consequences of unethical behavior, which can undermine a campaign's ability to win by throwing it "off-message." (Recall George W. Bush's campaign's one-week stall due to the furor raised by soft money issue advertising associated with the "RATS" ad discussed in chapter 1.) The DNC curriculum stresses that behavior that discourages

Code of Fair Campaign Practices for Democratic Candidates for Elective Public Office

—Democratic candidates shall conduct their campaigns with civility, honesty and decency, discussing issues as they see them, presenting their records and policies with sincerity, frankness and candor, and criticizing without fear or favor the record and policies of their opponents and their opponents' parties which merit such criticism, so as to engage in and encourage constructive debate on the issues of the day and to uphold the best in American tradition.

—Democratic candidates shall defend and uphold the right of every qualified American voter to full and equal participation in the electoral process.

—Democratic candidates shall not engage in, and shall condemn the use of, personal vilification, character defamation, whispering campaigns, libel, slander, negative innuendo, or scurrilous attacks on any candidate or his or her personal or family life.

—Democratic candidates shall not participate in, and shall condemn the use of, campaign material of any sort which misrepresents, distorts, or otherwise falsifies the facts or misleads the electorate regarding any candidate, as well as the use of malicious or unfounded accusations against any candidate which aim at creating or exploiting doubts, without justification, as to his or her morality, loyalty and patriotism.

continued next page

turnout and participation and therefore impacts the legitimacy of the electoral and representational process is unethical. And it emphasizes the fact that unethical behavior damages reputations, destroys careers, and can cost huge amounts in legal fees. This is consistent with some Republicans' perspective on ethics: public exposure damages the professional, the party, and the campaign; thus ethical behavior should be a self-enforcing and self-rewarding value in our political culture.

Ethical dilemmas in political campaigns are often complex and multifaceted where competing normative "goods" create institutional tension. "Ethical relativity" is taught by the use of creative and realistic hypothetical case studies in campaign management covering a range of reasonable scenarios: circumventing campaign spending limits, covering up in-kind

—Democratic candidates shall not participate in, and shall condemn, any appeal to prejudice and discrimination based on race, sex, age, color, creed, national origin, religion, ethnic identity, sexual orientation, economic status, philosophical persuasion, or physical disability.

—Democratic candidates shall not engage in, and shall condemn, any dishonest or unethical practice which tends to corrupt or undermine our American system of free elections or which hampers or prevents the full and free expression of the will of the voters.

—Democratic candidates shall not seek, and shall immediately and publicly repudiate, support deriving from any individual or group which resorts, on behalf of their candidacies or in opposition to that of their opponents, to the methods, practices and tactics which they condemn.

—Democratic candidates, in conducting and financing their campaigns, shall abide by the letter and spirit of all relevant statutes and regulations regarding campaign practices.

—Democratic candidates shall, to the extent reasonably possible, assure that their representatives and staffs, as well as they themselves, adhere to this Code.

As adopted March 8, 1986, and amended October 9, 1993.

Source: Democratic National Committee.

contributions, kickbacks, sexual harassment, the use of information gathered by opposition research on personal, sexual, financial, or business conduct, and collusion and coordination with ostensibly independent committees.

I experienced a very practical example of "ethical relativity" during my tenure as executive director of the DNC. In what was expected to be a very close election in 1976, we were particularly concerned about the then candidate Jimmy Carter's weakness in the key Democratic stronghold of New York State where we ran fourth, following Senator Scoop Jackson (D-Wash.), Representative Morris Udall (D-Ariz.), and votes cast as "uncommitted" in the primary. Our concerns were compounded by the fact that Carter had no relationship with New York's—or the nation's—

critical Jewish community, and former senator Eugene McCarthy had filed as an independent candidate on the New York presidential ballot. We feared McCarthy would siphon off as many as 500,000 disgruntled liberal and Jewish votes, very likely costing Carter the state.

As a former New Yorker, I understood the complexity of the state's filing procedures, its cumbersome petition process involving each of its congressional districts, and the fact that petitions were gathered in a problematic fashion. I proceeded with a legal effort to have McCarthy removed from the New York ballot, after Robert Strauss, then DNC chairman, said I could proceed if I raised the funds for the legal challenge myself. Ultimately, McCarthy was thrown off the New York ballot because of insufficient proper petition signatures, and Carter went on to win New York by fewer than 400,000 votes. Had McCarthy remained on the ballot in New York, Carter pollster Pat Caddell believes Carter would have lost the state and Gerald Ford (R-Mich.) would have been elected president.

I had weighed the normative "good" of providing voters the broadest and fairest ballot choice against the pragmatic "good" of advancing my party's interests, and pragmatism won the day. (A similar effort successfully challenging Ralph Nader's presence on the New Hampshire ballot alone would have cleanly elected Al Gore President in 2000.) It is not surprising that in the 2000 New York Republican primary, Governor (and Bush supporter) George Pataki (R-N.Y.) followed the exact same petition-challenging route to knock Senator McCain off the ballot in many of New York's thirty-four congressional districts. Reformers, liberals, and most New York Democrats condemned the effort as undemocratic and unfair. Ethics, in the heat of a campaign, is not always a right-wrong decision but rather reflects myriad shades of gray. Ethics training nonetheless can make us aware of the ethical questions and consequences of our actions.

A strong case can be made for including a comprehensive ethics component in all party education and training. By sensitizing students of political management to ethical dilemmas they will encounter and the range of available options and consequences, it is far more likely that in times of ethical crisis, decisionmakers will pause and think before committing themselves to an improper course of action. Such introspection would be most effective in building a more ethical political culture.

The RNC has yet to initiate an effort to incorporate ethics in its educational and training programs. In 850 pages of text in six training manuals, the word *ethics* does not appear.

Toward a More Ethical Political Party System

Political science has long argued that the most fundamental building blocks of a free society are organized political parties competing in free and fair elections, conducted pursuant to the rule of law. Party building and the encouragement of nongovernmental organizations have proved fundamental in fostering democracy in the former Soviet bloc and the transitional world. To the extent parties perform their functions transparently and are respected by the polity, civic culture is strengthened and political culture legitimized. To the extent they are perceived as unethical, corrupt, or irrelevant, democracy's infrastructure is undermined, as in America today. Americans have lost faith in the parties' ability to be meaningful players in their lives.

The national parties should be made stronger and more effective in communication and organization, building their constituent parties from the bottom up through education, training, and technology. State parties, the fundamental rational political units of America, should eschew their roles as money launderers circumventing election laws.

It is unclear whether the proposed McCain-Feingold or Shays-Meehan legislation, which include bans on soft money, will be passed by this Congress and signed into law by the president. Has party exploitation of the Winograd soft money loophole passed a point of no return? If new campaign finance legislation ever does pass, it inevitably will include a total ban on soft money. But the original concerns of the Association of State Democratic Chairs, echoed in 2001 by the Congressional Black Caucus, are relevant to the parties' future in America.

Congress and the president should ban the use of soft money for issue advertising and advocacy, while preserving its role in financing specifically designated party-building activities as originally intended: party building (including technology and physical infrastructure), registration, and voter mobilization. (How much more vital would American political parties be today if only 10 percent of the $1 billion in soft money raised in the last decade had been so invested?) Were individuals, corporations, and labor unions to commit themselves to increasing political participation in America, our civic culture could be strengthened enormously.

The parties initially should consider internal efforts to deal with the ethical challenges. Codes governing the conduct of nominating campaigns for federal office, especially presidential nominations, could be promulgated by both political parties. At national conventions, presidential candidates who refused to comply with the code, behaved unethically, or misrepresented the views of their opponents would be sanctioned by the national parties. At national conventions, sanctions could be enforced by denying delegates floor access and hotel and trailer accommodations. Over the years, the Democratic Party has been unsuccessful in efforts to enforce compliance with delegate selection rules principally because the national party invariably has relented. This need not be the case in the future.

The Democratic and Republican Parties should consider agreeing jointly and publicly to commit themselves to a single code of fair campaign practices in the conduct of their activities and political campaigns. Unilateral action by either party will prove ineffective; only in tandem can the parties make this system work. They should create a joint task force to identify the steps to be taken to restore the public's confidence in them as ethical institutions worthy of public pride, not shame and disgrace.

Enforcement of such a code would be external—by the press and the public—rather than by any arm of the government, including the FEC. Such public enforcement, with the media as the fundamental mechanism of accountability, has proved effective in reviewing the fairness and accuracy of campaign advertising, with television and radio routinely refusing to air inaccurate, misleading, or distorting spots.

An analogous enforcement procedure succeeded in the fall of 2000 when a bipartisan presidential debate commission headed by former RNC chair Frank Fahrenkopf and former DNC chair Kirk promulgated sites, dates, and procedures for presidential and vice presidential debates, which the Bush campaign initially rejected. At one point it was unclear whether any debates at all would be held and whether any would be sponsored by the Presidential Debate Commission. The press all but uniformly condemned the Bush position and Bush, then governor, soon discovered that the attempt to manipulate the interparty agreement was generating strong public disapproval. The Bush campaign quickly reversed its position, adopting the bipartisan commission's recommendations only due to "press and public" pressure, in essence a successful enforcement mechanism. Those recommendations collectively could serve as a model for any number of agreements on fair campaign practices and ethics.

In addition, the press's role in matters of political ethics could be expanded. One could reasonably argue that if the media were really committed to restoring ethics to our political discourse and building more ethical political parties, they would offer free media time to major party candidates (see chapter 12) and could withdraw such time if they or a neutral third observer determined that a campaign violated the ethical standards agreed to by both parties. Such enforcement would give would-be violators of campaign practices and ethics pause.

The Democratic Party's attempt to incorporate meaningful ethics in its education and training curriculum through the Brown-Tulley Institute is a positive development that should be expanded at state and national levels. It also should be considered seriously for inclusion in Republican Party education and training. Ethical political parties should be a matter of civil consensus, not partisan debate.

These small steps alone may not reverse our national parties' deterioration in the eyes of our citizenry, but they should be viewed as a significant beginning in coming to grips with the ethical dilemmas facing the parties in the new millennium. If championed by party reformers and respected media critics, such attempts to implement meaningful ethical reform might well generate real support, as did presidential candidate McCain's call for reform as a central theme during the 2000 cycle. By strengthening parties and the public's faith in our political system, these reforms could expand our civic culture and relegitimize the foundations of our American democracy.

Notes

1. See Traugott's chapter 13 in this volume for a discussion of the declining trust in government and general cynicism.

2. Angus Campbell and others, *The American Voter* (University of Chicago Press, 1960).

3. Please see the Federal Election Commission press release, "FEC Reports Increase in Party Fundraising for 2000," May 15, 2001.

4. Some have attempted to understand the soft money loophole and where it came from, but do so in an incomplete manner. Anthony Corrado examines the FEC regulations allowing for the loophole in "Party Soft Money," in Anthony Corrado and others, eds., *Campaign Finance Reform: A Sourcebook* (Brookings, 1997). The discussion that follows is designed to be an addition to his and similar accounts.

5. Morley Winograd, interview by author, Washington, July 2000. In fact the Republicans did use this provision much more effectively in 1980, as predicted. See Elizabeth Drew, "Politics and Money—Part II," *New Yorker*, December 13, 1982.

6. Federal Election Commission. "FEC Reports Increase in Party Fundraising for 2000" (2001; www.fec.gov).

7. Much of the information for the above section came from lengthy discussions with Morley Winograd in July of 2000. Winograd, as has been noted, chaired a major Democratic Party reform commission in the 1980s, was Michigan Democratic State Chairman and president of the Association of State Democratic Chairs, and headed the "reinventing government" office in the Clinton-Gore White House.

8. Elizabeth Drew, *The Corruption of American Politics* (Woodstock, N.Y.: Overlook Press, 1999), p. 8.

9. Federal Election Commission, "National Party Transfers to State/Local Party Committees, January 1, 1999–December 31, 2000" (2000; www.fec.gov).

10. Drew, *Corruption of American Politics*, p. 58.

11. Paul Kirk, telephone interview by author, July 17, 2001.

12. See Nelson, Medvic, and Dulio in chapter 5 of this volume for discussion of political consultants' awareness of their own code of ethics.

13. Kirk's chairmanship lasted from 1985 to 1989.

14. 527 committees, so named after a little-known section of the tax code, are tax-exempt political organizations that can receive and disburse monies for political purposes. During 2000 legislation in Congress required all 527 committees to disclose their activities.

15. This conclusion is drawn from a discussion during a meeting of media consultants in conjunction with the Improving Campaign Conduct project at American University.

16. Kirk, interview.

17. Much of the curriculum at the Brown-Tully Institute has been designed and taught by Brad Knott under American University's grant from The Pew Charitable Trusts. The Knot curriculum undoubtedly is the most important political ethics training initiative to be attempted in the United States.

CHAPTER NINE

INTEREST GROUPS

From Campaigning to Lobbying

JAMES A. THURBER

Interest groups and lobbyists are increasingly having an impact on the quality of American campaigns and elections as they become more influential. Their participation in campaigns includes promoting candidates and issues, raising money, and swaying voters. In addition, many groups provide critical campaign services such as issue advocacy advertising, polling, advice about media strategy, organizing get-out-the-vote (GOTV) strategies, and general tactical guidance for candidates.[1] However, scholars have focused on their monetary contributions to campaigns, especially through political action committees (PACs).[2] Less is known about the more subtle and nontransparent assistance to candidates, such as issue campaigns waged by groups or nonmonetary contributions provided by political parties.[3] The services provided by professional campaign consultants, which are paid for by lobbying groups, are also difficult to measure, although they are often a key part of winning modern elections. It is the variety of services consultants provide in campaigns that sets the foundation for the powerful roles many are beginning to play in postelection governing.

The metamorphosis of the campaign consultant to lobbyist plays a key part in access and lobbying battles after candidates become elected public officials. The nonregulated election activities (outside the campaign finance and lobbying laws) of interest groups present ethical dilemmas for campaign consultants turned lobbyists and candidates turned elected offi-

cials. Are the overlapping worlds of interest groups and lobbyists in elections and their influence on the outcomes of public policy debates undermining campaigns and ultimately American democracy?

Ethical Problems of Interest Group Activity

Lobbying is the third largest enterprise in our nation's capital after government and tourism,[4] with the 15,000 full-time professional lobbyists
registered by Congress representing virtually every type of interest in
America.[5] However, the number of persons employed in Washington who
are either lobbyists or associated with them in some way has been estimated at 91,000.[6] This industry is not confined to Washington, as there
are thousands more individuals lobbying state legislatures, city councils,
and executive branches at every level of American government. Similarly,
3,000 to 4,000 people are also full-time campaign professionals at the
national level, but many more thousands are part-time campaign consultants for local and state politicians.[7] Hundreds and even thousands of people
involved in campaigns later lobby politicians, and this presents a problem
for democracy because of the lack of transparency in the relationship between elected public officials and campaign consultants–lobbyists.[8] As the
campaign consultant-lobbyist's identity blurs, so may his or her loyalty to
the cause and the candidate. Participation in the democratic process of
campaigns and elections should be encouraged but must be distinguished
from questionable secret linkages among campaign consultants, lobbyists, and candidates.

The several "dilemmas" presented by interest group activity in contemporary election campaigns include (1) the huge sums of money put
into the process by interest groups; (2) interest groups' use of issue advertising; (3) interest groups' contributions to what has been termed the permanent campaign; (4) conflicts of interest; and (5) the norm of reciprocity
that exists between those in government. Many of the subsequent problems listed are directly related to the first—the immense amounts of money
that fund campaigns, so well documented in Makinson's chapter 10 in
this volume. The enormous amount of money raises serious ethical questions about corruption in financing elections.[9] Evidence of the increasing
cost of elections is found in the fact that spending in all presidential and
congressional campaigns, including soft money and issue advertising by
interest groups, reached approximately $4 billion in the 2000 electoral
cycle, double the campaign expenditures of four years earlier.[10]

A second problem is that the amount of issue advertising and independent expenditures can dwarf the input from constituents and less well-funded groups. The result is a narrowing of public policy options because only those groups that have sufficient resources are heard. This may undermine the "common good" through the maximization of narrow interests.

Third, interest groups feed certain aspects of the "permanent campaign," defined by Heclo as "the combination of image making and strategic calculation that turns governing into a perpetual campaign and remakes government into an instrument designed to sustain an elected official's popularity."[11] This results in an unrelenting demand from incumbents for campaign funds, which are more easily collected from particular interest groups than from broad-based networks; candidates can also collect much-needed campaign dollars in larger amounts from interest groups because higher contribution limits apply to interest groups' PACs ($5,000 for each candidate each election) compared to individual donations ($1,000). In an era of partisan parity, within both Congress and the electorate, the permanent campaign creates the need for advice from campaign consultants–lobbyists beyond the strategy of conducting a winning campaign to include which issues and policies to embrace in order to win the next election. National politics has thus gone past the stage of campaigning to govern and has reached the "more truly corrupted condition of governing to campaign," with campaign consultants and lobbyists playing a central role in the phenomenon.[12]

Fourth, when interest groups participate in election campaigns through money or services and also hire or are their own lobbyists, it introduces serious ethical questions of conflict of interest about who is paying for what and with what consequences for public policymaking. Who are the lobbyist-consultants loyal to, the issues and lobbyists or the candidates and campaign consultants? Ethicist Tom DeCair of the Josephson Institute of Ethics argues that "the appearance of conflict can be as damaging as a real conflict." If campaign consultants are also lobbying candidates for special interests, the line of loyalty to the campaign and the special interest becomes blurred, creating real conflicts of interest.[13]

Fifth, problems stem from a pervasive norm of pluralist democracy and political life generally—reciprocity. Reciprocity is one of the strongest embedded norms in public life. It is directly related to ethical dilemmas that occur in the linkage among consultants, lobbyists, and elected public officials. Reciprocity can be defined as: "To return in kind or degree; the mutual or equivalent exchange or paying back of what one has received; a mutual exchange; mutual dependence, action or influence; a mutual exchange of privileges."[14] Reciprocity is expected in personal relationships and it is a strong influence on political relationships in campaigns, lobbying, and policymaking.

The drive for political self-preservation (reelection) is central to these ethical dilemmas involving reciprocity. Candidates with the most campaign resources are often able to hire campaign professionals with the best reputations, thus improving their probability of winning elections.[15] Most of these campaign contributions (money, volunteers, and services) come from powerful businesses, unions, associations, and interest groups.[16] Campaign consultants with the best reputations also help generate campaign funds, thus helping to build incumbency advantage.[17] These consultants are successful during an election year and also in off-election years because their business volume relies on both campaigns and lobbying. Thus electoral success for consultants often leads to lobbying success, which in turn presents a dilemma. Where is their loyalty when consultant-lobbyists are simultaneously working for an interest group and several candidates for public office, especially when income is involved? What are the motivations of those giving campaign contributions and hiring campaign consultants who are also lobbyists? This linkage of mutual exchange is at the heart of contemporary politics in the United States, but may undermine the civic responsibility of the actors and reduce public trust in the policymaking process.

Campaign consultants and lobbyists are at the nexus of policymaking networks.[18] Both build relationships that help bring money to campaigns to help candidates win and to influence elected public officials. The influence starts in the campaigns and continues after elections. Relationships among campaign consultants, lobbyists, and public officials are mutually beneficial, but does that help the public? Does the advocacy relationship (protected by law) build an ethical blind spot and undermine the civic responsibility of the actors in the relationship? Is it ethical to have reciprocal relationships among consultants, lobbyists, and public officials when those alliances are not transparent and they seem to go against the public interest?

The close ties of campaign consultant–lobbyist–elected public officials may also foster cynicism toward government. Public complaints about the quality of election discourse and lack of trust in government is a sixth problem, which some say stems directly from interest group activity in elections.[19] The level of trust in our elections and governmental institutions has declined over the last three decades, and often the reasons given for this decline relate to the role of interest groups in campaigns and their strong influence in public policymaking generally.[20]

All of these ethical problems or dilemmas have serious consequences for public policymaking at all levels of government. The role of interest groups and lobbyists in fund-raising, delivering campaign services, and massive unregulated political expenditures that can lead to access and influence with public officials have immeasurable effects on the quality of American democracy.

Consequences

Some scholars and journalists have presented evidence that the primary consequences of these election activities are unequal access to elected public officials, conflicts of interest, lower voter turnout, and increased suspicion, cynicism, and even resentment among the public.[21] Interest groups and the lobbyists they hire have helped to transform electoral politics from party-centered to candidate-centered to the present "interest group–centered" system.[22] Interest groups have contributed greater and greater sums of money and services to candidates and parties in each campaign cycle over the last three decades. The passage of campaign finance reform legislation in 1971 and amendments in 1974, 1976, and 1979, various tax codes, numerous regulations and decisions by the Federal Election Commission (FEC), and a few court decisions have had little or no effect on this growth of influence.[23] As noted above, interest groups endorse candidates and contribute significant resources, both money and services, to help elect public officials. They do this not only to ensure electoral outcomes but to gain access to elected public policymakers. Unlike campaign cash contributions, analyzed in Makinson's chapter 10, issue advertising and volunteered services for campaigns are nontransparent, unregulated, and have no limits.

An example of the problem—a campaign consultant who helped elect a candidate and then became a lobbyist advocating for a specialized interest to the same public official—recently came to light in Los Angeles. As Los Angeles city commissioners debated whether a lucrative construction contact should be awarded to the House of Blues Concerts for a new theater, one of the firm's top lobbyists, Steve Afriat, played his "connection card." Afriat had been a campaign consultant to Los Angeles councilwoman Laura Chick; Councilwoman Chick became the House of Blues's chief backer on the city council. Mr. Afriat was so close to the councilwoman he listened in via speakerphone from her office during the deliberation about awarding the contract. Moreover, at the same time Afriat was lobbying Councilwoman Chick on behalf of the House of Blues, he was the political consultant running Chick's campaign for city controller.[24]

According to the *Los Angeles Times*, more than a dozen Los Angeles city hall lobbyists were campaign consultants for elected officials they lobbied afterward.[25] As a result of the exposure of this proliferation of lobbyists doubling as campaign advisors, the Los Angeles Ethics Commission *considered* barring elected officials from voting on issues involving lobbyists who also served as their campaign consultants.[26] However, the commission eventually declined to act on the issue. Lobbyists and elected public officials often defend this arrangement, saying they can keep their relationships as campaign consultants and candidates separate from their roles as lobbyists and politicians.

These alliances are prevalent at the federal, state, and local levels of government throughout the United States.[27] The reciprocal relationships among campaign consultants and lobbyists are often viewed skeptically by the media and voters.[28] However, in order to understand public policymaking in Washington or any state capitol, it is essential to understand the linkage among campaign consultants, top lobbyists, and interest groups.[29]

Tracing Interest Group Activity

One window into the world where campaign consultants, lobbyists, and elected public officials intersect is the contributions by interest groups *and* lobbyists to candidates' campaigns. *Fortune Magazine*'s top twenty-five lobbying groups and lobbyists (lobbying firms) in Washington contributed millions of dollars to candidates in the 2000 election campaign (see tables 9-1 and 9-2). Specifically, the top twenty-five lobbying groups (organized interest groups) contributed over $31 million in total during the 2000 election cycle and the top twenty-five lobbying firms spent over $4 million. Many of the top companies and associations give to both political parties and to all the candidates vying for the nomination on both sides of a campaign. The Center for Public Integrity calls them "double-dippers," as they give to both sides in an attempt to gain access to, or influence with, the eventual winner; obviously they do not give for ideological or partisan reasons.[30]

Table 9-1. *Fortune Magazine's Top 25 Lobbying Firms*

Rank	Firm	Total amount given during 2000 cycle (dollars)
1	Barbour, Griffith, & Rogers	191,251
2	Patton Boggs	389,457
3	Verner, Liipfert, Bernhard, McPherson, & Hand	316,175
4	The Duberstein Group	282,354
5	Akin, Gump, Strauss, Hauer, & Feld	235,890
6	Timmons & Co.	247,594
7	Baker, Donelson, Bearman, & Caldwell	n.a.
8	The Dutko Group	201,237
9	Podesta & Mattoon	n.a.
10	Clark & Weinstock	174,091
11	Quinn Gillespie	n.a.
12	Bergner Bockorny	n.a.
13	BKSH & Associates (Black, Kelly, Scruggs, & Healy)	n.a.
14	Cassidy & Associates	832,981
15	Williams & Jensen	270,258
16	The Wexler Group	n.a.
17	Hogan & Hartson	n.a.
18	Wilmer, Cutler, & Pickering	324,850
19	Van Scoyoc Associates	207,343
20	The Smith-Free Group	197,255
21	Greenberg, Traurig	n.a.
22	Washington Counsel	n.a.
23	OBC Group (O'Brien Calio)	233,209
24	PricewaterhouseCoopers	n.a.
25	Griffin, Johnson, Dover, & Stewart	n.a.

Sources: "The Power 25," *Fortune*, May 28, 2001; Center for Responsive Politics (www.opensecrets.org/ [December 20, 2001]).

Notes: n.a. denotes not available or not applicable. Fund-raising data are taken from the Center for Responsive Politics, which compiles fund-raising data for only the top contributors in each industry; contributions from others do not appear. The totals include contributions from state and local chapters of the parent organization. The totals include only contributions from registered lobbyists or firms; firms that engage in both legal and lobbying work are not necessarily included. The totals do not reflect contributions from individuals within associations or firms or from individual members of trade associations.

Campaign contributions are only one route to their power, however. Many of the top twenty-five groups and firms also contributed services (either in-kind or for a fee), such as strategic advice about finance, media, and grassroots activities, directly to the 2000 presidential and congressional campaigns. Almost all of the top twenty-five firms hired former prominent campaign activists who contributed their time to the campaigns in the 2000 cycle and other elections.[31] For example, several of the consultant-lobbyists helped candidates on behalf of interest group clients (such

Table 9-2. *Fortune Magazine's Top 25 Lobbying Groups*

Rank	Group	Total amount given during 2000 cycle (dollars)
1	National Rifle Association of America	3,084,296
2	AARP	n.a.
3	National Federation of Independent Business	n.a.
4	American Israel Public Affairs Committee	n.a.
5	Association of Trial Lawyers of America	3,637,450
6	AFL-CIO	2,210,636
7	Chamber of Commerce of the United States of America	n.a.
8	National Beer Wholesalers Association	2,126,661
9	National Association of Realtors	3,905,950
10	National Association of Manufacturers	n.a.
11	National Association of Home Builders of the United States	2,336,099
12	American Medical Association	2,081,519
13	American Hospital Association	1,616,269
14	National Education Association of the United States	2,685,428
15	American Farm Bureau Federation	n.a.
16	Motion Picture Association of America	134,201
17	National Association of Broadcasters	819,650
18	National Right to Life Committee	110,009
19	Health Insurance Association of America	n.a.
20	National Restaurant Association	869,034
21	National Governors' Association	n.a.
22	Recording Industry Association of America	466,243
23	American Bankers Association	1,714,395
24	Pharmaceutical Research & Manufacturers of America	454,332
25	International Brotherhood of Teamsters	2,886,490

Source: See table 9-1.

as for the National Rifle Association of America for Republican Party candidates and the AFL-CIO for Democratic Party candidates) with grassroots get-out-the-vote campaigns.[32] Both of these interest group organizations also purchased millions of dollars' worth of issue ads to assist the campaigns.[33]

The Association of Trial Lawyers of America contributed over $3.5 million and the American Medical Association and the American Hospital Association together over $3.6 million to candidates supporting their positions on the patient's bill of rights.[34] In the 1999–2000 electoral cycle, these organizations also hired several top lobbying firms to help candidates in the election and then to present their case to members of Congress.[35] These monetary and in-kind contributions (such as giving strategic campaigning advice, doing opposition research, producing media spots, paying for public opinion polls, sponsoring issue advocacy advertising to help candidates, engaging in get-out-the-vote grassroots organizing, building electoral coalitions among groups) and the alliance between the lobbyists and these groups helped to build strong ties to those in Congress, contributing to the reciprocity dilemma.[36]

Codes of Conduct

The exponential growth of campaign consultants and lobbyists during the last three decades has also created a proliferation of strong election campaign–lobbying alliances. The network of alliances is not unregulated—campaign consultants, lobbyists, interest groups, candidates, and elected public officials must all abide by local, state, and federal statutes. Members of Congress, for example, are bound by an extensive set of congressional ethics stemming from the Constitution, federal laws, party provisions, and House and Senate rules and codes of conduct. There are countless detailed laws and rules about campaign contributions, gifts, and lobbying practices that must be obeyed.

Lobbyists, campaign professionals, and political party professionals also have detailed codes of conduct (see below for the American League of Lobbyists Code of Ethics, chapter 2 for the American Association of Political Consultants Code of Ethics, and chapter 8 in this volume for a discussion of the Code of Fair Campaign Practices for Democratic Candidates for Elective Public Office). In addition, an independent body, the Woodstock Theological Center at Georgetown University, has developed a set of principles it judges important for the ethical conduct of lobbying. It was drafted with the help of lobbyists, academics, and other political professionals.[37]

Do these codes protect our elections and our democratic system from abuses by lobbyists and campaign consultants? Do the codes help protect the "public good"? What is the "public good" that should be preserved?[38] James Madison argues in *Federalist* 10 that factions or narrow interests undermine the rights of other citizens and that it is the duty of government to regulate the factions so that they do not do harm to others.[39] Madison continues by stating that factions are "adverse to the rights of other citizens or the permanent and aggregate interests of the community."[40] In *Federalist* 45 Madison emphasizes that the public good seems

American League of Lobbyists Code of Ethics

Article I—Honesty and Integrity

1.1. A lobbyist should be truthful in communicating with public officials and with other interested persons and should seek to provide factually correct, current and accurate information.

1.2. If a lobbyist determines that the lobbyist has provided a public official or other interested person with factually inaccurate information of a significant, relevant and material nature, the lobbyist should promptly provide factually accurate information to the interested person.

1.3. If a material change in factual information that the lobbyist provided previously to a public official causes the information to become inaccurate and the lobbyist knows the public official may still be relying upon the information, the lobbyist should provide accurate and updated information to the public official.

Article II—Compliance with Applicable Laws, Regulations, and Rules

A lobbyist should seek to comply fully with all laws, regulations and rules applicable to the lobbyist.

2.1. A lobbyist should be familiar with laws, regulations and rules applicable to the lobbying profession and should not engage in any violation of such laws, regulations and rules.

2.2. A lobbyist should not cause a public official to violate any law, regulation or rule applicable to such public official.

Article III—Professionalism

A lobbyist should conduct lobbying activities in a fair and professional manner.

3.1. A lobbyist should have a basic understanding of the legislative and governmental process and such specialized knowledge as is necessary to represent clients or an employer in a competent, professional manner.

3.2. A lobbyist should maintain the lobbyist's understanding of governmental processes and specialized knowledge through appro-

continued next page

priate methods such as continuing study, seminars and similar sessions in order to represent clients or an employer in a competent, professional manner.

3.3. A lobbyist should treat others—both allies and adversaries—with respect and civility.

Article IV—Conflicts of Interest

A lobbyist should not continue or undertake representations that may create conflicts of interest without the informed consent of the client or potential client involved.

4.1. A lobbyist should avoid advocating a position on an issue if the lobbyist is also representing another client on the same issue with a conflicting position.

4.2. If a lobbyist's work for one client on an issue may have a significant adverse impact on another client's interests, the lobbyist should inform and obtain consent from the other client whose interests may be affected of this fact even if the lobbyist is not representing the other client on the same issue.

4.3. A lobbyist should disclose all potential conflicts to the client or prospective client and discuss and resolve the conflict issues promptly.

4.4. A lobbyist should inform the client if any other person is receiving a direct or indirect referral or consulting fee from the lobbyist due to or in connection with the client's work and the amount of such fee or payment.

Article V—Due Diligence and Best Efforts

A lobbyist should vigorously and diligently advance and advocate the client's or employer's interests.

5.1. A lobbyist should devote adequate time, attention, and resources to the client's or employer's interests.

5.2. A lobbyist should exercise loyalty to the client or employer's interests.

5.3. A lobbyist should keep the client or employer informed regarding the work that the lobbyist is undertaking and, to the extent possible, should give the client the opportunity to choose between various options and strategies.

continued next page

continued from previous page

Article VI—Compensation and Engagement Terms

An independent lobbyist who is retained by a client should have a written agreement with the client regarding the terms and conditions for the lobbyist's services, including the amount of and basis for compensation.

Article VII—Confidentiality

A lobbyist should maintain appropriate confidentiality of client or employer information.

7.1. A lobbyist should not disclose confidential information without the client's or employer's informed consent.

7.2. A lobbyist should not use confidential client information against the interests of a client or employer or for any purpose not contemplated by the engagement or terms of employment.

Article VIII—Public Education

A lobbyist should seek to ensure better public understanding and appreciation of the nature, legitimacy and necessity of lobbying in our democratic governmental process. This includes the First Amendment right to "petition the government for redress of grievances."

Article IX—Duty to Governmental Institutions

In addition to fulfilling duties and responsibilities to the client or employer, a lobbyist should exhibit proper respect for the governmental institutions before which the lobbyist represents and advocates clients' interests.

9.1. A lobbyist should not act in any manner that will undermine public confidence and trust in the democratic governmental process.

9.2. A lobbyist should not act in a manner that shows disrespect for government institutions.

Source: American League of Lobbyists, Washington (www.alldc.org/ethicscode.htm [December 2001]).

Woodstock Principles for the Ethical Conduct of Lobbying

—The pursuit of lobbying must take into account the common good, not merely a particular client's interests narrowly considered.

—The lobbyist-client relationship must be based on candor and mutual respect.

—A policy maker is entitled to expect candid disclosure from the lobbyist, including accurate and reliable information about the identity of the client and the nature and implications of the issues.

—In dealing with other shapers of public opinion, the lobbyist may not conceal or misrepresent the identity of the client or other pertinent facts.

—The lobbyist must avoid conflicts of interest.

—Certain tactics are inappropriate in pursuing a lobbying engagement.

—The lobbyist has an obligation to promote the integrity of the lobbying profession and public understanding of the lobbying process.

Source: Woodstock Theological Center, Georgetown University (www. georgetown.edu/centers/woodstock/newweb/ethicspubpol.htm [November 15, 2001]).

to be a collective or communal interest that is different from the individual rights of special interests. He argues: "It is too early for politicians to presume on our forgetting that the public good, the real welfare of the great body of the people, is the supreme object to be pursued; and that no form of government whatever has any other value than as it may be fitted for the attainment of this object."[41] In chapter 2, Miller and Medvic elaborate on Madison's conception of the public good by asking whether self-interest or civic responsibility is a better campaign ethic. In other words, where do campaign actors' responsibilities lie: only to their own interests or to the broader body politic? They conclude that the civic responsibility conception of ethics is the best standard because it better serves the public good.

Do the codes of conduct for campaign consultants and lobbyists help to preserve the public good by focusing on civic responsibility? Codes of ethics can fall short of the goal of ensuring good behavior and in this case, clean campaigns. The American League of Lobbyists (ALL) and the American Association of Political Consultants (AAPC) codes attempt to apply general rules of political morality to specific professional behavior by articulating guidelines and regulations. However, compliance with these codes is always voluntary, which results in adherents "cherry picking" favorite provisions or ignoring the entire code. There are no enforcement mechanisms for these codes other than internal commitment and self-regulation by the professionals to their provisions.[42] Despite the fact that unethical behavior has occurred in campaigns, neither the ALL or the AAPC has censured members for breaking the codes of conduct.[43] The codes give no guidance about the ethical concern addressed earlier, the nontransparent connection of campaign consultants, lobbyists, and elected public officials.

The AAPC code does not apply to campaign finance, campaign services, and lobbyist-policymaker relationships. Its major emphasis is upon honesty, truthfulness, good business practices and refraining from "negative" attacks in campaigns. As shown in chapter 5, a large majority of consultants are aware of the AAPC code of ethics; however, few believe the code has had even a "fair amount" of influence on the behavior of campaign professionals. However, a significant majority (75 percent) of consultants believe there should be a code of ethics among campaign professionals.[44]

By comparison, the ALL code is very detailed and prescriptive, focusing on honesty and integrity, compliance with applicable laws, professionalism, conflicts of interest, confidentiality, business practices, and duty to governmental institutions.[45] Another important difference between the lobbyists' and consultants' codes is that the ALL codes of conduct address the question of reciprocity, not addressed by the AAPC code. However, the vast majority of lobbyists have no knowledge of the code or its contents.[46] Of thousands of ALL members, only a few hundred lobbyists sign the code of ethics.[47]

For all of these reasons, the mere presence of ethical codes does not seem to reduce public and media suspicion of lobbyists and campaign consultants.[48] Because of the quality of the codes and the lack of adherents to them, it is difficult to determine how the codes could make a difference.

Are the nontransparent (private) promises to stop or vote for legislation ethical if they are made by campaign consultants (who are later lobbyists) in the name of candidates who will later become public officials?

INTEREST GROUPS: FROM CAMPAIGNING TO LOBBYING

Do these agreements and connections create public cynicism and distrust of government when the secret relationships are later revealed? Is the norm of reciprocity in conflict with the public interest when elected public officials are lobbied by campaign consultants who also have interest groups as clients? Do the motivations, expectations, and deliverables in the mutual exchanges of privileges among campaign consultants, lobbyists, and candidates (public officials) undermine the public trust in government and ultimately our democracy? There are no clear answers to these questions. They are dilemmas to be resolved by consultants, lobbyists, and elected public officials, and the codes of conduct are of little help with the answers.

Conclusions

While most campaign consultants and lobbyists follow high ethical standards, a final judgment on their behavior depends on the criterion used—self-interest or civic responsibility. Special interest advocacy without concern for civic responsibility may undermine trust in government and democracy generally and may not serve the public good. Those involved in campaigning and lobbying have an obligation to enhance the democratic process and civic culture as stated in the ALL code of ethics. Who is to judge what is ethical advocacy behavior and what is civically responsible in our rough-and-tumble, winner-take-all politics? However, without rules and judges to hold the actors accountable, we must ask campaigners and lobbyists to hold themselves to a higher ethical standard. Do they? The codes of ethics help give them guidelines, but they are not enforceable and often ignored. The only protection and constraint in a pluralist representative democracy against the negative aspects of election and advocacy campaigns may be transparency and the competition from other campaign actors, lobbyists, and groups.

A free and objective media to cover the battles, transparency of the campaign-advocacy-government connection, and strong norms of conduct by the campaign professionals, lobbyists, and elected public officials—with the voter as the judge—may be the best solution to the problems of interest group activity in elections. Ethical standards and a system of checks and oversight are necessary in our nation's democratic process if our governmental institutions are to maintain their institutional legitimacy. But can this be done simply through competition, the free press, and general guidelines for ethical behavior?

If campaign consultants, lobbyists, interest groups, and elected officials must abide by statutes, rules of the House and Senate (or other governmental bodies), and codes of ethics, then why is their activity in elections and lobbying troubling? Large sums of political contributions find their way to the nation's capital and to every state capital through election campaigns and lobbying. Public distrust and concern about ethical behavior may stem from the influence of this money and other resources flowing into election and lobbying campaigns by specialized interests, thus undermining the "public good." The corrosive effects of distrust and negative opinions about campaigns and government may come from the dilemma of clearly defining what is good and bad about campaigning and advocacy for our democracy.

The activities of campaign consultants and lobbyists often present inconsistent alternatives of what is good or bad for our democracy or for themselves as professionals. The AAPC and ALL codes of conduct do not help these actors out of this dilemma and in fact often seem to contribute to it.[49] What is good for campaign advocacy (by campaign consultants) or issue advocacy (by lobbyists) is not always what is good in terms of civic responsibility (protection of our democratic values) in elections. Similarly, what is good for civic responsibility will not always be beneficial from the perspective of a campaign or issue advocate.[50]

Like all private citizens, interest groups are guaranteed a right to free political speech with which to lobby for their public policy goals. But they also have a civic responsibility to the overall democratic system. However, ultimately the ethical behavior of consultants and lobbyists should support the common good. The common good is the enduring well-being of the political community as a whole. The common good comprises a "broad range of human goods to which people are jointly committed and for which they accept final responsibility."[51] As the preamble of the U.S. Constitution makes clear, America is not a collective for individual or group benefit, but a carefully balanced network of free institutions deliberately designed to secure the common good through competition and division of power. The founders articulated the common good in memorable terms: "to form a more perfect Union, establish justice, insure domestic tranquility, provide for the common defense, promote the general welfare, and secure the blessings of liberty for ourselves and our posterity." The ultimate public good is for campaign consultants, lobbyists, interest groups, and elected officials to rise above private interests and desires in order to discern what is good for the country as a whole. This public-spirited frame of mind is tough to achieve but an indispensable ingredient of ethics, civic virtue, and good campaign conduct. It is a fundamental condition of a sustainable democratic civilization.

Notes

1. See James A. Thurber and Candice J. Nelson, eds., *Campaign Warriors: Political Consultants in Elections* (Brookings, 2000); David A. Dulio, "For Better or Worse? How Political Consultants Are Changing Elections in the United States" (Ph.D. diss., American University, 2001); Stephen K. Medvic, *Political Consultants in U.S. Congressional Elections* (Ohio State University Press, 2001) for analyses of the role of campaign consultants in elections.

2. For a thorough discussion of the money involved in election campaigns, see Larry Makinson, chapter 10 in this volume.

3. For an analysis of the relationship of consultants and political parties in U.S. elections, see David A. Dulio and James A. Thurber, "The Symbiotic Relationship between Political Parties and Political Consultants: Partners Past, Present, and Future" (paper presented at "The State of the Parties: 2000 and Beyond" conference, the Ray C. Bliss Institute, University of Akron, Akron Ohio, October 11–13, 2001).

4. Allan J. Cigler and Burdett A. Loomis, eds., *Interest Group Politics*, 6th ed. (Washington: CQ Press, 2002), p. 11.

5. Donald R. Wolfensberger, "Factions and the Public Interest: Federalist No. 10 in 2001" (paper presented at a seminar of the Woodrow Wilson Center's Congress project, "Congress, Lobbyists, and the Public Interest," Woodrow Wilson International Center for Scholars, Washington, 2001), p. 1.

6. Allan J. Cigler and Burdett A. Loomis, eds., *Interest Group Politics*, 5th ed. (Washington: CQ Press, 1998), pp. 10–11.

7. James A. Thurber, Candice J. Nelson, and David A. Dulio, "Portrait of Campaign Consultants," in James A. Thurber and Candice J. Nelson, eds., *Campaign Warriors: Political Consultants in Elections* (Brookings, 2000): 10–36; Dennis W. Johnson, *No Place for Amateurs: The Professionalization of Modern Campaigns* (Routledge Press, 2001).

8. See Ronald J. Hrebenar, Matthew J. Burbank, and Robert C. Benedict, *Political Parties, Interest Groups, and Political Campaigns* (Boulder, Colo.: Westview Press, 1999), pp. 251–70. The exact number of lobbyists involved in campaigns each election cycle is estimated to be in the thousands by party and campaign activists and interest group representatives in Washington, D.C.; however, a definitive number has not been established. The number involved in campaigns varies over time and is dependent upon competitiveness of the presidential and congressional races.

9. Michael J. Malbin and Thomas J. Gais, *The Day after Reform: Sobering Campaign Finance Lessons from the American States* (Albany, N.Y.: Rockefeller Institute Press, 1998); Robert K. Goidel, Donald A. Gross, and Todd G. Shields, *Money Matters* (Lanham, Md.: Rowman & Littlefield, 1999); David Magleby

and Candice J. Nelson, *The Money Chase: Congressional Campaign Finance Reform* (Brookings, 1990).

10. Burdett Loomis, "The Industry of Politics," University of Kansas, Department of Political Science, November 2001, p. 1.

11. Hugh Heclo, "Campaigning and Governing: A Conspectus," in Norman Ornstein and Thomas Mann, eds., *The Permanent Campaign and Its Future* (American Enterprise Institute and Brookings, 2000), p. 3; and see Sidney Blumenthal, *The Permanent Campaign* (Simon & Schuster, 1982), p. 7, for definition of the permanent campaign.

12. Heclo, "Campaigning and Governing," p. 34.

13. Tom DeCair of the Josephson Institute of Ethics, quoted in Patrick McGreevy, "Lobbyists' Dual Role Alarms Critics," *Los Angeles Times,* February 11, 2001, p. B-2.

14. *Webster's New Ninth Collegiate Dictionary* (Springfield, Mass.: Merriam-Webster, 1983), p. 983.

15. See Stephen K. Medvic, *Political Consultants in U.S. Congressional Elections* (Ohio State University Press, 2001); or Dulio, "For Better or Worse?"

16. Makinson, chapter 10.

17. See Dulio, "For Better or Worse?"

18. James A. Thurber, "Political Power and Policy Subsystems," in B. Guy Peters and Bert A. Rockman, eds., *Agenda for Excellence* (Chatham, N.J.: Chatham House, 1996), pp. 38–75.

19. Jeffrey H. Birnbaum, *The Money Men: The Real Story of Fund-Raising's Influence on Political Power in America* (New York: Crown, 2000); Kenneth R. Mayer and David T. Canon, *The Dysfunctional Congress? The Individual Roots of an Institutional Dilemma* (Boulder, Colo.: Westview Press, 1999).

20. Haynes Johnson and David S. Broder, *The System: The American Way of Politics at the Breaking Point* (Boston: Little Brown, 1996); Gary C. Jacobson, *The Politics of Congressional Elections* (Longman, 2001), pp. 86–88.

21. See David S. Broder, *Democracy Derailed: Initiative Campaigns and the Power of Money* (Harcourt, 2000); Diana Dwyre, "Campaigning outside of the Law: Interest Group Issue Advocacy Activity," in Cigler and Loomis, *Interest Group Politics*; Hrebenar, Brubank, and Benedict, *Political Parties*; Kathleen Hall Jamieson, *Dirty Politics: Deception, Distraction, and Democracy* (Oxford University Press, 1992); Mark J. Rozell and Clyde Wilcox, *Interest Groups in American Campaigns: The New Face of Electioneering* (Washington: CQ Press, 1999); Stephen Ansolabehere and Shanto Iyengar, *Going Negative: How Political Advertisements Shrink and Polarize the Electorate* (Free Press, 1995).

22. Rozell and Wilcox, *Interest Groups in American Campaigns*, ch. 1.

23. Connor, *Ethical Conduct of Lobbying*, p. 2.

24. McGreevy, "Lobbyists' Dual Role Alarms Critics," p. B-1.

25. Ibid., p. B-3.

26. Patrick McGreevy, "Ethics Panel to Study Limits on Lobbyists at City Hall," *Los Angeles Times*, March 21, 2001, p. B-2.

27. Evidence of this is documented by many scholars and journalists, such as Thurber, "Political Power and Policy Subsystems"; Jeffrey H. Birnbaum, *The*

Lobbyists: How Influence Peddlers Get Their Way in Washington (Times Books, 1992); Hrebenar, Burbank, and Benedict, *Political Parties,* Charls E. Walker, "A Four-Decade Perspective on Lobbying in Washington," in Paul S. Herrnson, Ronald G. Shaiko, and Cylde Wilcox, eds., *The Interest Group Connection: Electioneering, Lobbying, and Policymaking in Washington* (Chatham, N.J.: Chatham House, 1998); Paul Herrnson, "Interest Groups, PACs, and Campaigns," in Herrnson, Shaiko, and Wilcox, *Interest Group Connection,* pp. 37–51.

28. Broder, *Democracy Derailed,* ch. 3.

29. Loomis, "Industry of Politics," p. 2; Birnbaum, *The Money Men.*

30. A discussion of double-dippers and a list of the major ones can be found on the Center for Public Integrity website: www.publicintegrity.org/reports/bop2000/dd_candiates.htm (December 20, 2001).

31. Based on personal interviews with principals from several of the top twenty-five lobbying firms, September–October 2001.

32. Ibid. For further evidence of this activity, see case studies in David B. Magleby, ed., *Election Advocacy: Soft Money and Issue Advocacy in the 2000 Congressional Elections* (Brigham Young University, Center for the Study of Elections and Democracy, 2000).

33. Dwyre, "Campaigning outside of the Law."

34. Magleby, *Election Advocacy,* p. 2.

35. Six-month lobbying reports from secretary of the Senate/clerk of the House for registered lobbyists, clients, issues lobbied, and expenses incurred, Legislative Resource Center, 1999–2001.

36. Burdett Loomis, "The Never Ending Story: Campaigns without Elections," in Norman J. Ornstein and Thomas E. Mann, eds., *The Permanent Campaign and Its Future* (Brookings, 2000), pp. 162–84.

37. See James L. Connor, *Principles for the Ethical Conduct of Lobbying* (Georgetown University, Woodstock Theological Center, forthcoming).

38. See Connor, *Ethical Conduct of Lobbying,* pp. 2–3, for a discussion of lobbying and the public good.

39. James Madison, "No. 10," in *The Federalist Papers,* 2d ed. (New York: New American Library, 1962), p. 79.

40. Madison, "No. 10," p. 83

41. Madison, "No. 45," in *Federalist Papers,* p. 289.

42. This was emphasized by participants in several focus groups and public forums organized by the Center for Congressional and Presidential Studies, American University, with campaign professionals in 2000 and 2001.

43. The ethics committees and leadership of the ALL and the AAPC report never having censured their members for breaking the codes of conduct as of November 2001.

44. Thurber and Nelson, *Campaign Warriors,* p. 193.

45. See Lobbying Disclosure Act of 1995.

46. Statement from Howard Marlowe, former president of the American League of Lobbyists, January 1999, and study by Professor Edward B. Arroyo, Senior Fellow, Ethics in Public Policy, Woodstock Theological Center, Georgetown University, October 2001, in Connor, *Ethical Conduct of Lobbying."*

47. Howard Marlowe (former president of the ALL), interview by author, Washington, October 2001.

48. See CCPS voter survey of campaign activity, November 2000.

49. See Connor, *Ethical Conduct of Lobbying*, pp. 2–7, for a discussion of lobbying and the common good.

50. See Miller and Medvic, chapter 2, for a discussion of this distinction.

51. Connor, *Ethical Conduct of Lobbying*, p. 2.

CHAPTER TEN

INTEREST GROUPS

What Money Buys

LARRY MAKINSON

Interest groups have been around as long as politics has been around, but the nature of their influence and their effect on the ethical undertones of election campaigns have evolved in critical (and not particularly positive) ways in the modern era of dollar-dominated campaigning. Traditional broad-based organized interest groups—labor, big business, activists on issues like gun control or abortion, and so on—have been joined by influential groups whose areas of interest are much narrower and much less visible to the public at large. As money becomes an ever more important prerequisite to winning, the power of that second tier of interest groups is on the rise.

Unlike the groups that represent large blocs of voters, these interests may represent a single industry, one company, or even a single individual seeking special treatment that would not normally be available. While they may occasionally use the services of a public relations firm to paint a benign rationale for their petitions to the government, more often they operate in a very restricted universe, running lobbying campaigns that are essentially invisible to all but the participants. Their ability to persuade lawmakers of the merits of their case in such campaigns often relies on money—specifically, campaign contributions—as a primary motivator.

Chiquita Banana, to take one example, encountered a problem several years ago. In 1993 the European Union slapped a fat tariff on bananas from Central America, effectively making Chiquita's bananas prohibitively expensive for the European market.[1] Chiquita's chairman, Carl Lindner, is one of the nation's most generous campaign contributors, and has been for years. Lindner is a Republican. His problem arose during a Democratic administration, that of Bill Clinton. Once Lindner started making major soft money donations to the Democratic Party—$250,000 in 1993, then $250,000 in the 1997–98 cycle, and $620,000 in 1999–2000—the Clinton administration took up his case and energetically fought the EU tariff.[2] This escalated in 1999 when the United States applied sanctions of its own against a variety of European goods (in the process causing substantial financial harm to the small U.S. importers of those goods). Finally, in April 2001 the tariff war ended on terms favorable to Chiquita—a settlement, ironically, that may have come too late to save the company. While there was some press coverage of the Chiquita case—including a cover story in *Time Magazine* that exposed the political price paid by companies without political connections that had been caught in the crossfire—it was hardly a matter that captured the public's attention.[3]

There have been other examples of spectacular quid pro quos after major donations involving both Democratic and Republican administrations. Indeed, some of the more blatant examples have given momentum to the movement to outlaw so-called soft money contributions, which can be given without limit. But those examples are hardly unique, and it does not take a six-figure contribution to win political influence in Washington, D.C. Fund-raising luncheons, breakfasts, and dinners, held virtually every day in the nation's capital, thrive on the unspoken but universally understood premise that the swiftest way to a politician's heart is through a check to the reelection campaign.

The ever-escalating cost of running campaigns has fed this trend and made virtually every member of Congress carefully solicitous of the interests of two crucial sets of constituents—the voters back home in the district and the "cash constituents" who supply the money it takes to run. Traditional interest groups can be found among both sets of those constituents—sometimes simultaneously—but the ethical implications in responding to them may be quite different.

If a politician caters to the needs of, say, the National Rifle Association or the Sierra Club—large groups with politically active members—he or she may do so for a variety of reasons. The ideal motivation would be basic agreement with the group's philosophy. In that case, it is natural for the politician to approach the group and seek an endorsement or a contribution. The fact that the group's support can help the election campaign is a political benefit that compromises neither the candidate's political position nor the ethical standards expected of a candidate seeking public office. That is the way politics is supposed to work, after all. Enlisting interest groups to work on a politician's behalf is an accepted and legitimate practice—all the more so since the politician will likely make the interest group's position known to the broader public (although, as James Thurber points out in the previous chapter, the nontransparency of some of these activities can be problematic). Candidates do this every day. They advertise their positions on issues of interest to broad groups of the electorate. They respond to questions from the news media or from voters directly. They fill out questionnaires that probe their positions on a variety of subjects. In short, they make no secret of their positions on issues that are followed closely by key interest groups; indeed, those issues may become an integral part of the candidate's platform.

But philosophical agreement is hardly the only reason a politician will seek out a contribution or endorsement. And no candidate has a predetermined position on *every* issue that has an interest group behind it. What of the candidate who seeks the support of an interest group simply because he or she wants its political support and is willing to adapt to its position to get it? Conversely, what are the implications of an interest group seeking to influence a candidate who may never have given its issue a second thought? Is the candidate right to seek the group's support and money? Is an interest group right in aiming for a "campaign-season conversion" of a candidate who has never spoken publicly or privately about its particular issue?

In the context of political campaigning, arguments could be made that both those practices are acceptable, even if they are not ideal. Certainly interest groups have a right to try to persuade candidates to their point of view, and they well understand that one motivating factor to align with them may be that it is in the candidate's political interest to do so. Candidates, too, should be granted some leeway in expanding their repertoire of policy positions in an election year, as long as their new positions do not conflict with their overall political philosophy. Additional leeway could even be given for candidates to change their position over time. Human beings do change their opinions, after all—even politicians. Likewise, politicians may sometimes sublimate their personal views for those of important blocs of their constituents. Plenty of Democrats in western states align themselves with the positions of gun rights advocates, just as Republicans in the Rust Belt may take positions on union issues that would be anathema to their party brethren elsewhere. Positions that are politically expedient are not necessarily unethical.

That is not to say that every position taken by a politician carries with it an ethical seal of approval. Conceivably, some positions could be unethical, or at least adopted for unethical reasons. Stating one position to an interest group in order to gain support or a financial contribution and expressing an opposite position to another group, the media, or the public at large would be an example of deceitful and unethical behavior. But few successful politicians are as blatant as that. More commonly, a candidate may deliver a crystal clear endorsement of an interest group's position when speaking to its members, but deftly equivocate or evade the issue altogether when speaking to an unsympathetic audience or to the public at large. Such behavior may not be exemplary but it is not surprising, and its ethical color is a shade of gray.

More troubling are private promises made to interest groups that are never mentioned publicly at all, with the mutual understanding of the interest group and the candidate that they would not be popularly received if they were widely known. Other election-season behavior that would be clearly unethical would be such things as secret contributions that were never reported. But that would also be illegal, so its ethical nature would not even be in question. The converse is not true. Just because an action is legal—or at least not illegal—does not mean it is ethical.

This is a particularly important distinction in the area of financing election campaigns. The rules governing contributions speak only to the amount of money that may be given and restrictions covering who can give. Universal prohibitions in the United States include secret contributions, money given through "straw donors" who are reimbursed by the true, but undisclosed, donor, and money that comes from foreign nationals who are not permanent U.S. residents. Beyond that, states and local governments may add rules of their own—contribution limits, restrictions on corporate or union giving, prohibitions on giving during the legislative session, and so on. No mention is made of the motivations behind the transactions, nor of expectations implicit with the contribution.

The lines between campaign contributions and bribery—or for that matter, extortion—would seem to be clear. Bribes are secret, they tend to go straight into the pocket of the politician rather than to the election campaign. And the kicker is: something of value is promised, and delivered, in return. But contrast that with a political contribution from, say, the Beer Wholesalers political action committee (PAC), and the ethical lines may be more subtle. We could just as easily be talking about the Realtors PAC, Microsoft, or Citibank. The point is that all these groups have a multitude of business interests affected by decisions made by Congress, all are active donors, and all are making political contributions as an extension of their business strategies rather than for reasons of patriotism, civic involvement, or even as an expression of the organization's political philosophy.[4]

The contribution is reported. Both the candidate and the PAC must file documents with the relevant election agency. These reports go into a filing cabinet or a computer database and are available to anyone who wants to pore through them. That is not the same as saying the contribution is widely known to the electorate. Unless the news media or the candidate's opponent makes it an issue, the circle of people who even know there was a contribution is generally very small. This fact is well understood by both the candidate and the donor.

The contribution goes to the candidate's reelection campaign, not to his or her pocket. This means it cannot be used as a down payment on a new car or to pay next month's mortgage. Of course, it may help the politician win the job that *will* pay for those things. And it may advance the politician's career—something presumably important to the person running for office. Political ambition may not be synonymous with economic gain, but is the contribution less appreciated? A further point: Though it is prohibited at the federal level, some states do allow elected officials to convert their campaign funds to personal use when they retire.

Finally, there is the matter of motivation, expectations, and deliverables. If the beer wholesalers' lobbyist slips $500 into the politician's pocket in return for a vote to reject tightening the blood alcohol limits for drunk drivers, that is a bribe. If the lobbyist delivers a PAC check to the politician's reelection campaign, in return for an expectation—or even an election-year promise—that the politician will vote against tightening the limits, it is not a bribe. But the practical result of that $500 investment may be the same. One important difference is that with the contribution both parties can hold their heads high. The candidate has "voted his conscience" and the beer wholesalers have "participated in the political process." Granted, the contribution does not carry a money-back guarantee if the politician votes the other way. But both parties understand implicitly the political price to be paid for unmet expectations. Unless the politician plans to retire, he or she will likely be going back to the beer wholesalers next election season asking for more. The wholesalers might decide to give again or they might not: or worst of all, they could give to the incumbent's opponent.

There is an extra dimension to this contrast between bribes and contributions that is important to the discussion: It does not affect all interest groups and all candidates uniformly. If the Sierra Club or National Right to Life gives $1,000 to a congressional candidate in an open-seat race where no incumbent is running, then they are clearly hoping to help boost that candidate into the winner's circle on election night. If they give to a challenger, they are doing the same, only with much greater odds against them.

But what of the contributions delivered to incumbents? The political calculus can be far different in that case, as can the motivation and thus the ethical implications. Political donors—particularly PAC directors, lobbyists, and other political insiders acting on behalf of a specific interest group—are not in the business of dispensing their money simply on principle. Don Quixote was not a PAC director, and he would not last long in the job. The job of a PAC director is to wisely invest the group's limited resources to maximize the political return. Given the choice between an ideologically pure newcomer and a most-of-the-time friendly incumbent, PAC directors will overwhelmingly give their cash to the politician who is already in power. In the 2000 elections, PACs representing ideological and single-issue groups (like the Sierra Club and the NRA) gave twice as much to incumbent officeholders as they did to challengers. Labor PACs gave more than three times more to incumbents than to their opponents. And for every dollar that business PACs—the most pragmatic of political donors—gave to challengers, $18.83 went to incumbents.[5]

Not coincidentally, the reelection rate in 2000 for incumbents in the House of Representatives was 97.8 percent—a level only slightly higher than the average over the past two decades. Even in the tumultuous elections of 1994, when Republicans unexpectedly took control of the House of Representatives, 90.2 percent of incumbents seeking reelection won. Reelection rates in the Senate are generally lower and much more volatile in contentious election years, but even there the great majority of incumbents are safely returned to office every election year. In 2000 the rate was just under 80 percent.[6]

For a political operative trying to maximize resources, the implications of those statistics are compelling. Except in a handful of cases each election year, the people already in office are extremely likely to remain in office. They may not need an interest group's contribution to win reelection, but they will undoubtedly be grateful for it. And when Election Day is over and the legislative season begins again, they will very likely be in a position to assist the interest group in realizing its agenda.

Given the stratospheric reelection rates of members of Congress—and similar rates can be found in many state legislatures—a reasonable observer might ask whether campaign contributions are truly given (or needed) to help elect incumbents at all. Could they rather be based on the *assumption* that the incumbent will win reelection, and given not to ensure that election but to lobby that politician when he or she returns to the corridors of power? There can be no doubt that this is exactly the way many lobbyists and PAC directors view their contributions. The patterns in campaign contributions over the past decade provide compelling evidence that for business PACs in particular, pragmatism—not ideology— rules. For one thing, all industries and nearly all individual PACs spread their campaign dollars to both sides of the aisle. For another, the patterns in their giving shift as power shifts in Washington. Until 1994 Democrats and Republicans received nearly equal amounts from business PACs. After the 1994 elections, when the Republicans took control of Congress, the money shifted dramatically in the GOP's favor. In 1996 Republicans started drawing two-thirds of all business PAC dollars, a pattern that has held ever since.[7]

Several years ago the Center for Responsive Politics undertook a project that entailed interviewing outgoing members of Congress on the effects of money in the current political system. Nearly all of them complained about the time they had to spend fund-raising; many complained about the uncomfortable position dialing for dollars puts them in; several talked about the money's influence in winning favorable legislation on Capitol Hill.[8] A question that was sometimes posed to the lawmakers after the interview was finished was "Why do you think these people gave you all this money in the first place?" Remarkably, many members responded to this question with blank stares, commenting they had never thought about that before! But given the prevailing system for funding their reelection campaigns, is that so surprising?

Think of it as the Santa Claus Syndrome. The tendency of a powerful lawmaker never to think about the motivation of his or her biggest funders is not unlike that of a six-year-old not to think too critically about the contradictions inherent in Santa Claus. How does this big fat man slide down all those chimneys, how does he make it to the home of every boy and girl on the planet in a single evening, dispensing unlimited gifts from a single bulky bag in a sleigh drawn by flying reindeer? It is a lot less complicated just to take the gifts, be happy, and leave it there. In fact, politicians have every motivation to do precisely that, and to interpret all these gifts not as a sop to ensure their loyalty, but as appreciation for a job well done in serving the broad interests of the American people.

Which brings us to a crucial question about the ethics of interest groups in modern political campaigns: Is it a part of their fundamental strategy to intentionally exploit the inherent human weaknesses of the politicians they support? Again, this applies not to all contributions, but particularly to those made by interest groups with narrow issues of little or no interest to the public at large. Are they giving these contributions with the hope that the recipient will have a moral lapse and give something of value in return for the interest group's generosity? If so, these interest groups are engaging in unethical behavior themselves and encouraging politicians to do the same.

And what of their ultimate goal? Do campaign contributions actually influence votes? Do the politicians on the receiving end really deliver? Answering that question is not easy for several reasons. Nearly every substantive bill on Capitol Hill—and the same is certainly true of state legislatures and other lawmaking bodies—is attended by complicated crosscurrents of pressure. The party leadership may have one position, the member's state, region, or hometown industry may have a special perspective, other members may horse-trade votes on issues important to them. And then there is the money.

Because of these complexities, the Center for Responsive Politics has found relatively few examples of clear straight-line correlations between money and votes. The great majority of congressional votes these days follow party lines. On the other hand, when one party gets substantially more money than the other from a particular industry, it almost always supports that industry's legislative agenda. Likewise, on bills that are of interest to a specific industry, those voting for it are nearly always found to have collected substantially higher contributions from the industry—on average—than those voting against it. That is not the same as saying the money influenced their vote, or that every member who got more money voted with the industry, but such is the case far more often than not.

Some issues in Congress—particularly major pieces of legislation such as banking or telecommunications deregulation—involve competing groups of deep-pocketed donors. Issues like that are manna from heaven for law-makers seeking reelection funds and often drag on for years as the details are hashed out between key members of Congress and lobbyists for the competing interests. Meanwhile, those on both sides of the issue spend millions on lobbying and campaign contributions as incumbents restock their war chests for the next election.

One very clear correlation the Center for Responsive Politics has found in its decade-long research into the patterns of money in federal elections is that committee assignments in Congress have a great bearing on the makeup of contributions going to a particular member. It is a fact of mod-ern political life that the first place members of Congress go for money for their reelection campaigns is to the industries and interest groups that fall under their specific jurisdiction. Members of defense-related committees, for example, rely on defense contractors as major financial supporters, agriculture committee members are heavily supported by agribusiness, banks give most heavily to members of the banking committee, and so on. Committee and subcommittee chairmen have historically been the big-gest recipients of industry money, but the pattern is clear even among rank-and-file members. These patterns have held for as long as the center has conducted its research, and undoubtedly prevailed long before that.[9]

That fact helps explain a large part of the motivation behind the con-siderable jockeying for plum committee assignments that occurs every two years between Election Day and the start of the new Congress. Members understand that a seat on one of the "money committees" like Ways and Means or Appropriations makes fund-raising considerably easier.

The implications of all this—both on public policy and on the ethics of contemporary elections—are sobering. And the pressures for this to con-tinue, and even accelerate, are growing stronger with each new election cycle. The greater the importance of raising cash in running successful campaigns, the more contentious these conflicts—especially for lawmak-ers trying hard to do an ethical job of representation.

Running for office these days is like opening a new business. A seat in the U.S. House of Representatives cost an average of $833,000 in the 2000 elections. In competitive races decided by less than 10 percent, the average was $1.7 million. Senate seats averaged more than $7.6 million (though that figure was skewed by record-setting campaigns in New Jer-sey and New York).[10] Whatever the motivations of a would-be candidate, whatever their party affiliation or position on the issues, the one matter that must be addressed before any other is where is the money going to come from to finance the enterprise? If the money does not come from the candidate's own pocket, it is going to have to come from someone else's. And the motivations of those contributors will not always be ethically pure. That is, self-interest—even at the expense of the broader public interest—may often be the rationale behind a large contribution to a candidate for public office.

All members of Congress face a potential conflict of interest between representing the interests of their cash constituents and those of their actual constituents. To the extent that the two overlap—say, for a farm-state member who sits on the agriculture committee—the conflicts may be reduced. But what of the farm-state member who sits on the banking committee? Or the member representing a poor inner-city district who cannot raise funds locally and has to depend on out-of-district interests with decidedly different political agendas than the hometown constituents?

It is commonly argued by practitioners of the current system that campaign contributions buy only one thing: access. In fact, a contribution buys much more. Not only does it help provide entrée into an incumbent's office, a chance to make the donor's pitch, it also buys a sympathetic hearing. That is not the same as guaranteeing a vote, but it is important.

Consider the following situation. Representatives of a major East Coast bank receive an invitation for a fund-raiser from a member of the House Banking Committee. A week later, the executives team up with their lobbyist in Washington and meet with the congressman to lay out the bank's position on amendments to a bill regulating mergers in the financial sector. The congressman listens attentively but makes no commitments. It is quite possible that the most important feature of that meeting—whatever details are discussed—is not what is said out loud, but what is understood implicitly by both parties. This bank—which may or may not have a presence in the congressman's district—supported the congressman with a $5,000 PAC contribution in the last election. Fund-raising season never ends in the House of Representatives, so the member is already stockpiling funds for next year's election. No word of a challenger has yet emerged, but there is always the odd chance that some unknown millionaire will jump in, so it pays to be prepared. The congressman's goal is to amass at least half a million dollars in his campaign account by January 1 of the election year.

The member is duly grateful for the contribution that came in last year. He is hopeful that the bank will be good for at least another $5,000 for

the contest ahead. He understands—as does the lobbyist—that sophisticated donors do not show up one day with a contribution, looking for a
vote the next day. Instead, they build relationships. They know they cannot win every vote, even if they give a contribution. But both the lobbyist
and the congressman also understand that if the bank is not getting a
decent return on its investment, it will put its PAC money elsewhere next
time.

Will $5,000 make or break the campaign war chest? Certainly not. But
the fact of life is that the congressman, like any politician, would prefer to
have the money than not to have the money. He would also prefer a friendly,
mutually beneficial relationship to an adversarial one. The lobbyist is a
likable chap, he presents a decent argument for his case. The issue is ob-
scure enough that it is not likely to cause any notice in the district, no
matter how the congressman votes. And what position did he have on
banking mergers anyway when he ran for the seat and took the oath of
office? Frankly, it is not an issue he is focused on or expended any political capital on one way or the other. Another $5,000 in his campaign ac-
count—even though the subject did not come up when the lobbyist came
to visit—would be one more step toward the half million. The vote comes
up in a week: What is he going to do?

Upon such decisions as these is our political system built. The system
does not require politicians to be evil, to break the law, or to violate their
promise to represent the people by selling them out to the highest bidder.
All it requires is that politicians be human, that they react as any human
being would react when approached by a generous supporter who comes
asking for help. If the politician does only that and no more, the $5,000
contribution may well tip the congressman's decision on a vote that could
otherwise go either way. Bribes are not necessary when that is the system
that finances our elections. A refined sense of ethics, however, is.

What money may be buying is not simply a vote here and a vote there,
but an ethical blind spot: a subtle incentive not to think too deeply about
the ethical implications of accepting funds from interest groups that are
seeking favors. To the bank executives and their lobbyist, the $5,000 po-
litical contribution may simply be written off as a cost of doing business,
an investment whose hardheaded logic and potential return can be programmed into a spreadsheet. That is a thought, however, that they are
likely to keep to themselves. To the congressman, it may be seen as a
thank you for listening, a professional courtesy, a tangible endorsement
of the honorable idea that his years of public service are appreciated.

The question the congressman may never ask, as he turns out the light and goes home—or heads off to another fund-raiser on the way home—is whether he would have even let the lobbyist and executives in the door if they had not come bearing the unspoken promise of gifts. The congressman may never ask whether arguments on the other side of the issue might have been sought out from quarters that did not hire lobbyists, will not attend the fund-raiser—quarters that, frankly, will not be heard.

The way the system is structured, clear-cut ethical questions may only rarely arise; the nature of ethical questions surrounding interest group activity is much more subtle. If the bankers had suggested that their potential gift would be tied to the congressman's vote, they would likely have been booted from the office. So they do not say it, and everyone closes with handshakes and smiles.

To consider the ethical implications of a vote, the candidate has to step back and look not simply at the situation before him or her—Do I seek this contribution? Do I deliver the votes that are expected?—but at the larger picture. Does this system produce equitable decisions? Can the infusion of money shift the likelihood of a favorable outcome for the interest group infusing the money? Who is being represented here, the people or the organized interests? And what implications does this have for the public's perception of how government works?

Those are questions that may never be asked; indeed, all the encouragement of Santa Claus Syndrome militates against it. To deeply consider the implications of questions like these, politicians—and interest groups as well—have to be ethical entrepreneurs. They have to go beyond answering the questions on the table and think about their answers to questions that are never asked.

In the rough-and-tumble world of electoral politics, ethics is likely the last subject on anyone's mind. It is not on the minds of the politicians, nor the consultants, nor the party fund-raisers, and certainly not the interest groups. Winning is the ultimate prize, and visions of the "good" that can be done once the politician is safely in office tend to discourage paying too much mind to troubling ethical questions faced along the way—all the more so if acknowledging them might make winning more difficult.

Introspective, ethical campaigns probably succeed far less often than slash-and-burn offensives that hold to the letter of the law but do not dwell on ethical niceties. As long as there is a large (and growing) gap between what is legal and what is ethical, this problem will continue. As long as amassing more money than the other guy is the key to winning elective office, even the most ethical politicians will be tempted to put on blinders when receiving checks from donors whose intentions may not be the loftiest. In such an environment, ethics to politicians—and especially to interest groups trying to influence politicians—will be regarded as a luxury item. If you are going to win anyway, you will feel better if you can do it with a squeaky-clean conscience. If there is any chance that you might not win, a strict adherence to ethical ideals may be the first thing to be cast aside.

Notes

1. The new EU-wide tariff (designed to protect former European colonies) was set at 20 percent for imports under 2.2 million tons from Costa Rica, Nicaragua, and Venezuela and 30 percent from other Central American countries. Once the annual quota of 2.2 million tons was met, the tariff jumped to 250 percent. This replaced a system whereby each country set its own tariff. In Germany, Europe's biggest banana importer, bananas had been allowed in duty-free (*Congressional Research Service Report RS20130—The U.S.-European Banana Dispute*, updated 1999).

2. These and all campaign finance figures in this chapter were calculated by the Center for Responsive Politics, a nonpartisan research organization in Washington, D.C., that tracks campaign contributions in federal elections. The center's website, www.opensecrets.org, features a vast amount of information on the patterns in campaign contributions in American elections.

3. Donald L. Barlett and James B. Steele, "Big Money & Politics: Who Gets Hurt?" *Time Magazine*, February 7, 2000, p. 42.

4. This latter point is especially telling, since most business groups routinely split their contributions to members of both political parties, even shifting the proportions of those contributions as the parties rise or fall in power in Washington. For example, contributions shifted noticeably toward the GOP after the Republicans took control of both houses of Congress in the 1994 elections.

5. Author's calculations. For further discussion of the pragmatism of PACs and other campaign finance trends in the 2000 elections, see Larry Makinson, *The Big Picture: The Money behind the 2000 Elections* (Washington: Center for Responsive Politics, 2001).

6. For reelection rates between 1954 and 1998, see Norman J. Ornstein, Thomas E. Mann, and Michael J. Malbin, eds., *Vital Statistics on Congress: 1999–2000* (Washington: AEI Press, 1999). For 2002 election rates, see Makinson, *The Big Picture: The Money behind the 2000 Elections*, viii.

7. Larry Makinson, "The Great PAC Flip-Flop of 1996," in *The Big Picture: Who Paid for the Last Election?* (Washington: Center for Responsive Politics, 1997). A later analysis of yearly industry-by-industry giving patterns can be found in Makinson, *The Big Picture: The Money behind the 2000 Elections*, 53–77.

8. Martin Schram, *Speaking Freely: Former Members of Congress Talk about Money in Politics* (Washington: Center for Responsive Politics, 1995).

9. When sending out invitations to fund-raisers, many members of Congress prominently highlight their committee assignments—particularly when targeting their appeals to lobbyists, PAC directors, and corporate executives whose interests fall within the committee's jurisdiction.

10. Author's calculations.

CHAPTER ELEVEN

THE MEDIA

The Form and Content
of Political Communication

ROBERT E. DENTON JR.

To address campaign ethics from a "media" perspective is a daunting task for several reasons. The first is the sheer complexity of the topic. Political campaigns are above all "mediated" events. Few Americans experience campaigns firsthand. We come to know the candidates and the issues through media portrayals of elections. In America, television has become the primary medium and tool of both political campaigning and governing. To complicate matters more, how we form political attitudes and images of candidates' competence, leadership abilities, and character depends largely on the mediums we view and the messages we receive. Seldom does one message alone determine how we establish political preferences; in some cases, years of media exposure condition specific responses during campaigns. In the complexity of the media's creation and portrayal of electoral politics, just where does one look for ethical considerations?

Second, there are many players involved with the media in campaigns: candidates, consultants, reporters, editors, and so on. Some of these players are examined in other chapters in this volume. Each has some role in determining the media portrayal of a campaign, and there are certainly no uniform considerations of media ethics among all the players.

Third, we should remember that there are many media involved in campaigns, from bumper stickers to political advertising, from the two-minute news package to the highly controlled (and entertaining) talking head political shows. But at the heart of this consideration is the notion that media are more than content. Authors of more traditional textbooks in mass communication argue that technology itself has no inherent values. The ethical concerns or decisions lie not in the machinery but in the people who use the machinery. While true, this rationale is too simplistic and only part of the story. Of course intentionality is a variable of ethics, but so is capability or access. For example, many works on political communication target television as the source of numerous social and political ills: reduced voter turnout, decline of political parties, decline of political participation, reduction of issue discussion to sound bites, automatic re-election of incumbents, increased use of symbolic rather than problem-solving strategies of leadership, and increase of general public distrust and cynicism, to name only a few. Are these concerns of medium, content, "publisher," access, control, or socialization (that is, how we *use* a medium)?

Fourth, as noted by Dale Miller and Stephen Medvic in chapter 2, there really is no single set of standards, criteria, or behavior that defines political campaign ethics, much less media ethics. Yes, all related professionals have generated laundry lists of "codes of conduct and ethics." However, despite the philosophical distinctions provided by Miller and Medvic, such codes are simply window dressing and not very informative, as chapters 5 and 9 illustrate with respect to political consultants and interest groups. We all know that we should tell the "truth" in political ads. But do we need to tell the "whole truth and nothing but the truth"? While what is said may be true, what is not said may be more useful in voter decisionmaking. Again as Miller and Medvic observed, when a claim is made that an opponent voted a certain way, information left out might be important: whether the vote was in committee, on the floor, for a specific bill, or an amendment. Or consider the attack ad that claims an opponent cast the "deciding vote" on an issue that passed by one vote. Who is to say it was the deciding vote? Consider, too, journalism's distinction between "objectivity" and "fairness." In order to meet the standard, one simply needs to present both sides of an argument or issue, regardless of whether the dissenting voice is legitimate, logical, reasonable, representative, or in any way valid. Does such reporting inform the citizenry?

Because of the variety, purposes, and contexts of media used in campaigns, I explore the ethical dimensions of four areas: the media as essential elements of campaigns in a democracy, television as a mode of communication, general media usage in political campaigns, and the role of journalism in covering campaigns. In the first area, the ethical standard is how the media inform and educate, generating a knowledgeable citizenry capable of making "reasoned" choices. The second discussion recognizes how the medium of television influences who runs and who is elected. The ethical standard, again, is the nature of citizen participation and the quality of electoral outcomes. The third area of discussion explores how campaigns use various media. The ethical challenge is simply one of "truthfulness." The final area of discussion focuses on the practice of contemporary journalism. I conclude with some suggestions on how media, broadly defined, may enhance political campaigns.

The Media's Role in Democracy

Historically, the critical characteristics of a democratic form of government include accountability, information, a free marketplace of ideas, and the notion of collective deliberation. Because citizens delegate authority to those who hold office, politicians are answerable to the public. Elections are just one method of accountability. In America, news journalism serves as another check on political power and authority. The "watchdog" function is a long-standing tradition of the American press, as detailed by Paul Taylor in the following chapter. Information is critical for citizens to make informed judgments and evaluations of elected officials. Obviously, incomplete or inaccurate information can lead to bad public decisions. A free marketplace of ideas is vital to a thriving democracy. Diversity of thought and respect for dissent are hallmarks of the values of freedom and justice. When multiple viewpoints are heard and expressed, the "common good" prevails over "private interest." Finally, democracy is a process of what Dennis Thompson calls "collective deliberation" on disputes of issues and fundamental values.[1] It is national and public debate that determines the collective wisdom and will of the people. It may be revealing to consider the impact of the media on the basic characteristics of democracy.[2]

Accountability

The media increase the accountability of politicians when they provide sufficient information to enhance public awareness and decisionmaking. But in many cases, the media have been co-opted by politicians as instruments of advocacy. Politicians surround themselves with media professionals who advise on ways of nurturing the proper image, persona, or personality. It is very easy for politicians to manipulate media access and control. Thus media portrayals are more beneficial for politicians as a mode of self-promotion than for the public as a channel of information.

Constant exposure to television results in the sharing of common "TV stimuli" by everyone in society.[3] This creates a reservoir of common media experiences. The way politicians "connect" with citizens is to present stimuli that "resonate" with information already stored within the experiences of individuals. "Most people's experiences with TV and radio stimuli are often more real than first-hand, face-to-face experiences."[4] We make inferences about politicians based not on objective experience but on previously stored knowledge, likes, dislikes, and so on. Television especially encourages focus on personalities rather than on abstract issues. Personalities are more salient and easier to understand than issues.

For candidates, the process of image projection and media manipulation is rather easy. Pollsters identify the desired qualities, and candidates act accordingly. Candidates, of course, need the help of media consultants and pollsters to project the desired image to the public. Once elected, officials use the media for image maintenance and control.

One result is the creation of a short-term political environment. The reactive, emotional nature of today's politics makes it too costly to endorse long-term, controversial policies. One problem of democracy, according to our founders, is the potential impact of the momentary passions of the people on policy. The short-term focus of the media further distorts the information necessary for political judgment and exacerbates one of democracy's most dangerous characteristics.

The politics of popularity results in "plebiscitary leadership." Samuel Kernell, for example, makes the argument that politicians "going public" is a strategic adaptation to the information age. "Going public," according to Kernell, is "a leadership style consistent with the requirements of a political community that is increasingly susceptible to the centrifugal forces of public opinion."[5] Thus "going public" occupies a prominent place in the strategic repertoire of all politicians.

Roderick Hart's studies reveal that presidents are talking to us more than ever before, primarily because of the mass media.[6] He concludes that "presidential speechmaking—perhaps presidential communication in general—has now become a tool of barter rather than a means of informing and challenging the citizenry."[7] Thus, as Iyengar and Kinder recognize, "To the extent that the president succeeds in focusing public attention on his accomplishments while distracting the public from his mistakes, he contributes to his popularity, and eventually, to the influence he can exercise over national policy."[8] The public is not only left out of the decisionmaking process of national policy but is also unaware of the manipulation. Authoritarian politics, according to Jean Elstain, can be carried out "under the guise of, or with the convenience of, majority opinion. That opinion can be registered by easily manipulated, ritualistic plebiscites."[9]

The greatest danger in the politics of popularity is the encouragement of demagoguery. Demagogues, primarily motivated by self-interest and self-promotion, play up false issues to divert public attention from true issues, relying heavily on propaganda, capitalizing on a contemporary social issue or problem.[10] Robert Entman argues that "the media now provide an overwhelming temptation for politicians and other political figures to engage in demagoguery." He claims that "the media feed a spiral of demagoguery, diminished rationality in policymaking, heightened tendency toward symbolic reassurance and nostalgic evasion of concrete choices, and ultimately misrepresentation of the public."[11]

The media play a part in the democratic process through their role in the origination and circulation of information and opinion; the quality of that information and opinion is vitally important. Ethical journalism serves the public interest and facilitates the democratic process. However, as we explore in greater detail later, contemporary news values may not enhance democracy. Thomas Patterson thinks "the press is in the news business, not the business of politics, and because of this, its norms and imperatives are not those required for the effective organization of electoral coalitions and debate. Journalistic values and political values are at odds with each other."[12] He argues the proper organization of electoral opinion is when individuals look at the world as a whole and not in smaller pieces, when media organizations provide incentives for the public to identify and organize interests for policy representation, and when media organizations are held accountable for their successes or failures in assisting the public in its electoral endeavors. Traditionally, the public has empowered the press to serve as the collective watchdog over elected officials. If the public is unable or unwilling to hold officials accountable for their actions, the press is there, on a daily basis, to ensure fair representation. As Paul Taylor attests in the next chapter, journalists have long considered themselves "the first line of defense" against unethical politicians.

Despite the perception of an adversarial relationship between the media and government officials, those officials still benefit more from mass media presentations than do the general public or critics of elected offi-

cials. In a study by Leon Sigal it was shown that government officials
provided 75 percent of all news stories; less than 1 percent were based on
a reporter's own analysis.[13] In addition, 90 percent of the stories were
based on the messages of key actors in the stories. Seldom do politicians
speak for themselves. Seldom do they have to. Reporters act as narrators
and interpreters assessing the motives or consequences of political actors
or events. And political realities are constructed to conform to the demands of the medium, demands that seem best satisfied by melodrama.

Regardless of the uneasy nature of the relationship between the media
and elected officials, they desperately need each other. The result of this
symbiotic relationship is a constant battle of access and control. To use a
medium effectively implies control, planning, and proper execution. Thus
public accountability of elected officials is lessened by the inequalities of
power and access to the medium of television. Journalists are now part of
the spectacle, less concerned with the quality of leadership than with the
latest Nielson ratings, circulation, or market share.

Information

In order for the public to make "good" decisions, it needs "good" information. Miller and Medvic argue in chapter 2 that those involved in the
campaign process have a duty to create an informed electorate. Shanto
Iyengar and Donald Kinder argue that television news is "an educator
virtually without peer that . . . shapes the American public's conception of
political life in pervasive ways." In their original agenda-setting research,
they found "those problems that receive prominent attention on the national news became the problems the viewing public regards as the nation's
most important."[14] Successful politicians who can control the media can
control the public's perceptions. The more removed and less interested an
individual is in politics, the greater the influence of television.[15]

As the public becomes ever more reliant on the media for political information and as the media increasingly simplify that information, the
ability to recognize and appreciate complex social issues declines. The
result, according to Jarol Manheim, is "a continuing qualitative reduction
of the intellectual content of political discourse among the mass of American citizens which may enable an elite which preserves the requisite knowledge, skills, and resources more effectively to manipulate the polity."[16]

Studies show that Americans are poorly informed about politics. Very
little is learned from newscasts. The nature of news may well contribute
to this problem. "Sound bite journalism" provides very little opportunity

for citizen understanding or education. In addition, the highly negative coverage discourages viewer attention, and the emphasis on drama, scandal, and personalities decreases the significance of stories covered.[17] Michael O'Neil observes: "mass information is not the same as knowledge, and sound bites are not the same as wisdom."[18] Along this line of reasoning, Michael Schudson suggests there is a difference between an "informational citizen" and a genuine "informed citizen." The "informational citizen" is one who is saturated with bits and bytes of information; the "informed citizen" is one who not only has access to information but can fully understand that information and formulate clear choices among policies, issues, and candidates.[19]

As already mentioned, there is a constant attempt to control the news by politicians. An official's press secretary is the immediate link with the media. Although the function of the press secretary is to serve as a conduit of information, he or she must attempt to control the agenda as well as what is said and what is not said. The only "information" an elected official is interested in sharing with the public is what serves the interests of the politician. In a more active sense, politicians are always taking every opportunity to "plug" accomplishments, thus infusing the news with self-serving commercials. Thus there is growing concern that the media are simply unreliable in providing sufficient and accurate political information for citizens to make electoral or policy decisions.

The Free Marketplace of Ideas

With the advent of cable television, the number of media outlets continues to increase but the diversity of programming does not, especially in terms of "hard" news and public affairs programming. While there appears to be more such programming, the shows are really entertainment and offer many of the same talking heads giving reactions and opinions rather than investigation, genuine analysis, or perspective. The proliferation of cable channels and programming simply results in further segmenting audiences by specific likes or dislikes, making program-specific audiences more narrow and less diverse. One can certainly find something for everyone, but there is less crossover, discussion, or exchange of ideas. As Dan Rather, anchor of CBS Evening News, observed, "you better decide what audience you want, because the days of getting all of the audience is [sic] virtually over."[20]

Because of the general lack of access and the competition for control, the media actually discourage the notion of an open and free marketplace

of ideas. Consider, for example, the early stages of a presidential campaign season, with many candidates competing for time and attention.
Should all candidates be covered equally? Every day? Obviously, this is
not possible, but such a dilemma limits the service of news programming
contributions to the marketplace of ideas and does not keep the public
fully informed for decisionmaking.

The media give form and substance to world events. They construct
our political realities, telling us who is good or bad, right or wrong, strong
or weak, just or unjust. Media snapshots of the world become the album
of both our knowledge and our memories of the outside world. In addition to telling us what to think about, the media also tell us how to think.
With the reporting of the facts comes a subsequent judgment. There is
always a conclusion, point, or reason for a presentation, but there is little
or no time for synthesis or analysis. Awareness is valued more than understanding. Television especially demands a "perspective" and discourages
ambiguity, innovation, and diversity.

From a historical perspective, Daniel Hallin thinks that public trust
and perceived media bias are related.[21] It started with the decline of public trust in officials in the mid-1960s. Both Vietnam and Watergate contributed to this erosion, as did the social movements of the sixties and
economic slump of the 1970s. Hallin argues that with the decline of confidence in government and public institutions, journalists assumed the role
of watchdog, challenging the words, statements, and actions of politicians and government officials. While assuming this role, journalists also
started interpreting events, attempting to provide context and perspective.[22] And further, for Hallin, tabloid television has substituted the ethic
of objectivity for one of emotional involvement. "The journalist must show
that he or she shares the emotions of the viewer." In essence, "it has become conventional wisdom that a story needs a point of view to connect
with the audience."[23] Hence the perceptions of media bias are correct.

The pressure for ratings often surpasses the values for news and politics. The mass media are first of all businesses. They require audiences in
order to make money and turn a profit. Ratings are of great concern to
news personalities, and news programming is very expensive. As Dan
Rather acknowledges:

> Well, there's no joy in saying this but one, the ratings do have a lot
> to do with it, ratings being our version of circulation. . . . The basic
> problem is that there's always someone in every news room to say,

look at our market research. . . . The view basically is, give people
what they say that they're interested in, and you will get a larger
audience. And I will say that the preponderance of the evidence so
far leans in that direction.[24]

Another result of this heavy reliance on polls and market research is that
political actors no longer formulate their policies on rational argument and
persuasion but rather on media-dominated concerns and public opinion.

In this type of environment, Davis and Owen argue that public discourse is compromised.[25] Today political news is replaced by sensational
stories. Debates about issues and leaders are reduced to nearly gossip.
The impact on the public is clear. When people perceive they are powerless to impact government or policy, they are no longer motivated to learn
about issues. Constant exposure to stories that play on our emotions and
rather trivial, myopic concerns tend to turn the public against government. Tabloid journalism may also erode society's moral boundaries by
focusing on personal tales of bad behavior. Some even argue that the tendency of individuals to use the media for public confessions about personal actions tends to excuse them, as if confession is the same as judgment and consequences.

The product of journalism is not ideas but news.[26] Politicians and journalists have separate and distinct motives, neither of which contributes to
the genuine exchange of philosophies or ideas.

However, news journalists and politicians need each other. The result
is an act of symbiotic engagement. According to Christopher Arterton, it
is like watching a tennis match without the benefit of actually playing the
game.[27] As spectators to the spectacle, we have lost access, control, and
involvement in the process of democracy. This leads to the final element
of consideration.

Collective Deliberation

It is ironic that as the speed of communication and information increases,
political interests, awareness, and public participation become less satisfying. At best, citizens become directly involved in the day-to-day affairs
of state by watching television news. But the privatization of politics has
made us passive observers rather than active participants in the political
process. The emphasis on citizen involvement has moved from action to
reaction, from initiation to response. Television may well have helped us
to become politically lazy. We may watch debates, but we seldom engage

in them. Our political discussions are most often confined to close, like-minded friends. As citizens, we seldom genuinely deliberate and debate, in the classical sense. Even fewer citizens watch political campaign debates or issue shows. At best, through television we have established a "plebiscitary democracy" where mass public opinion is sovereign. But collective opinion is not the same as collective wisdom. The speeding up of counting votes and opinions does not address the quality of those votes and opinions.

Although television is highly involving, it does not encourage critical involvement in information. The medium literally reduces the message and prepares the viewer for its nearly automatic reception. This process is similar to consuming a great deal of food of little nutritional value. The meal is satisfying but critically deficient. As a personalizing medium, television presents a world of personalities who organize our reality and articulate our social agendas. Walter Cronkite's infamous nightly statement ending his newscasts, "And that's the way it is," reinforced the certainty of his perception of the day's events. Humans fear isolation; television provides a pressure to conform. Television is an individual medium that produces mass responses.

The Case of Television

Television has become the primary medium and tool of both campaigning and governing. Indeed, television news is the prime source of information for the public. The electorate receives 65 percent of its political information through television programming.[28]

From its inception, television was heralded as the ultimate instrument of democracy. It was, as no other medium, destined to unite us, educate us and, as a result, improve the actions and decisions of the polity. Television requires no special literacy. It is readily available. In fact, we spend more time viewing television than engaged in interpersonal communication. As a source of timely public information, it provides the greatest *potential* for understanding ourselves, our society, and even the world.

With the development of national cable systems, satellite delivery systems, and other television technologies, scholars and pundits predicted a major transformation of American society. The medium of television was to become the vehicle of direct democracy, promising electronic voting, more civic programming, and greater citizen participation. The medium provides instant access to any event or to any location on the planet and even in the stars. However, what we have experienced is declining rates of voting, increasing levels of cynicism, and lower levels of political knowledge.

Television as a medium of political communication raises two considerations: its inherent elements as a medium of communication (editing, camera movement, narrative forms, and so on) and the content of its political communication. Of course, the separation between form and content is difficult at best. However, because of the pervasiveness, complexity, and subtleness of the medium, it is useful to consider the unique nature of television followed by a brief examination of the contents of campaign communication and the newsgathering process.

David Altheide and Robert Snow posit that the media collectively are a form of communication with a logic of its own. Media logic is the interactive process through which media present and transmit information.[29] Elements of the logic include organization, style of presentation, focus on elements of behavior, and the grammar of the medium used. These elements impact social institutions such as politics, religion, or sports to create a unique "media culture." The major point is that when media are used to present the form and content of an individual or institution, the very form and content of the individual or institution are altered. A key part of this process is the audience's perception and interpretation of a particular medium's messages. As a technology, the modern media carry a connotation of rationality. Audiences view the information shared as accurate, objective, and current. Pictures and visions make the world understandable and shape the environment. What is projected affects what is seen. People, of course, see things differently.

Along similar lines of argument, Roderick Hart thinks television "certifies" a special way of seeing and hence a special way of knowing. He argues that television "occupies too much of our emotional lives. Increasingly, television tells us what to feel, when to feel it, and how and why as well."[30] More specifically, television helps us to feel intimate, informed, clever, busy, and important. In terms of politics, "television acts as an emotional referee in political life, ruling out some emotions, ruling in others. But television's prized emotions are counterfeit."[31] Hart claims that television makes us feel good about feeling bad about politics. He further argues that television has traded political wisdom for the emotions of intimacy, discernment, cleverness, activity, and importance.

Television, as a medium, especially tends to reduce abstract or ideological principles to human, personal components. Political issues and actions are linked to individuals. We have choices not among policies as much as between actors. Victims, villains, and heroes are easier to identify and address than complex issues, causes, or ideas. Television is especially a "personalistic" medium. With television the presenter dominates. It is a medium for actors and animate objects.

Noel Carroll is concerned about the inherent impact of the features of realism, escapism, and hypnotism on the political process by television.[32] The small-screen image is realistic in the sense that its image is processed in the same way we view ordinary objects, as opposed to the way we read or process words.[33] Watching television imbues whatever it presents with the aura of being natural, an actual representation of the way things are. Perceptual realism tends to convince viewers of the veracity of what they are seeing. This speaks to the power of visual stereotypes. From an ethical or moral perspective, television discourages reflection or consideration of alternatives. "The rapid succession of structural articulations, like cutting, does not allow the spectator the time to imagine moral alternatives; one is so occupied in simply attending to the visual array that there is no space for the moral imagination to take root."[34]

The notion of escapism implies that one is replacing one activity with another that may well be more beneficial or rewarding. Political participation reduced to watching ads is qualitatively different and less committed than actually going to political rallies, attending candidate debates, or passing out candidate literature. Thus in simplistic terms, according to many critics, politics becomes an activity of style over substance, image over reality, melodrama over analysis, belief over knowing, awareness over understanding.

Of course candidates talk about issues and policy, but there are media-created differences. For one, if you place a contemporary campaign speech beside one of the 1940s, you find that the contemporary speech is much shorter, probably only about one-third as long, and it is composed of much shorter paragraphs.[35] The longer paragraphs of yesteryear contained arguments, attempts to convert the audience; contemporary short paragraphs contain assertions and conclusions, attempts to give the audience a position to identify with while simultaneously providing a ten- to twenty-second pithy "bite" for the evening news.

Additionally, some contemporary campaign speeches are given purely to establish image. When a liberal gives an antiwar speech to the American Legion convention or a conservative attacks affirmative action at a meeting of the NAACP, neither expects to convert the audience. Rather, the speeches are given for image reasons, to prove their courage, to prove that the speakers can stand up to those opposed to their positions, to prove they are not "wishy-washy." Electioneering politicians no longer try to convert through argumentation; rather, they attempt to say something we in the audience can identify with, to project an image by what they say, to communicate something about their personalities by the audiences they choose to address. Dennis McQuail observes, "when we think of television as a means of political communication we are now more likely to think of it as a means of political marketing and would-be manipulation rather than as a valued participant in the democratic process."[36] Candidates are groomed for the media, and campaign events are coordinated with television coverage.

I have argued elsewhere that the Reagan presidency was the first true "primetime" presidency.[37] The critical dimensions of the primetime presidency include: the message fits the medium in both form and content; industry demands for news are carefully crafted by the incumbent; and today's president must be, if not an actor, at least media savvy or, even better, a "media celebrity." It is nearly impossible to separate the influence and interaction among elected officials, broadcast journalism, and television as a medium of communication. Numerous agenda-setting, media-priming, and framing studies have demonstrated that media coverage shapes how the public thinks about politics.[38] Its collective influence is almost seamless.

Michael O'Neil thinks television profoundly impacts the balance of power between citizens and politicians, magnifying public demands and conflicts and increasing the velocity of action and reaction beyond the limits of thought.[39] The implications of how television is changing politics include a new TV politics driven by money and special interests rather than by party loyalties, a huge industry of media manipulation, the micromanagement of public opinion in the cause of fragmenting single issues, and a shift from deliberative debate to policymaking by polls and television.[40]

According to surveys, the American public has become disenchanted with media coverage of politics. Viewership of the network evening news continues to decline, a trend that started in the 1970s. In general, the public perceives the coverage as too adversarial, too cynical, too obsessed with character issues.[41] James Fallows finds that the media "increasingly present public life mainly as a depressing spectacle, rather than as a vital activity in which citizens can and should be engaged."[42] If this trend continues, many scholars fear citizens will become more cynical and frustrated and will opt out of the democratic political process.

There are media differences in terms of individual political behavior. Heavy newspaper readers and television news viewers tend to vote more, have greater political interests, and be more involved in the community than nonviewers or nonreaders.[43] In fact, the more involved individuals are in public affairs, the more they find radio, magazines, and friends influential. However, those who are motivated to learn about politics and expert opinions tend more often to be readers of newspapers.[44]

There are differences of style and content as well. Television, as the primary source of political information for most Americans, especially impacts the style and content of political discourse and subsequent information. Political speech is increasingly familiar, personalized, and self-revealing. For example, Reagan's use of contractions, simple, often incomplete sentences, informal transitions, colloquial language, and frequent stories transformed his "formal" Oval Office addresses into conversations with the American people.[45] His skillful adaptation to the camera simulated direct eye contact with individuals in his audience. It has all the appearance of conversation. This conversational style "invite[s] us to conclude that we know and like" politicians who use it.[46] Ronald Reagan first excelled at this style, which stands in marked contrast even to the conversational style of Franklin D. Roosevelt, for example. However, Bill Clinton, through his "mediated conversational style," excelled at both adaptation and conversational style, especially in the town hall meeting format.

It is important to note, however, that mediated conversation does not parallel the process of human communication. We know, for example, in the media interview format, that questions to be asked are often known ahead of time, and politicians rehearse desired responses before a mediated event. In some cases, topics and areas of discussion are issues of negotiation. In addition to lacking spontaneity, the partners in the interaction, whether it is the audience or the interviewer and politician, are not equal in terms of control, power, or reciprocity in any phase of the conversation. There is not a mutual exchange of asking questions, voicing opinions, or stating facts. Politicians may make themselves "physically" available but not accessible in terms of openness and a willingness to share and disclose feelings, beliefs, and attitudes. Likewise, there is little commitment to the interaction and from a politician's perspective, the "conversation" is more often a means to a political end. In short, there is no intrinsic value to the conversation. Although interaction takes place, it is, quite simply, a different kind of interaction.

Interviews on television differ greatly from those in print. On television, how one responds is as important as the content of the response. Was there a hesitation, a shift of the brow, an expression of emotion? Remember the shot of George H. W. Bush, in the 1992 Richmond presidential candidate debate with Clinton and Perot, taking a quick glance at his watch? This simple action was perceived as a rather callous, cavalier attitude toward the audience and the event.

Personal characteristics conveyed primarily in nonverbal communication influence viewer perception of specific performances. How viewers measure a politician's cooperative attitude, equality, humility, warmth, interest, similarity and friendliness, and sincerity and honesty affect how likely they are to vote for a candidate as well as their subsequent perceptions of his or her credibility and judgments about his or her competence, sociability, and character.[47] The secret, therefore, is for a politician to present a controlled response best suited for the medium of television. "More than print," Meyrowitz says, "electronic media tend to unite sender and receiver in an intimate web of personal experience and feeling."[48] The public's reactions are personal and "real," shaped by feelings and intuitions as much as by rational analysis and interpretation.

Mediated political conversation fails to properly inform and educate the public on political matters. It encourages citizens' continued emphasis on character rather than substance of policy.[49] Ferrarotti observes that "as we are informed, we know everything about everything, but we no longer understand anything. It is purely cerebral information that does not manage to touch the deeper levels of human beings."[50] For Roderick Hart, "television miseducates the citizenry but, worse, it makes that miseducation attractive."[51] In reality, the public does not know what it thinks it knows, and the public does not care about what it does not know.

Staged mediated political conversations offer a mode of discourse that Neil Postman characterizes as "accessible, simplistic, concrete, and above all, entertaining." He argues:

> the problem is not that TV presents the masses with entertaining subject matter, but that television presents all subject matter as entertaining. What is dangerous about television is not its junk. Every culture can absorb a fair amount of junk, and, in any case we do not judge a culture by its junk but by how it conducts its serious public

business. What is happening in America is that television is transforming all serious public business into junk.[52]

Perhaps the most damaging aspect of mediated conversations is the public's open acknowledgment that all political talk is performance. Sanford Schram argues that the public's recognition that all politicians are ultimately "acting" merely leads to acceptance of the ability to perform as the essential qualification for office: "the quest for personal leadership becomes a self-destructive quest in which all pretenders are found to be just that. In the end, the grammar of electronic electioneering teaches people to be content with their inability to find a 'real leader' and to be comfortable with elected officials who are comfortable faking it."[53] For Collins and Skover, we are on the border of equating "amusement with enlightenment, fantasy with fact, and the base with the elevated."[54]

Media and Electoral Politics

Royce Hanson makes an interesting comparison of campaigning that draws on the moral principles and metaphors of war as well as democratic governance.[55] He views campaigns as surrogates for civil war, with ballots substituted for bullets. The vocabulary of a campaign is rich in the language of warfare (victory and defeat, attack and counterattack, strategy and tactics, rallying the troops). However, there are interesting differences of ethical considerations between war and democracy. For example, during war, ethical constraints are relaxed. It is not unethical to mislead the enemies, spy on them, withhold information from one's own citizens and soldiers to protect strategic advantages. However, democracy demands ethical principles. Voters must have access to the information necessary to make informed decisions. The ethics of democracy demand that information be truthful enough to ensure quality of decisions.[56]

In campaigns, "truth" is assumed to emerge from the competition between candidates. Hanson notes that unlike trials by jury, campaigns follow no rules of evidence. No one is under oath. Everything is admissible and everything is deniable. Under the rules of political engagement, we expect candidates to present views and positions most favorable to their campaign and most damning to their opponents. It is important that truth and collective wisdom emerge from the campaign process. There's an old adage that states, "If there is such a thing as truth, it results from the clashing of ideas." As mentioned earlier, democracy thrives in a genuine "marketplace of ideas." Thus democracy condemns political and governing strategies of lying and secrecy. Misinformation is dangerous to informed choice. A campaign is the means to governing, and governing is the implementation of the candidate's promises and the fulfillment of constitutional duties. These duties include obligations to be truthful and to address issues of public concern.

While there are numerous media in campaigns whose "truth" could be assessed, two broad categories raise special ethical concerns: the Internet and political advertising.

Internet and New Technologies

Computers, fiber optics, and satellites have introduced an era of high-speed communication that greatly impacts the creation, collection, and dissemination of information. It is the "new media," which include the proliferation of cable options and news magazine shows, talk radio, electronic town meetings, and the Internet, that promise to enhance the public's understanding of political issues and motivate citizen participation. They provide services to mass audiences, transcending time and space constraints of traditional media. In addition, the "new media" bypass national and international boundaries, opening all the world to Americans.

Davis and Owen identify several major differences in the potential and actual influence between the "new media" and traditional media.[57] First, they vary in their approach to political news, which influences the content of the news reported. The new media have an anti-institutional bias. Historically, the mainstream media had, as part of their mission, public service and an obligation to cover governmental affairs. The new media have profit and entertainment as their primary concern. Thus, because the new media cover politics as entertainment, their focus is more on personalities and human-interest stories than issue education. Their coverage is more personal, colorful, and conflict-oriented. Second, the new media are populist in content and coverage. The focus is on conflict and crime, with an antiestablishment, anti-incumbent slant. Finally, the new media are less concerned with more customary standards of ethics than traditional media. There is certainly less objectivity or even fairness in presentation. Members of the new media are more ideological and willing to use their positions to advance specific people or causes.[58]

The Internet is becoming one of the defining scientific and social innovations of this century. The "information superhighway," as labeled by politicians and the media, has the ability to link people and resources in a way that was never previously possible. Users can share data, communicate messages, transfer programs, discuss topics, and connect to computer systems all over the world. The potential of the Internet as a tool for retrieving information is almost limitless. As a result of the freedom of expression allowed on this unique network, the possibilities for learning and enrichment are endless. But with a network so large (and a territory so uncharted), there is great concern about the material readily available to anyone accessing the net. And it is clear that our laws and social expectations have not kept up with the rapid changes in communication technologies.

The role of the Internet in politics is still evolving and uncertain. It is a medium, however, that no politician can ignore. Indeed, well over 100 million American adults accessed the Internet specifically for election information during the 2000 electoral season.[59] It ranked behind television but just ahead of newspapers as the primary source of obtaining political news.[60] With each campaign cycle, we learn more about the uses of the Internet and those who use it for political purposes. Currently, most candidate sites have video, press releases, issue statements, merchandise for purchase, contribution opportunities, and opportunities to receive weekly e-mail bulletins.

Kevin Hill and John Hughes argue the Internet has the potential to change the flow of political information and thus revolutionize the process of political communication.[61] Before the Internet, the flow of political information was primarily one way, from media to public. The Internet now allows individuals to become in effect "broadcasters," providing unfiltered information not shared by more mainstream media channels. Hill and Hughes found that Internet "activists" tend to identify themselves as Democrats (though they vote between the political parties), oppose government regulations of personal activities, and are more politically active and knowledgeable than the general population.[62]

There are several concerns related to the Internet. The greatest is privacy. Gary Selnow warns that "through site tracking, computers can monitor user progress on a Web site and infer from these movements the issues that might interest the user."[63] One may also scan recent sites visited and provide a user profile of the visitor. Another general concern is simply the presentation of inaccurate and misleading information. For every legitimate, "official" site, there are several parody or even hateful sites. During the Virginia governor's race of 2001, the Republican Party of Virginia created a website to criticize Mark Warner, the Democratic nominee for governor, called www.whichWarner.com. Perhaps the most vicious and thus misleading are those maintained by individuals. It costs only $70 to obtain an unclaimed Internet address. During the 2000 presidential campaign, a counterfeit site emerged as www.gwbush.com. It looked official but contained comic and parodic attacks on Bush. Increasingly, campaigns have demonstrated fear that subversive individuals or groups will spread gossip, rumors, and lies to sway unwary voters.

The increased use of the Internet will pave the way for a new type of political consultant whose job it is to master the Internet spin control. The Internet relies on the use of experts who understand that campaigns also have access to e-mail discussion groups and virtual information portals to rebut information. Finding Internet specialists with the tools to monitor the Internet and the knowledge to intervene appropriately on behalf of a campaign will be critical to future electoral success. In earlier days, campaigns had twenty-four to forty-eight hours to respond to attacks or criticisms. Today, with the speed of communication technologies, twenty-four-hour news channels, and especially individual instant access to the Internet, news cycles have become a matter of minutes. On the Internet, campaigns respond to criticisms before they have been publicly uttered—the "dialogue [is] essentially constant."[64]

Political Advertising

Political advertising has come under strong attack in recent years. Today, political ads are the primary source of campaign information for the vast majority of voters. Research indicates that political ads educate viewers about issues, influence voter perceptions about candidates, and especially influence late-deciding or undecided voters.[65] However, as Miller and Medvic noted in chapter 2, all campaign ads are misleading to some degree.

Lynda Kaid provides one of the most comprehensive analyses of some of the ethical concerns related to political advertising.[66] Content aside, Kaid expresses concern about the use of ads as a means of "buying access to voters." This becomes an increasing concern with corporate or organizational issue and advocacy advertising. Without question, the greatest expense of most campaigns is advertising. It is a simple fact that those with abundant resources are most able to get their message out to the general public. If, as some argue, that money equates with free speech, then some politicians and organizations have more "free speech" than others.

An enduring criticism of political advertising is the dependence on emotion and strong visuals to convey meaning rather than a more rational, logical discussion of issues. Another criticism is that political spots tend to oversimplify issues, thus debasing and even trivializing the electoral process. It is nearly impossible to fully explain the complexity of most issues in thirty or sixty seconds. As a result, most ads are superficial, and many contain half-truths and some distortion of information.

A growing concern among scholars is the use of media manipulation to enhance or even alter reality. The most common uses of television technology include editing techniques, special effects, visual imagery, or dramatizations and computerized alteration techniques. Examples of each abound. In some cases, the "morphing" technique of transforming objects or candidates (such as the Pinocchio effect of an opponent's nose growing, implying the lack of truthfulness) may be humorous. In other cases, however, such techniques are misleading. As noted in chapter 1, in the 1996 U.S. senatorial campaign in Virginia, incumbent John Warner (R) aired an ad that replaced the face of the then senator Chuck Robb (D) with that of his opponent, Mark Warner, in a group shot of "liberals." Surely all would agree this is more than simple distortion.

Scholars have recently investigated the role and impact of attack or negative ads. They have found that such political ads influence voters because they are more compelling, memorable, and believable.[67] However, Stephen Ansolabehere and Shanto Iyengar find that the heavy reliance on negative political ads results in lower voter turnout and general public cynicism. "Attack advertisements resonate with the popular beliefs that government fails, that elected officials are out of touch and quite corrupt, and that voting is a hollow act. The end result: lower turnout and lower trust in government, regardless of which party rules."[68]

Another concern is inadequate or incomplete information. Even when the source of allegations is disclosed in negative advertising, for example, the references are on the screen for just a matter of seconds and are often out of context. Finally, often messages are ambiguous or inconsistent. Visual impressions may lead viewers to "see what they want to see."

Journalism

Especially within the last decade, there has been a growing concern about the practice of journalism in America. Criticisms of the press range from distortion to bias to even outright lying. Generally, the public increasingly thinks the press has become too powerful, too negative, and too biased in its news coverage. A Harris survey conducted in early 1999 reported that 52 percent of Americans "don't trust" journalists and just 22 percent think they have "high ethical standards."[69]

It is important to remember from the outset that news is a human communication endeavor. "News" is selected, created, and communicated by people. News is much more than just facts. It is a story, an argument, a process of the "symbolic creation of reality." News stories influence how readers and viewers perceive reality. Cole Campbell of the *Virginian-Pilot* acknowledges: "news is not a scientifically observable event. News is a choice, an extraction process, saying that one event is more meaningful than another event. The very act of saying that means making judgments that are based on values and based on frames."[70] As observed by Kathleen Jamieson and Karlyn Campbell, "news is gathered, written, edited, produced, and disseminated by human beings who are part of organizations and who have beliefs and values. . . . These beliefs, values, functions, and interests are bound to influence the messages these networks publish and broadcast."[71] Thus Thomas Patterson concludes: "we get a picture that is not value-neutral but is instead embedded with the values of journalism and its particular biases and refractions. Some of these pictures inform our judgment, but more of them mislead us about what is at issue in campaign politics."[72]

News and the truth are not the same thing. News reporting is just one version of the facts—a created sequence. Some aspects are magnified, others are downplayed. Likewise, the notion of objectivity does not address the issue of truth. Rather, it simply acknowledges the attempt to present both sides or perspectives of an issue.

A review of the recent plethora of books about television news reveals four major areas of concern. First, how the medium covers people, places, and events has been questioned. Some argue that the coverage is largely irrelevant to the average citizen. Journalists tend to ask questions for themselves rather than reflect the interests of citizens. They maintain what is called a "within the beltway" mentality rather than connect to the average citizen. For example, during the 2000 presidential primary, former senator Bill Bradley (D) focused on his initiatives in health care and education. The media, however, focused on his personality and personal health issues of irregular heartbeats.[73]

For James Fallows, the problem is journalists have moved away from their central values. In essence, "mainstream journalism has fallen into the habit of portraying public life in America as a race to the bottom, in which one group of conniving, insincere politicians ceaselessly tries to outmaneuver another."[74]

Entertainment values encourage "tabloid journalism," which has become the mainstay of news today. "The tabloid reporting style is designed to heighten readers' and viewers' sensory experience with the news. The details of stories are presented in graphic form. Tabloid news is written in dramatic, engaging, and readable prose presented in short paragraphs and set off with attention-grabbling headlines and visual accompaniments. TV tabloids feature quick cuts between plots and subplots, highlighting conflict and crisis."[75] As former anchor and journalist for ABC News David Brinkley acknowledges, "the one function that TV news performs very well is that when there is no news we give it to you with the same emphasis as if there were news."[76] In the last five days of the 2000 presidential campaign, news about candidate George W. Bush's drunk-driving conviction generated twice the number of stories than coverage of the Republican convention.[77]

The growing trend of "checkbook journalism," paying sources for news and exclusive interviews, has become so widespread that even more traditional and "legitimate" news outlets are forced to make "indirect" payments to sources in the form of "consultant fees," travel and entertainment expenses, and so on. Such practices may well increase the entertainment and dramatic value of a story, but they raise questions of conflict of interest, source integrity, and motivation.[78]

The second concern of most critics is how the negative coverage of both campaigns and daily events has contributed to public alienation from the political process. Especially since Richard Nixon, journalists have added their own negative spin and interpretation of events and issues. In 1996, for example, journalists got six times more airtime than the candidates they were covering. The dominant news value in campaign stories is conflict, not issues.

This negative, antipolitical bias of the press is an alarming historical trend. A study by Thomas Patterson shows that "candidates of the 1960s got more favorable coverage than those of the 1970s, who in turn received more positive coverage than those of the 1980s."[79] The overall change is dramatic. Of all the evaluative references to Kennedy and Nixon in 1960, 75 percent were positive. Network news portrayals of recent presidential campaigns reveal an alarming trend toward negative coverage. During the 1992 presidential campaign, more than 80 percent of the network news stories on the Democratic Party were negative, as were 87 percent of all references to the Republican Party.[80] During the 1996 campaign, 53 percent of television news stories about President Bill Clinton and 59 percent of stories about Senator Bob Dole (R) were negative.[81] This trend of negative coverage has occurred in news magazines as well. Thus for Patterson, "there can be no doubt that the change in the tone of election coverage has contributed to the decline in the public's confidence in those who seek the presidency."[82]

Third, much of the criticism of contemporary journalism focuses on the coverage of politics and political campaigns. Perhaps the most recent study of the influence of television coverage of campaigns is provided by Cappella and Jamieson. They argue that the contemporary journalistic culture and its focus on strategy, conflict, and motives encourage public cynicism.[83] Specifically, they claim that voters exposed to news framed in terms of campaign strategy report higher levels of cynicism than those who saw it framed in the more traditional problem-solution story formats.[84] Strategy coverage is composed of several characteristics: winning and losing is the central concern; the language of war, games, and competition dominates; stories involve performers, critics, and audience; the performance, style, and perception of the candidate is prominent; and polls and the candidates' standing in them are heavily weighted.[85] During the 2000 primary season, only 13 percent of news stories focused on issues, while 80 percent focused on campaign strategies and tactics, or who was ahead in the horse race.[86]

For Cappella and Jamieson, strategic coverage of campaigns and government is problematic because it "invite[s] the attribution of cynical motives to political actors in campaigns and public policy debates, not because voters are distanced from the process but precisely because they are drawn into it and, through a rational analysis of the politicians whose motives they have come to know, reject the actors and ultimately the process."[87] The result is a "spiral of cynicism" in which "reporters and politicians justify their own cynical discourse by saying that it is required by the other. By producing the predicted discourse, each reinforces the assumption the other brought to the exchange."[88]

Finally, Richard Davis and Diana Owen are concerned about the rise of an elite corps of "celebrity journalists" who increasingly become integral parts of news stories and events.[89] They have their own "star system" and compete for airtime. They enjoy celebrity status in terms of pay, perks, fan clubs, and huge speaker fees. Connected with this trend is the rise of the interpretive content of news. Each story has a slant. Each has also become shorter in order to accommodate more segments for viewer interest. In addition, there is a growing number of individuals who move from political jobs into the newsroom. These partisan pundits have become a mainstay of morning and Sunday news magazine shows. There is no expectation or pretense of objectivity or independence. These "pseudo" journalists "masquerade as reporters on newscasts and talk shows."[90] Note that such individuals as Oliver North, G. Gordon Liddy, Patrick Buchanan, George Stephanopoulos, and Jesse Jackson, to name just a few, all have or had their own shows and appear as political analysts. Recall that some "celebrity" journalists appear in movies as well as in product commercials. How are we expected to know what is real and whom to believe?

In summary, Thomas Patterson demonstrates well that journalistic values and political values are at odds with one another, which results in a news agenda that misrepresents what is at stake in voters' choices. Journalistic values introduce an element of random partisanship into campaigns, which works to the advantage of one side or the other. Election news, rather than serving to bring candidates and voters together, drives a wedge between them.[91]

> The problem is that the press is not a political institution. Its business is news and the values of news are not those of politics. Election news carries scenes of action, not commentary on the values reflected in those scenes. Election news emphasizes what is controversial about events of the previous twenty-four hours rather than what is stable and enduring. The coverage is framed within the context of a competitive game rather than being concerned with basic issues of policy and leadership. It projects images that fit story lines rather than political lines. Election news highlights what is unappetizing about politics rather than providing a well-rounded picture of the political scene.[92]

Conclusion

There is a constant struggle between republican and democratic principles of self-rule. For well over two hundred years, America has moved toward a more "inclusive" democracy: greater participation of women, minorities, and the young. Yet during this time of increased opportunity for participation, citizen interest, awareness, understanding, and voting have declined. Have the media contributed to this decline?

One can certainly argue that the media have changed the fundamental nature, structure, and function of American politics. It is not an overstatement to claim that the media influence who runs, who is elected, and the very nature of contemporary democracy. Without being too deterministic, there is some cause for concern.

Does media coverage honestly depict candidates and elected officials, or does it serve as the instrument of the image makers? Campaigns today no longer reveal a depth of issue knowledge or understanding—simply issue awareness. Political debate is more an exchange of predictable sound bites. The background and experience of candidates are less important than their ability to attract media support and public popularity. As professional politicians, our leaders no longer reflect the diversity of occupations and accompanying expertise of the general public. Gone are the true and mature laborers, businessmen, educators, and professionals who once composed state and national legislators. The media have given birth to a new type of American politician and opened Washington to "career" politicians. Politicians use the media to confirm rather than to challenge, to present rather than to engage the public. National audiences require generic appeals and predictable responses.

Political leadership today tends to be charismatic rather than programmatic. Does this style of leadership help policy formation and execution? Can today's "media celebrities" support strong measures to deal with the debt, social security, campaign finance reform, health care, and so on? Probably not. One of the concerns of Michael Rogin is the "false intimacy of the modern, personified state."[93] The media encourage us to look at politicians in informal contexts and allow the politicians to demonstrate concern for citizens. This two-way mirror contributes little to leadership, governing, or program development.

The mass media are the instruments of mass production. Just as each Barbie and Ken doll is the same in millions of households, so we all see the same manufactured politician. The foundation of democracy is the notion of choice. Primarily because of the media and the way they cover campaigns, candidates in general increasingly look the same, sound the same and, unfortunately, act the same. Public offices become products for public consumption.

One of the most important developments in American politics since 1980 has been the professionalization of political communication. Without doubt, the kingmakers of contemporary politics are the new breed of political and media consultants. Once limited to the continuing cycle of campaigns, they now find themselves on the permanent staffs of elected officials. These professional politicians have become the link between electoral politics and campaigns, leaders and the public.

It has become rather common and almost expected for academics to attack the media's campaign and political coverage. My motive is not to demonize the media or claim that they are responsible for all our social ills. From a social perspective, the media were supposed to take a largely uneducated, uninformed electorate and transform it into model democratic citizens. This, I fear, they cannot do. The responsibility belongs not to the media—designed, after all, primarily as entertainer and conveyer of goods—but to the citizens.

The central task is how to cultivate an active, democratic citizenry in light of the heavy dependence on the media, and television in particular. Yes, the media, broadly defined, can help to enhance informed decisionmaking. Specifically, it would help if during campaigns the media would:

—Cover voters' concerns over candidate concerns

—Cover the entire campaign, big and small events alike

—Cover "issues" more and "politics" less

—Cover commonalities, not just differences, among the candidates

—Let the candidates speak for themselves

—Spend less time predicting and more time seeking audience understanding

—Spend less time covering how candidates are "playing the game" and more on their stand on issues

—Give citizens information and tools to participate in campaigns by providing additional links, references, and other sources for further information and inform citizens of opportunities for participation in public discussion and involvement in campaign issues and events

—Provide free airtime to candidates as a public service

—Provide unnarrated coverage of campaign events

—Expand length of news packages to include more of actual events and exchanges

As citizens, we need to have a greater understanding of the role, function, and power of the media in our society. As social and scientific technologies rapidly increase, we must carefully plan for their usage within the context of democratic values. More than a decade ago, veteran news icon Walter Cronkite suggested in a speech at the University of South Dakota: "We could benefit by a journalism course for consumers. If we could teach people how to read a newspaper, how to listen to radio and watch television . . . we could create an understanding of media, of the individual strengths and weaknesses of each medium. We could lead them away from a dependence on television, back to good newspapers, magazines, and books."[94] I would add to his suggestions the need for more exposure to multiple sources of information, more self-reflection, analysis, and attention to the affairs of state. In the end I concur with Miller and Medvic: civic responsibility and initiative, which surely transcend any medium, should once again become the keystones of our social and political life.

Notes

1. Dennis F. Thompson, *Political Ethics and Public Office* (Harvard University Press, 1987).

2. The argument pertaining to the media's role in democracy may also be found in Robert E. Denton Jr., "Dangers of 'Teledemocracy': How the Medium of Television Undermines American Democracy," in Robert E. Denton Jr., ed., *Political Communication Ethics: An Oxymoron?* (Westport, Conn.: Praeger, 2000), pp. 91–124.

3. Tony Schwartz, *The Responsive Chord* (Anchor Books, 1973).

4. Ibid., p. 44.

5. Samuel Kernell, *Going Public* (CQ Press, 1986), p. 212.

6. Roderick Hart, *Verbal Style and the Presidency* (Orlando, Fla.: Academic Press, 1984); Roderick Hart, *The Sound of Leadership* (University of Chicago Press, 1987).

7. Hart, *Sound of Leadership*, p. 212.

8. Shanto Iyengar and Donald Kinder, *News That Matters* (University of Chicago Press, 1987), p. 122.

9. Jean Elstain, "Democracy and the Qube Tube," *Nation*, August 7, 1982, p. 108.

10. Richard L. Johannesen, *Ethics in Human Communication*, 4th ed. (Prospect Heights, Ill.: Waveland Press, 1996), pp. 134–35.

11. Robert Entman, *Democracy without Citizens* (Oxford University Press, 1989), pp. 126, 128.

12. Thomas Patterson, *Out of Order* (Vintage Books, 1993), p. 36.

13. See W. Lance Bennett, *News: The Politics of Illusion* (Longman, 1983), for details on the studies.

14. Iyengar and Kinder, *News That Matters*, pp. 2, 16.

15. Ibid., p. 60.

16. Jarol Manheim, "Can Democracy Survive Television?" in Doris Graber, ed., *Media Power in Politics* (CQ Press, 1984), p. 134.

17. Richard Davis and Diana Owen, *New Media and American Politics* (Oxford University Press, 1998), p. 166.

18. Michael O'Neil, *The Roar of the Crowd* (Times Books, 1993), p. 195.

19. Michael Schudson, "Creating Public Knowledge," *Media Studies Journal*, vol. 9, no. 3 (Summer 1995), p. 28.

20. Dan Rather, CNN: *Crossfire*, June 24, 1999.

21. Daniel Hallin, "A Fall from Grace," *Media Studies Journal*, vol. 12, no. 2 (Summer 1998), pp. 42–47.

22. Ibid., p. 44.

23. Ibid., p. 46.

24. Rather, *Crossfire*.

25. Davis and Owen, *New Media and American Politics*, p. 104.

26. Entman, *Democracy without Citizens*, p. 11.

27. Christopher Arterton, *Media Politics* (Lexington, Mass.: Lexington Books, 1984), p. 25.

28. Lynda Lee Kaid and Dorothy K. Davidson, "Elements of Videostyle: Candidate Presentation through Television Advertising," in Lynda Lee Kaid, Dan Nimmo, and Keith R. Sanders, eds., *New Perspectives on Political Advertising* (Southern Illinois University Press, 1986), pp. 184–209.

29. David Altheide and Robert Snow, *Media Logic* (Beverly Hills, Calif.: Sage, 1979), pp. 9–10.

30. Roderick Hart, *Seducing America* (Thousand Oaks, Calif.: Sage, 1999), p. vii.

31. Ibid., p. 155.

32. Noel Carroll, "Is the Medium a (Moral) Message?" in Kieran Matthew, ed., *Media Ethics* (London: Routledge, 1998).

33. Ibid., p. 138.

34. Ibid., p. 148.

35. Kathleen Hall Jamieson, *Eloquence in an Electronic Age: The Transformation of Political Speechmaking* (Oxford University Press, 1988).

36. Dennis McQuail, "New Roles for New Times?" *Media Studies Journal*, vol. 9, no. 3 (Summer 1995), p. 16.

37. Robert E. Denton Jr., *The Primetime Presidency of Ronald Reagan* (Praeger, 1988).

38. Joseph Cappella and Kathleen H. Jamieson, *The Spiral of Cynicism* (Oxford University Press, 1997), p. 56.

39. O'Neil, *Roar of the Crowd*.

40. Ibid., p. 131.

41. Davis and Owen, *New Media and American Politics*, p. 44.

42. James Fallows, *Breaking the News* (Random House, 1997), p. 8.

43. Ibid., p. 6.

44. Bruce Pinkleton and Erica Austin, "Media and Participation: Breaking the Spiral of Disaffection," in Thomas Johnson and others, eds., *Engaging the Public* (Lanham, Md.: Rowman & Littlefield, 1998), p. 78.

45. Jamieson, *Eloquence in an Electronic Age*, p. 166.

46. Ibid.

47. Michael Pfau and Jong Kang, "The Impact of Relational Messages on Candidate Influence in Televised Political Debates," *Communication Studies*, vol. 42, no. 2 (1991), p. 124.

48. Joshua Meyrowitz, *No Sense of Place* (Oxford University Press, 1985), p. 96.

49. Sandord Schram, "The Post-Modern Presidency and the Grammar of the Electronic Engineering," *Critical Studies in Mass Communication*, vol. 8 (1991), pp. 210–16.

50. Franco Ferrarotti, *The End of Conversation: The Impact of Mass Media on Modern Society* (New York: Greenwood Press, 1988), p. 13.

51. Hart, *Seducing America*, p. 12.

52. Neil Postman, *Amusing Ourselves to Death* (Penguin, 1985), p. 15.

53. Schram, "Post-Modern Presidency," p. 215.

54. Ronald Collins and David Skover, *The Death of Discourse* (Boulder, Colo.: Westview Press, 1996), p. 203.

55. Royce Hanson, "Reading Lips and Biting Sound: The Ethics of Campaign Communications," in Lawson Taitte, ed., *Morality of the Mass Media* (University of Texas Press, 1993), pp. 157–206.

56. Ibid., p. 158.

57. Davis and Owen, *New Media and American Politics*.

58. Ibid., pp. 17–20.

59. Lee Rainie and Dan Packel, "More Online, Doing More," the Pew Internet & American Life project (February 18, 2001; www.pewinternet.org [June 2001]).

60. BIGResearch, "Public Policy & Media Influence Study" (February 2001; www.bigresearch.com [June 2001]).

61. Kevin Hill and John Hughes, *Cyberpolitics* (Lanham, Md.: Rowman & Littlefield, 1998), pp. 21–22.

62. Ibid., p. 243.

63. Gary Selnow, "Internet Ethics," in Denton, *Political Communication Ethics,* p. 205.

64. Jeremy Derfner, 25 January 2001. "So, Was It a Net Election?" *Slate* (January 25, 2001; slated.msn.cx/netelection/entries/01-01-25 97767.asp [May 2001]).

65. Montague Kern, *30-Second Politics* (Praeger, 1989), p. 5.

66. Lynda Kaid, "Ethics and Political Advertising," in Denton, *Political Communication Ethics,* pp. 146–77.

67. Michael Pfau and Henry Kenski, *Attack Politics* (Praeger, 1990), p. xiii.

68. Stephen Ansolabehere and Shanto Iyengar, *Going Negative* (Free Press, 1995), p. 148.

69. Harris Survey, *The Polling Report, Inc.*, January 9, 1999.

70. Quoted in Fallows, *Breaking the News*, p. 262.

71. Kathleen Hall Jamieson and Karlyn Campbell, *The Interplay of Influence* (Belmont, Calif.: Wadsworth, 1992), p. 30.

72. Patterson, *Out of Order*, p. 208.

73. Thomas Hollihan, *Uncivil Wars* (Boston: Bedford, 2001), p. 77.

74. Fallows, *Breaking the News*, p. 7.

75. Davis and Owen, *New Media and American Politics*, p. 96.

76. Quoted in ibid., p. 260.

77. Marjorie Hershey, "The Campaign and the Media," in Gerald Pomper, ed., *The Election of 2000* (New York: Chatham House, 2001), p. 65.

78. Davis and Owen, *New Media and American Politics*, p. 96.

79. Patterson, *Out of Order*, p. 20.

80. Ibid., p. 18.

81. Diana Owen, "The Press Performance," in Larry Sabato, ed., *Toward the Millennium: The Election of 1996* (Boston: Allyn & Bacon, 1997), p. 207.

82. Patterson, *Out of Order*, p. 22.

83. Cappella and Jamieson, *Spiral of Cynicism*, p. 31.

84. Ibid., p. 96.

85. Ibid., p. 33.

86. Hollihan, *Uncivil Wars*, p. 89.

87. Cappella and Jamieson, *Spiral of Cynicism*, p. 37.

88. Ibid., p. 237.

89. Davis and Owen, *New Media and American Politics*, pp. 189–209.

90. Jim Squires, "The Impossibility of Fairness," *Media Studies Journal*, vol. 12, no. 2 (Summer 1998), p. 68.

91. Patterson, *Out of Order*, p. 52.

92. Ibid., p. 208.

93. Michael Rogin, *Ronald Reagan, the Movie* (University of California Press, 1987), p. 9.

94. Walter Cronkite, acceptance speech for the 1989 Allen H. Neuharth Award for Excellence in Journalism, University of South Dakota, October 27, 1989.

CHAPTER TWELVE

THE MEDIA

Watchdog, Guide, and Soapbox

PAUL TAYLOR

How can the media foster ethical campaigns? They can do so by serving as a watchdog, a guide, and a soapbox—each a distinct role that carries a different set of responsibilities. The media do a reasonably good job in the first role but function poorly in the second and third, a spotty record that leaves them implicated in the decline of modern political campaigns. They are not the heavies of the piece, but neither are they innocent bystanders. To understand why, one need only follow the money. Not the political money, the media money.

Before elaborating, I should make it clear that for the purposes of this chapter, I intend to load a lot of freight onto the term *ethical*. I mean for it to do more than describe campaigns that are guided by norms of honesty, accountability, and fair play. I mean for it also to describe campaigns that inform the public and help turn it into an engaged citizenry. This is the civic responsibility model that Dale Miller and Stephen Medvic describe in chapter 2. For those who find this broader requirement a semantic stretch, let me invoke a passage from John Stuart Mill. He wrote of "the moral part of the instruction afforded by the participation of the private citizen, if even rarely, in public functions. He is called upon, while so engaged, to weigh interests not his own . . . to apply, at every turn, principles and maxims which have for their reason of existence the common good. . . . He is made to feel himself one of the public, and whatever is for their benefit is for his benefit."[1] Mark me down as a Millian. By my lights, political campaigns perform their highest function when they frame public life as something larger than the sum of private interests. They have the opportunity to do so at the indispensable moment in any democratic process—the moment when citizens act out their sovereignty and choose their leaders. At their best, "campaigns make a population a citizenry," wrote political scientist Roderick Hart.[2] That is no small challenge in a politically placid era such as ours, and campaigns that meet it are ethical in the highest meaning of the term.

Modern campaigns fall well short of this ideal; they have lost their pride of place at the center of our national life. The benign explanation is that, except in times of crisis, Americans value their freedom from politics. The darker view is that modern campaigns have become so soaked in special interest money and synthetic speech that they repel rather than engage the public. Both diagnoses seem right to me, and the media are implicated in each. Increasingly driven by profits, they have retreated from the journalistic challenge of presenting campaigns as a compelling spectacle that can have a direct impact on the lives of their readers and viewers. The overnight ratings declare that politics is a turnoff; and for too many television stations, that is the end of the story. To compound the problem, as the broadcast media devote less time to substantive campaign coverage, candidates are forced to raise more money to get their messages out, fueling a money chase and ad bombardment that exacerbates the public's low opinion of the whole exercise.

The media do better when measured on fostering ethical campaigns in the narrower and more conventional meaning of the term, which involves promoting a political culture of integrity and openness. The difference is that the "watchdog" role that helps build such a culture is viewed in most media newsrooms and boardrooms as a fount of good stories and ratings, while the more civic-minded roles of "guide" and "soapbox" are not. Here is a closer look at how the media performed in these three roles in the 2000 campaign.

The Media as Watchdog

Journalists have always considered themselves society's first line of defense against hypocrites, demagogues, charlatans, and other unsavory or unethical types who from time to time aspire to political power. "A journalist is the lookout on the ship of state," the publisher Joseph Pulitzer wrote a century ago. "He peers through the fog and storm to give warnings of the dangers ahead."[3] For reporters covering presidential campaigns, translating this exalted mission into action can mean subjecting candidates to levels of scrutiny not normally found outside of psychiatry or proctology. Part of the drill involves a thorough review of the candidates' past records and résumés. But the real trophies seem to go to the reporters who seize on a current campaign gaffe or misstep as a pretext to probe the candidate's warts. These are the stories deemed in newsrooms to have the sort of immediacy and drama that attract eyeballs. (And even when a story originates with the unearthing of an embarrassing episode from a candidate's past, the reporting usually focuses, for the same reason, on how the candidate reacts to the revelation in the present.)

In the 2000 campaign, the media had George W. Bush in their crosshairs for lacking gravitas, and Al Gore for lacking authenticity. As is their custom, political reporters were on the prowl for real-time campaign events that would allow them to pick and probe at these suspected flaws. Sometimes, their peg seemed painfully thin. For example, Gore suffered a rash of bad press when he mistakenly claimed during the first presidential debate that he had toured disaster-stricken areas in Texas with the head of the Federal Emergency Management Agency (FEMA), when in fact he had accompanied the deputy head. Not a lot there, but the press had a field day. Similarly, Bush's verbal gaffes, his flunking of a reporter's pop quiz, and the persistent (but never proven) rumors of youthful drug abuse provided no end of fodder, not just for the campaign journalists but for the late-night comics.

Such "gotcha" coverage has grown commonplace over the past generation, and is the type of sensational and issue-free coverage of campaigns Robert Denton critiques in the previous chapter. This type of coverage also tracks a parallel decline in trust toward public officials and institutions. Is there a cause and effect relationship here? Yes, though it probably moves in both directions simultaneously. Would it be better if the press did not go overboard at the slightest provocation? Yes. But does this relentless scrutiny raise the ethical norms of those who seek and win public office? Yes again, I'd venture. It seems safe to assume (even if it is a negative that is impossible to prove) that lots of potential candidates who have skeletons in their closet never run for public office in the first place, fearing the press will pry open doors they would rather keep shut. On balance, this is a net plus for democracy, though it probably also explains why so many modern politicians seem so bland. (Former president Bill Clinton is the exception who proves the rule; politics in the age of gotcha

journalism is not a hospitable line of work for the charming rogue.) By
the same token, it also seems safe to assume that for those who do brave
the gauntlet, the fear of bad press restrains a lot of behavior that might
otherwise, in the heat of a campaign, become ethically challenged. Here
there actually is a bit of empirical evidence, and it comes from an unlikely
quarter—political advertising. In the popular mythology, ads that attack
the opponent are most likely to resort to deception, half-truth, and outright falsehood. But the popular wisdom happens to be wrong. Political
communications scholar Kathleen Hall Jamieson has studied television
advertising in presidential campaigns since 1952 and found that attack
ads are more truthful than ads that advocate on behalf of a candidate
without ever mentioning the opponent.[4] The apparent reason for the difference is that candidates and their consultants know that the media scrutiny of attack ads tends to be much tougher than the scrutiny of self-
promoting ads, and they adjust their communication norms accordingly.

In sum, the attack-dog instinct of the press leads to a certain coarsen-
ing of the political culture, it contributes to a prevailing cynicism about
government and elected officials, and on occasion it produces feeding fren-
zies that distort rather than illuminate the character of the candidates under scrutiny. But it also raises the level of ethical norms in politics and
public life. Moreover, if there were no attack-dog press, if instead we had
a reverential press that looked the other way, how much trust would the
public wind up having in public officials and institutions? None at all.
When it comes to this watchdog role, the late *Washington Post* editorial
writer Alan Barth had it right: better that the press bite the occasional
mailman than allow a burglar to sneak past.[5]

The Media as Guide

This is the meat and potatoes of campaign journalism. It consists of helping citizens to understand who the candidates are, what the issues are,
and how their Election Day choices will impact their lives. It rarely produces scoops or scandals, but when done well, it does produce an informed
electorate. Unfortunately, there is less of this sort of journalism than there
used to be, and in the case of the broadcast media, a lot less.

Back when Walter Cronkite was the most trusted man in America, broadcast television was the sea that political campaigns swam in. Its cameras
transformed debates and conventions and election nights into something
they had never been before—mass spectacles. Its anchormen served as tour

guides, deciphering the speeches, the platforms, the rituals, and the infighting for the politically uninitiated. During Cronkite's reign, CBS, NBC, and ABC together attracted 75 percent of the television viewing public to their nightly newscasts, and their attention to campaigns helped to cement politics at the center of our national life. "If it didn't happen on television," went a favorite political aphorism of the era, "it didn't happen."

Much has changed in the generation since then. Campaigns have lost both their novelty and lure as television events; today's audiences find them dull, even grating. The broadcasters have lost huge chunks of their audience, first to cable and more recently to the Internet. And politics has lost its preeminent place in society, struggling in the post–cold war age to hold its own against competition from soap operas, scandals, sports, stock markets, and soft news.

As politics has been downsized, so has political coverage. For decades, researchers have meticulously tracked the shrinking sound bite and the declining number of minutes that television broadcasters devote to substantive campaign coverage. According to the Center for Media and Public Affairs, a Washington-based research group, the three nightly network newscasts devoted 28 percent less time to coverage of the 2000 campaign than they had to the 1988 campaign, the last time there was an open-seat race for the presidency. Coverage of the national party conventions was down by roughly two-thirds from 1988. Just 12 percent, a record low, of all presidential campaign coverage on the network newscasts in 2000 was devoted to the candidates' own words. (Reporters received 74 percent of election news airtime and all other sources—voters, pundits, campaign staffers—the remaining 14 percent.) The length of the typical presidential candidate sound bite on the nightly newscasts also hit a record low—7.8 seconds. And finally, of all the campaign stories that the networks did air, 71 percent focused on the horse race rather than on the issues.[6]

Broadcast news executives insist that this scale-back is justified both by the sharp decline in audience interest and the sharp increase in the availability of political information on cable and the Internet. Their defense, in so many words: "Let 'em eat cable." But not everyone has access to cable or the Internet, and those who do must pay a monthly fee for the service. Do we really want to become a "subscription democracy" where citizens who want a front row to their presidential campaign have to pay a fee?

It is one of the paradoxes of the information age that as more political information has become more available on more kinds of media, fewer and fewer citizens have chosen to partake of it. Polls taken throughout 2000 showed a decline in citizen interest in that campaign compared to previous ones, even though it was apparent from Labor Day forward that the presidential race was headed for a tight finish. And because people were not interested, they did not take the time to learn. In a nationwide survey taken just two days before the election, Harvard University's Vanishing Voter project found that fewer than half of those polled could answer simple questions about Bush's views on taxes, abortion, and gun control, or Gore's position on Medicare prescription drug plans, Social Security, school vouchers, or affirmative action.[7] These results came at the end of a campaign in which fewer people than ever in the television era followed the campaign on broadcast television, and more people than ever followed it on cable and the web.[8] The lesson seems clear: If politics cannot win the battle for eyeballs in the broadcast world, it cannot recover in the narrowcast world.

Suppose, however, that the real problem is not the media; it is that campaigns have indeed become dull, candidates wooden, conventions scripted, and debates programmed. Is it the media's job to fix them? No. But it *is* the media's job to make what is important interesting. Political campaigns are important; they have a direct bearing on the very things that most citizens hold most dear—their health, their security, their financial well-being, their children's education, and so on. Campaigns also have all the ingredients to be interesting—character, plot, drama, a suspenseful ending, and an important underlying purpose. Yet somehow, when it all gets tossed into the media blender, it comes out as "bad television." This says more about television that it does about politics.

I had the opportunity in early 2001 to serve as one of the judges for the inaugural Cronkite Award for Excellence in Broadcast Television Journalism sponsored by the Annenberg School for Communication of the University of Southern California.[9] We reviewed scores of tapes of 2000 campaign coverage from local stations and national networks. The most sobering aspect of our work was the number of entry letters that began with some variant of the following: Such and such station had decided to make a substantial commitment to campaign coverage in 2000 despite the prevailing industry wisdom that politics is "ratings suicide," that it makes for barely "watchable" television, and that campaigns are "more trouble to cover than they are worth." The most gratifying aspect of our work was the number of entries that gave the lie to these bleak assessments. From the biggest and best-known of our award recipients (NBC's

Meet the Press) to the smallest (WGME-TV in Portland, Maine, and KTRV-TV in Boise, Idaho), broadcast news organizations demonstrated during the 2000 campaign that good political coverage can not only inform the public, it can also make good television. And there was not a lot of rocket science involved.

The most compelling pieces we viewed were the ones in which reporters focused on issues and explained how they affected the lives of ordinary citizens. It was probably no coincidence that several of the top awards were for stories that dealt with ballot initiatives rather than candidate races—for example, WGME-TV's superb treatment of a physician-assisted suicide ballot measure in Maine. Reporting on a ballot question seemed to free reporters from the drearily familiar tactical and horse race frame that so often smothers their candidate coverage; it also forced them to explain issues in ways that candidate coverage rarely does. Citizens have never been drawn to politics by a sense of civic duty (even though civic engagement is one of the happiest by-products of their participation in the democratic process). Nor are they attracted for more than a fleeting moment by the horse race, the infighting, the tactical thrust and parry. They are drawn, ultimately, because they believe it is something that can make a tangible difference in their lives. Great political journalism explains how.

Unfortunately, in today's profit-obsessed media culture, pieces of this kind have become the exception. They require a serious investment of journalistic talent, imagination, and enterprise at a time when most local stations and the national networks have gone in for the eye candy of the soft, the shallow, and the sensational. Campaigns need not be ratings suicide. Indeed, they present journalists with the ultimate opportunity to provide "news you can use." They are the only story for which the viewers themselves get to choose the ending, and in so choosing, shape their futures. Broadcasters not only have failed to respond to this challenge, it is no longer clear if they even recognize it.

The Media as Soapbox

If the television industry has become reluctant to serve as a journalistic guide, it has grown positively allergic to the idea that it should provide a forum or soapbox so candidates themselves can communicate their ideas to the broadest audience possible. Here again, a few statistics from the 2000 campaign tell the story. During the primary season, the Democratic

and Republican candidates held a total of twenty-two television debates—
of which just two aired on commercial broadcast networks, neither of
them in prime time (the twenty others were shown nationally only on
cable or public television, where they drew tiny audiences). The network
coverage of the summer conventions was down by nearly 80 percent from
1988, as one anchor after another took turns pummeling the conventions
as "infomercials" unworthy of even the minimal coverage they received.
And in the fall, for the first time ever, two of the four national networks
(NBC and Fox) chose not to carry the general election presidential debates. Instead, they counterprogrammed with sports and entertainment.

This retreat from coverage of the traditional "big event" campaign forums coincided with the broadcast media's refusal to embrace a recommendation that it provide a new series of short formats for candidate discourse in the final weeks of the campaign. The recommendation came
from a blue-ribbon White House advisory panel charged with updating
the public interest obligations of television broadcasters in the digital era.
It called on national networks and every local television station to volun-
tarily provide five minutes a night of candidate discourse—be it in the
form of interviews, minidebates or issue statements—in the month preceding all elections. The hope was that five minutes a night would be long
enough for candidates to get into substance and short enough for a disengaged public to keep watching. But even though the panel was cochaired
by CBS president Leslie Moonves and included several other leading broadcasters, the great bulk of the industry (including Moonves's own CBS)
ignored its recommendation. According to research by Annenberg Schools
at the Universities of Pennsylvania and Southern California, the network
newscasts devoted an average of just sixty-four seconds a night to candidate discourse in the month before the election, and the typical local television station devoted just forty-five seconds a night.[10]

That is not to say there was not a veritable blizzard of political communication on these stations, though. There was a billion dollars' worth,
which went to pay for a record 1.2 million political ads that ran from
January 1 through November 7, 2000.[11] Campaign 2000 was the television industry's third best advertising client that year—behind automobiles
and retail stores but well ahead of movies and fast foods. In the closing
months of the campaign, the unprecedented spike in demand for paid political ad time led stations in markets with hotly contested races to double
and sometimes triple their ads rates for political and nonpolitical adver-

tisers alike. This gouging forced candidates to raise more special interest money. And the more they raised, the more gouging they faced.

Let us follow the bouncing ball here. We the public give broadcasters free and exclusive rights to our public airwaves in return for their commitment to serve the public interest. Come election time, they turn around and sell back chunks of airtime to candidates, triggering a money chase and ad blizzard that help to sour the public on political campaigns. Meantime, the news departments of these same broadcaster license holders do not cover the campaigns. The public does not give a damn, they say. Bad television, they say. And so candidates who want to be seen and heard on television have to run more ads.

This vicious circle enriches the broadcasters while it impoverishes democracy. Every industry has an obligation to maximize profits, but the broadcasters have a couple of other obligations as well. One of them is the public trustee role they take on when they receive their free government licenses. The other is their responsibility as journalists. "The news is not a product like any other," the *Economist* magazine editorialized a few years ago. "People learn about how they are governed by what they read in the newspapers and what they see on the television news. Unless voters know something about how they are governed, they cannot have an intelligent opinion about it. And without intelligent opinions about government, you cannot have a healthy democracy."[12] Nor, it might have added, ethical campaigns.

Notes

1. John Stuart Mill, "Considerations on Representative Government," in *Collected Works of John Stuart Mill* (University of Toronto Press, 1977), p. 412.

2. Roderick P. Hart, *Campaign Talk: Why Elections Are Good for Us* (Princeton University Press, 2000), p. 11.

3. Cited in Paul Taylor, *See How They Run: Electing the President in an Age of Mediaocracy* (Knopf, 1990), p. 9.

4. Kathleen Hall Jamieson, Paul Waldman, and Susan Sherr, "Eliminate the Negative? Categories of Analysis for Political Advertisements," in James A. Thurber, Candice J. Nelson, and David A. Dulio, eds., *Crowded Airwaves: Campaign Advertising in Elections* (Brookings, 2000).

5. Alan Barth, *The Rights of Free Men* (Knopf, 1984), p. 322.

6. Center for Media and Public Affairs, "Campaign 2000 Final: How TV News Covered the General Election Campaign," *Media Monitor*, vol. 14, no. 6 (November–December 2000; www.cmpa.com/Mediamon/mm111200.htm).

7. Vanishing Voter project, "Knowledge of Candidates: Issue Position Questions" (www.vanishingvoter.org/data/cand-knowledge.shtml).

8. Robert Denton discusses the potential problems of Internet coverage and journalism in chapter 11.

9. Readers interested in this competition can find out more about it by going to www.entertainment.usc.edu or www.reliablesources.org/award.html.

10. See the Norman Lear Center, Annenberg School for Communication at the University of Southern California, "Local TV Coverage of the 2000 General Election" (February 2001; www.entertainment.usc.edu); or the Annenberg Public Policy Center, the University of Pennsylvania, "Are Voluntary Standards Working? Candidate Discourse on Network Evening News Programs" (December 20, 2000; www.aapcpenn.org/political).

11. Alliance for Better Campaigns, *Gouging Democracy: How the Television Industry Profiteered on Campaign 2000* (Washington, 2001).

12. *Economist,* vol. 348, no. 8075 (1998), p. 13.

CHAPTER THIRTEEN

THE CITIZENRY

The Electorate's Responsibilities

MICHAEL W. TRAUGOTT

Citizens sometimes face complex issues about how to choose between satisfying their own self-interest or the greater social good. While this may not be a broad definition of an ethical dilemma, these circumstances do place citizens in difficult moral positions. For example, they may face a choice between a candidate who promises to reduce their own taxes and one who promotes programs to improve the educational system under current tax rates. Or they may face the dilemma of supporting an interest group that promises to promote a cleaner environment but engages in tactics that distort or misrepresent the circumstances of a particular ecological event to advance its cause. Such choices pit personal interests against an ethical position about how broader political or policymaking affairs should be conducted (see the discussion of the self-interest and civic-mindedness models in chapter 2).

These normative considerations have to be viewed in the context of the actual behavior of citizens in the United States. For example, voting is generally seen as the most common and widespread form of political behavior. While there is clearly an imperative to participate in elections, turnout in the United States has been declining—approximately 16 percent from 1960 to 2000, leading to a situation in which only about half of all of the citizens of voting age actually vote. Other forms of political participation, such as attending a political meeting, working for a political candidate, or giving money to a campaign, are reported by less than 10 percent of the American public.[1]

Any discussion of the ethical issues citizens confront has to focus on the interaction between the substance of the dilemmas and the time or context in which they occur. Do the issues arise at particular points in the campaign, or are campaign-related dilemmas just a special case of the ethical issues that citizens can face at any time? A discussion of ethical issues almost always centers on normative principles; therefore, this chapter focuses on what citizens *ought* to be doing rather than the construction of an accurate description of what they *are* doing.

Any discussion of political matters at the individual level is significantly complicated by the overriding filter of partisanship, which can prevent a reasoned assessment of the merits of a particular issue. The prism of partisanship is so strong that individuals sometimes take unanticipated positions that seem to fly in the face of objective evaluations of evidence. Nowhere was that more recently clear than in the public debate among political elites and the citizenry about former president Bill Clinton's behavior in his relationship with Monica Lewinsky. Democrats and Republicans at both levels had characteristically different views of the political ramifications and consequences of the president's behavior. Democrats initially gave the president the benefit of the doubt and praised his handling of the situation, although his personal standing suffered with successive disclosures. Republicans, on the other hand, started with more critical evaluations of his performance and low assessments of him personally, and both sets of evaluations deteriorated. The example indicates that the general ethical standard expected of an elected official or candidate varies according to the citizen who is doing the evaluating.

It is important to sort out systemic issues that affect the entire population (such as the continuing decline in trust in government) from issues associated with particular institutions (such as the "check-writing" scandal in the 103d Congress that affected the 1992 elections) and from individual issues that face particular members of Congress (such as Gary Condit [D-Calif.] and his alleged affair with Chandra Levy).[2] While the repeated occurrence of problems of personal misconduct may accumulate over time in ways that generalize from assessments of an individual member of Congress to the entire institution, these have to be considered as two distinct consequences.

At the same time, citizens face a dilemma in deciding whether and how to deal with the intersecting trends of increasingly negative news about governmental institutions and the more personalized and negative campaigns that some candidates for office run. In ethical terms, this often requires a considered evaluation of an elected official's professional competence as distinct from his or her personal life. Take, for example, the impact of all kinds of negative news on citizens as it accumulates over time and has an effect on their trust in government.

There has been an overall decline in the public's trust in government over the last thirty-five years.[3] According to the America National Election Studies (ANES), this began in 1966 and continued essentially unabated, with the exception of a slight upturn in the Reagan years. There has been an equivalent decline in the public's perceptions of the responsiveness of government across this time period,[4] but there has not been an associated shift in the public's approval of the performance of the U.S. Congress.[5] The latter measure has always reflected relatively low assessments, and there is some suggestion that public approval of the performance of Congress increased somewhat after the 1994 election.[6] So assessments of the public response to ethical concerns will vary according to what aspect of government is being measured.

Responsibilities during the Campaign

Perhaps the easiest way to discuss the ethical dilemmas that citizens face and their alternatives for dealing with them is to start with election campaigns. During such a period of heightened candidate activity and media coverage, citizens have at their disposal an unusually large and rich information base to use for evaluating candidates and policies. Compared to the noncampaign period, citizens have a clearer picture of how the candidates differ, which organized interests support them, and how their competence and past behavior may be relevant for service in office.

There are suggestions that contemporary citizens have both more and qualitatively different information than citizens of even twenty or twenty-five years ago had, although the magnitude of these differences is unclear. For one thing, journalists now pursue stories in an increasingly adversarial way at the same time that the general tone of campaigns has become more negative.[7] In addition, the increase of cable news outlets and the Internet as a source of news has meant that there is more information available. The content of the information itself has changed—it is often more personal and more negative.[8] This is not to say that such coverage is completely unwarranted. But it raises ethical considerations for citizens that they often did not face in the past, requiring them to make judgments about qualifications for the job and fitness to serve in relation to assessments of a candidate's personal morality compared to their own.

In the case of former presidential candidate Gary Hart and Donna Rice in the 1984 presidential primary campaign, the disclosures came early (in May) and when the nomination was still in doubt. There was direct photographic evidence, and the candidate faced the press without strong support from his family. In light of earlier claims he had made about the state of his personal life, his withdrawal was inevitable. How different things were at about the same point in the political process in the 1992 presidential primaries when the relationship between the then presidential candidate Bill Clinton and Gennifer Flowers was disclosed. This time it was the *Star* rather than the *Washington Post* that broke the story, and Clinton issued a strong initial denial that was followed by a television interview in which he appeared with his wife. She expressed support for him and their marriage at the same time that she acknowledged they had experienced personal difficulty in the past.

Survey data collected at the time suggest that there was a very strong partisan dimension underlying citizens' evaluations of Clinton.[9] While Americans generally believed that Clinton's marital infidelity should not be an issue (by a 4-1 margin), they were sharply divided over whether an untruthful Clinton should withdraw from the race. A majority of Democrats (52 percent) believed he should stay in, while a majority of Republicans (60 percent) thought he should get out. For a significant amount of time in a much more drawn-out story, the same phenomenon occurred with public evaluations of Bill Clinton after his affair with Monica Lewinsky was exposed and then confirmed. The durability of the story was due in part to how politicized it became, culminating with impeachment proceedings in Congress. Also there was a special prosecutor, Ken Starr, already in place investigating some of the Clintons' real estate transactions who could take up the charge of obstruction of justice. A daily stream of information from these events kept the story alive.

As much a result of different survey methods as changing times and the public's growing realization that politicians are people who lead complicated personal lives, too, we learned a lot in the Clinton-Lewinsky-Starr episode about the public's ability to segregate feelings about performance in office from assessments of character and personal conduct. Clinton's approval ratings remained very high for a second-term incumbent, buoyed by the support of Democrats and Independents. But the constant news coverage of his problems took a toll on the public's assessments of him personally, as even his most loyal partisans acknowledged that they expected a higher standard of conduct for the person holding the highest elective office in the land.

In the case of the presidency, it is often difficult to distinguish the officeholder from the office. But this same phenomenon faces citizens in a more complicated way when they have to distinguish assessments of the Congress from evaluations of their own representatives. This is most often described in terms of the dilemma captured in Richard Fenno's question, "Why do Americans love their congressmen so much more than their Congress?"[10] Many members of Congress actually run against their institution, suggesting to their constituents that they need to be returned in order to keep an eye on their less trustworthy colleagues. In this way, they are trying to benefit personally from increased public distrust at the institutional level, but in doing so they may be contributing to higher levels of general public distrust of government.

Welch and Hibbing describe another dimension of contemporary campaign styles that contributes to declining levels of trust.[11] They cite the increasingly negative tone of campaigns and the tendency of candidates to separate themselves from opponents by routinely levying charges of impropriety or corruption. The consequence is that campaigns focus less on issues and more on "moral character, personal finances, utilization of perquisites, family life, daily habits, and related matters."[12] So citizens are developing different perceptions of political institutions and those who serve in them as a result of these concurrent trends in reporting and campaign styles.

Monitoring Candidate Behavior

One of the most important functions that citizens have in a campaign is being critical consumers of the candidates' ads. This is obviously related to staying informed about the candidates and their issue positions. The ethical element of this comes when citizens believe that one candidate is mischaracterizing the opponent's issue positions or producing false or unwarranted charges about the opponent's voting record or personal life. Such charges represent a problem in both the short and long term. In the immediate campaign, the false claims can have an impact on the outcome, especially in a tight race. But in the longer term, repetition of such incidents can decrease citizens' level of system support and increase their levels of cynicism.

Under such circumstances, a citizen has an obligation to let the offending candidate know that he or she believes a misrepresentation is taking place and expects it to stop. Because events in a campaign happen so rapidly and most negative behavior happens at the end of the campaign when there is little time left for response, the citizen may have to decide relatively quickly that he or she also needs to inform friends and other likely voters of the belief that misrepresentation is taking place. This is especially important if the citizen is confident that misrepresentation is occurring and the candidate acknowledges the citizen's concern but refuses to change or modify the ad.

Another important opportunity for citizens is in monitoring the behavior of candidates or interest groups that engage in unethical campaign tactics (Rourke deals with this more fully in the following chapter). As others in this volume have noted (Maisel in chapter 3; Nelson, Medvic, and Dulio in chapter 5; and Whitney in chapter 6), one of the most common of these techniques, being used with increasing frequency, is "push polling." This is a technique that simulates an interview in a legitimate poll but actually is a negative persuasion telephone call.[13] In some campaigns, hundreds or even thousands of calls are made from phone banks, usually just before Election Day. The very nature of the technique is to hide the calls from public scrutiny. The only way to divulge the fact that a candidate is using push polling is to have citizens report the calls they receive to the media. There are no public bodies that can review a particular circumstance and produce a binding decision that requires a campaign to stop the practice. The only antidote is widespread public disclosure through the media and a demand for commentary by the offending campaign. Such disclosures require citizens to step forward and describe the calls they received. In conjunction with news organizations, citizens can reduce the likelihood of such negative campaign practices.

In a few cases, citizens in a local area might have to decide about the difference between their evaluations of a candidate's personal life and his or her competence and service to the constituency. This is a complication because the candidate's behavior may be unethical or even immoral according to the citizen's personal standards, but his or her service to the constituency may be excellent. If citizens decide that ethical considerations override their satisfaction with the quality of representation they have been receiving, then they have an obligation to make their feelings known to the candidate. This can often influence whether the candidate seeks reelection. Such an expression of citizen concern does not always produce the same outcome. In 1994 news organizations withheld information about Senator Robert Packwood's (R-Oreg.) personal life at the end of the campaign, and he was reelected. But the disclosures and citizen feedback were salient enough that he resigned shortly thereafter. In the case of Representative Gary Condit, information about his personal life became public in the course of an investigation into another matter. After extended deliberation, he decided not to resign and faced a primary challenge that he lost.

Monitoring Press Behavior

Citizens have an obligation to monitor press behavior in the same way that they monitor candidate behavior. As critical consumers of press coverage of the campaign, citizens must be on the alert for bias, favoritism, or the simple lack of coverage of a particular candidate or issue. This can raise an ethical dilemma for citizens when their preferred candidate is the beneficiary of imbalanced coverage because registering a complaint may work against their candidate's interest. But the preservation of balanced campaign coverage is an important democratic value, and a citizen's own candidate could suffer from such treatment in a future campaign.

Biased coverage occurs when the content of the coverage misrepresents a candidate's positions or inaccurately describes his or her personal characteristics and suitability for office. This is a factual distortion. Favoritism reflects an imbalance in the coverage when one candidate receives a greater quantity of coverage than another. This is a common occurrence in many races because one candidate has more resources than the other and can support more activity like rallies or produce more media events like press conferences. Some campaigns, especially those for legislative offices where there is a poor fit between media markets or circulation areas and the geographic area of the district, involve strong incumbents from a majority party running against poorly financed and supported challengers. These "invisible challengers" may receive no news coverage at all.

How can citizens deal with such circumstances of unbalanced coverage? They have to make their concerns known to the media organizations. That means writing or calling newspapers and radio and television stations to express concerns about the quantity or quality of the campaign coverage. Editors and producers have to learn that audience members are paying attention to the way they cover politics and feel strongly enough to express their dissatisfaction. Media organizations are generally feeling the pinch of declining audiences and increased competition from a more heterogeneous set of competitors—cable TV, the Internet, specialist newsletters, and the like. The rise of the "civic journalism" movement is a reflection of and response to these trends, clearly suggesting that news organizations are much more likely to pay attention to such complaints than they were just a few years ago.[14]

Monitoring Interest Group Behavior

Interest groups have become much more active in American politics recently, engaging in a wide range of independent campaign activities, as noted by James Thurber in chapter 9. This is especially true in the area of "soft money" activities, where they raise and spend ever-increasing amounts of money on advertising without contacting the parties or their candidates.[15] This kind of activity is especially significant ethically, as these organizations are not required to report the source of their funds or how they spend them. Larger and larger amounts of money are being spent on television advertising, but interest groups also spend a great deal on direct mail campaigns and often hire or place staff in locations where important campaigns are under way.

The issue is not how much these groups spend but the kinds of things they buy. When they purchase airtime on television, for example, their messages are broadcast to large segments of the electorate. Then it is much more likely that problematical messages will come to the attention of large numbers of citizens or to journalists who can report on dubious messages. But when the money purchases direct mail, these messages are usually delivered in a highly targeted way, often below the radar screen of activists who publicize potential problems. And sometimes the money is spent on dishonest and unethical campaign techniques such as the push polls discussed above.[16]

These circumstances again place a burden on citizens to act as watchdogs and disclose inappropriate or unsavory campaign techniques to the media. Sometimes this can be as simple as indicating the kinds of mailings, phone calls, or personal contacts they have received. At other times, citizens may have to step forward and become personally involved in the disclosures. The best way to dissuade candidates from using unethical techniques or messages of dubious authenticity is to publicize their existence widely. Interest groups, like candidates, need to understand that if they engage in certain inappropriate behaviors or techniques they will be reported and endure widespread public censure.

Casting an Informed Vote

At the end of the campaign, citizens have to decide whether to become voters. While this is a clear moral obligation of citizenship, it does not typically present an ethical dilemma. The closest circumstance to that involves deciding whether to cast an informed vote. The problems of gathering information, in terms of cost and inconvenience, are best encapsulated in Downs, whose work guided the field for quite a while.[17] More recent theoretical and empirical developments suggest that voters can produce quite rational decisions about candidates by using cognitive shortcuts.[18] Voters do not require large stores of information to cast votes, but how much information should they reasonably be expected to seek in order to cast their vote? Electing representatives to pass laws and establish policy is arguably one of the most important and lasting decisions (at least in the midterm) that citizens make. It has real consequences for how their city, state, or nation functions.

First and foremost among the shortcuts that voters use is party identification. Even though overall levels of strength of partisanship have declined in the American electorate and this psychological attachment to party does not provide the stability it once did, it remains the strongest predictor of candidate choice. But what are the consequences when a voter takes the shortcut of looking for the candidate who represents his or her party in lieu of collecting additional information about policy positions, and the result is a vote for a pro-life candidate when the citizen is pro-choice? Or what if the candidate is for increased government spending when the citizen wants a decrease in taxes? The self-interest principle suggests citizens should cast the most informed vote they can, using the maximum amount of resources they can expend to become informed.

Responsibilities on Election Day

The major decision that citizens face at the end of the campaign is whether to participate in the election. I use this particular terminology because the meaning of Election Day is changing rapidly. More and more voters are finding it a convenient option to vote early at a mobile site, through registration as a "permanent absentee voter," or by mail. More than one-quarter of all the votes in the 2000 election were cast before November 7.

These trends present two potential ethical problems for citizens. The first is the long-standing issue of whether to vote at all, given the difficulties of becoming informed, especially with the increased number of candidates and issues that now appear on ballots. The United States has many more elections for more offices than any European democracy or Japan. The difficulties of obtaining information have increased substantially by this fact alone. The movement toward more convenient voting procedures is directed at reducing the trouble of getting to the traditional polls on Election Day, but it has no effect on the information deficit. Recent changes in election procedures have been driven by the significant decline in voter turnout in the United States since 1960. In one sense, Americans' answer to this dilemma is already known, and attempts are being made to deal with it.

But the more convenient voting procedures present another problem because citizens are given the opportunity to vote alone rather than in the central public location of a precinct polling place. This may increase the prospects for fraud or the attempts of some to engage citizens in fraudulent behavior. When ballots are circulated widely by mail over extended periods of time, for example, rather than being under the central control of election officials at a polling place for several hours, several things can happen. In the most extreme case, they can be sold or bartered and cast by someone else. But more likely, citizens can be subject to pressure by family members or friends about how to vote. There is a potential loss of privacy that accompanies added convenience, and individual voters will face different circumstances and have differential abilities to ward off threats to the integrity of their votes.

Beyond these factors at the individual level, candidates and parties sometimes engage in activities deliberately designed to reduce turnout. Sometimes these are general techniques that serve multiple purposes, such as negative advertising campaigns, which simultaneously attack the qualifications of an opponent and raise levels of cynicism and disaffection in the electorate, leading people to stay away from the polls.[19] Under such circumstances, citizens face a series of important questions. They begin with evaluating the truthfulness of the claims made in the attacks. At this level, they can simultaneously assess the quality of the campaign and decide whether it affects their candidate choice. This provides an opportunity to make a conscious decision to participate as a reaction against the strategy to depress turnout. One way to view this choice is that citizens should deliberately choose to participate, to resist their growing cynicism with the process. If the claims about unethical or immoral behavior by a candidate are true, then citizens should actively participate in deciding the fate of that candidate rather than be turned off by the system and stay at home.

Responsibilities between Campaigns

While some may argue that the greatest ethical issues citizens face are associated with exercising their right to vote, there are also important and recurring occasions between elections when equivalent issues may arise. One of the most important is simply staying informed. Policies and laws will be proposed and debated that were never brought up during the campaign, so many citizens never gave them very much thought, if any, at that time. Elected officials have to produce actual laws or regulations about issues never discussed during the campaign; some would argue that electing independent representatives rather than instructed delegates will yield adequate results.

One element of citizen responsibility frequently overlooked is how constituents stay in touch with elected officials about issues they feel are important. The news media or interest groups serve some function in highlighting the positions of elected officials on issues that are either of general interest or important to specific segments of the population. But conveying personal opinions and the intensity of their feelings on issues is an important obligation of individual citizens in a democracy. There are now more means of doing this than ever before. In addition to letters and phone calls, various Internet-based options including e-mail are also readily available. Most elected officials and government agencies now have websites that include instructions about how to ask questions, provide views, or describe the quality of services rendered. More citizens need to take advantage of these opportunities on a regular basis rather than waiting until the next campaign starts.

Many citizens now find it easier and more effective to join organized political groups than to try to act alone. Interest groups have become increasingly important in American politics, partly due to the declining role of parties and partly as a result of the role of money in campaigns. Interest groups provide a means for aggregating individual interests in a way that often multiplies their influence. Furthermore, fund-raising through the interest group's membership can aggregate a critical campaign resource that is valuable enough to both incumbents and challengers that it can often guarantee access to discuss important issues, even if not directly affect a specific vote. The first decision is whether to join a group rather than take advantage of the "free rider" circumstance, whereby one can benefit from the organized activities of the collectivity but not expend any of one's own resources, including time. Olson described this problem most succinctly, and it has remained a focus of considerable research among democratic theorists because the phenomenon is so widespread.[20] While membership in organized groups seems to be on the rise (although this is itself a source of controversy in the "social capital" literature), the "free rider" problem remains.[21]

Group affiliation can present a problem for citizens if they discover that their organization is engaging in unethical behavior. This could include learning that it made illegal campaign contributions, produced a false and negative campaign ad about an issue or against a candidate, or organized a protest or demonstration that incapacitated a business or harmed another group of individuals. In this case, the citizens presumably still support the goals but may face an ethical dilemma about tactics. As a result, they will have to decide whether to retain their membership in the group as a way of promoting their interests or drop out as a form of protest.

Conclusions

Good citizenship carries with it many responsibilities, and they often present citizens with ethical and moral dilemmas that pit their self-interest against broader social and political concerns—the same dichotomy that Miller and Medvic outlined in chapter 2. Many of these surround a citizen's role as voter and are linked to evaluations of campaign behavior by candidates, parties, and interest groups as well as the media. But they also extend to the noncampaign period as well, especially with regard to staying informed and maintaining contacts with elected officials.

One of the most important issues for citizens is how to balance the demands of their daily lives with the high costs of staying informed and active in political affairs. The American political system places higher demands on its citizens, especially as they translate to voting obligations, than virtually any other democracy in the world. This is a special burden that citizens face in the United States, but in exchange they are granted potentially higher levels of involvement in government. Will American citizens accept the burden of self-governance, and will they shoulder it ethically?

Notes

1. Data from the American National Election Studies measuring these other forms of political participation can be found at www.umich.edu/~nes/nesguide/gd-index.htm#6 (March 23, 2001).

2. On the check-writing scandals, see John Alford and others, "Overdraft: The Political Cost of Congressional Malfeasance" *Journal of Politics*, vol. 56 (1994), pp. 788–801; Michael A. Dimock and Gary C. Jacobson, "Checks and Choices: The House Bank Scandal's Impact on Voters in 1992," *Journal of Politics*, vol. 57 (1995), pp. 1143–59.

3. See www.umich.edu/~nes/nesguide/graphs/g5a_5_1.htm (March 23, 2001) at the website of the National Election Studies for the full-time series.

4. See www.umich.edu/~nes/nesguide/graphs/g5c_3_1.htm (March 23, 2001) at the website of the National Election Studies for the full-time series.

5. See www.umich.edu/~nes/nesguide/graphs/g5c_4_1.htm (March 23, 2001) at the website of the National Election Studies for the full-time series.

6. It is worth noting that in the context of the attacks of September 11 and their aftermath, still another measure of public attitudes about political institutions—confidence in them—has shown a sharp upturn. Preliminary results from a study conducted by the National Opinion Research Center can be found at www.norc.uchicago.edu/projects/reaction/pubresp.pdf (March 23, 2001). It remains to be seen how durable these shifts will be.

7. On the adversarial nature of journalist coverage, see Larry Sabato, *Feeding Frenzy: How Attack Journalism Has Transformed American Politics* (Free Press, 1991).

8. Thomas Patterson, *Out of Order* (Knopf, 1993).

9. Michael W. Traugott and Jennifer Means, "Problems of Character: Was It the Candidate or the Press?" in Paul J. Lavrakas, Michael W. Traugott, and Peter V. Miller, eds., *Presidential Polls and the News Media* (Boulder, Colo.: Westview Press, 1995).

10. Glenn R. Parker and Roger H. Davidson, "Why Do Americans Love Their Congressman More than Their Congress?" *Legislative Studies Quarterly*, vol. 4 (1979), pp. 53–61.

11. Susan Welch and John R. Hibbing, "The Effects of Charges of Corruption on Voting Behavior in Congressional Elections, 1982–1990," *Journal of Politics*, vol. 59 (1997), pp. 226–39.

12. Ibid., p. 228.

13. Michael W. Traugott and Mee-Eun Kang, "Push Polls as Negative Persuasion Strategies," in Paul J. Lavrakas and Michael W. Traugott, eds., *Election Polls, the News Media, and Democracy* (Chatham, N.J.: Chatham House, 2000).

14. On the rise of "civic journalism," see Jay Rosen, *Getting the Connections Right: Public Journalism and the Troubles in the Press* (New York: Twentieth Century Fund, 1996).

15. David Magleby, ed. *The Other Campaign: Soft Money and Issue Advocacy in the 2000 Congressional Elections* (Lanham, Md.: Rowman and Littlefield, forthcoming).

16. "Push polling" is the only campaign technique that has received the simultaneous censure of the American Association for Public Opinion Research, the American Association of Political Consultants, and the National Conference of Public Polls.

17. Anthony Downs, *An Economic Theory of Democracy* (Chicago: Harper, 1957).

18. Samuel Popkin, *The Reasoning Voter* (University of Chicago Press, 1991).

19. Stephen Ansolabehere and Shanto Iyengar, *Going Negative: How Attack Ads Shrink and Polarize the Electorate* (Free Press, 1995); Gina M. Garramone and others, "Effects of Negative Political Advertising on the Political Process," *Journal of Broadcasting and Electronic Media*, vol. 34 (1990), pp. 299–311.

20. Mancur Olson, *The Logic of Collective Action* (Harvard University Press, 1965).

21. On social capital, see Robert Putnam, *Bowling Alone: The Collapse and Revival of American Community* (Simon & Schuster, 2000).

CHAPTER FOURTEEN

THE CITIZENRY

More than Voting

BRAD ROURKE

If liberty and equality are chiefly to be found in democracy, they will be best attained when all persons alike share in government to the utmost.

—Aristotle, *Politics*

In 1998 the phone in the Columbus, Ohio, office of the Institute for Global Ethics was ringing off the hook. We had set up a "voter action hotline" for citizens to complain about the behavior of political candidates. The response overwhelmed the voice mail system within a day. One caller was a woman from northwest Ohio. The message she left was also a plea for help: "I'm tired of all of this. . . . I'm tired of being the silent majority. . . . We've got to start letting people know how we feel." The desperation in her voice was palpable, and understandable. After all, aren't most citizens fed up with what they see as the eroding quality of campaigns? The caller, though, also pointed the way to a solution involving the relationship between citizens and candidates.

What role do citizens play in fostering ethical election campaigns? Reading narrowly, the answer is obvious: A citizen ought to vote her or his conscience, taking into account the candidate's campaign conduct as well as his or her issue positions. However, by valuing the franchise as the highest and best expression of civic engagement, this answer devalues the role of the citizen. As the caller from northwest Ohio understood implicitly, there is much more than voting, or not voting, at stake in citizenship. Today's ordinary, mainstream conceptions of what it means to be a citizen—and what the attendant obligations are—largely miss the mark because they lack a basis in ethics.

There are a variety of difficulties in American civic life, all of which tend to make it less likely that citizens will participate as they ought. What is needed, and what is possible to develop, is an ethics of citizenship that will help citizens resolve the dilemmas they face as members of the government. For if citizenship is a moral obligation and its exercise has a moral dimension, then it must be approached from an ethical standpoint. It is not enough to encourage more, or even more informed, voting. We must shift our sense of voting from "the most one is expected to do" to "the least of one's obligations."

To respond to the distressed caller in Ohio, we might first ask the question: "What are the ethical dimensions of *citizenship*?"

Things Are Not So Good

It is no secret that Americans, by and large, dislike most aspects of politics. Indeed, this thesis has become such a given among the politically knowledgeable that, like knowledge that the earth revolves around the sun, it is just something that "everybody knows." In our own work on public attitudes over the last few years at the Institute for Global Ethics,[1] we have seen this piece of conventional wisdom hold true. According to the institute's most recent national Civic Values Survey,[2] citizens are angry and disgusted with the state of their political system. Some of the symptoms of Americans' frustration with politics include:

—*We do not like officeholders.* Large majorities of Americans distrust government, elected officials, and politicians, with 67 percent of the voting public reporting that they can trust the government "only some of the time" or "almost never." They also believe that elected officials often do not behave ethically (60 percent agree) and have a hard time telling right from wrong (54 percent agree).

—*We do not like candidates.* Large numbers of respondents believe that "all or most" candidates twist the truth (59 percent) or lie outright (39 percent). Most Americans agree that campaigns have gotten worse with respect to "ethics and values" over the past twenty years (55 percent).

—*We do not like the press.* The distrust accorded to politicians is extended to the media as well. More than half the respondents strongly agree that "the media is just another part of negative, attack-oriented campaigning" (57 percent, with another 30 percent somewhat agreeing).

Added to this generalized disgust, there are also those who see the present system as actively pushing people out of the process. Many citizens have simply disengaged from political life; anecdotal evidence points to an upsurge over the last decade in the idea that *nonvoting* is a reasonable response to a system that has grown increasingly unresponsive to citizens' needs and on which a citizen can have little impact. According to Jack Doppelt and Ellen Shearer in their landmark work, *Nonvoters,* "[Some] see the nonvoting phenomenon as a reaction by the public to contemporary flaws in the political environment"; and conservative columnist George Will wrote the week before the 1996 presidential election, "Nonvoting is a sensible way for people who feel soiled by contemporary campaigning to express disgust."[3]

Meanwhile, ordinary citizens are not the only ones who are concerned with the state of politics in the United States. Even those most deeply involved with the system—among them political donors and political consultants—have strong reservations about the health of American democracy.[4]

So things are not so good. Both survey and anecdotal evidence paint the same sad picture of the American political process, a Hobbesian place where most do not vote, where those who do hold their noses in the voting booth, and where no one believes anything he or she hears. The situation is perhaps best described in a story taken from a 1997 conference sponsored by American University's Improving Campaign Conduct effort, at which "in one focus group, a woman was asked what one thing she would like to communicate to the political leaders of her state. Turning to the one-way mirror separating her from the consultants behind it, she raised one closed fist and extended her middle finger."[5]

Against this backdrop, one might ask, how can it be relevant to discuss the obligations of citizenship? How could citizens possibly "foster ethical campaigning"? Even if civic obligations exist, has not the electorate by and large abdicated its responsibility, either in disgust or sheer laziness? Not exactly. Mixed in with the foreboding of the political and academic elites and with citizens' feelings of irritation and resentment are positive signs of a citizenry that knows things can and should be better.

Americans believe honesty in public life is more important than accomplishments, and say they lose faith in politicians who lie. Seven in ten Americans strongly agree with the statement, "I prefer elected officials to be honest and fair in their dealings even if they are unsuccessful at getting the best results for the public," with another 25 percent somewhat agreeing. Further, an equal share strongly agree that "when a politician lies, I lose faith in him or her" (70 percent).

On the one hand, it is easy to dismiss such responses as manifestations of a phenomenon well known in survey research, the "halo effect." Respondents frequently seek to portray themselves as they would like themselves to be, rather than as they are—that is, they will say that they are in favor of good things and opposed to bad things. Whether they will act on those expressed sympathies is another matter. So in many cases, it is well to take responses to such "motherhood and apple pie" questions with a grain of salt. However, these data are relevant in this case. The discussion of ethics is at its core a normative, or even an aspirational, exercise, in which questions of what *ought* to be are just as important as questions of what *is*. Evidence of a desire to do the right thing on the part of the public makes a difference, because it speaks to a capacity to do better.

Defining the Question

The question of the ethics of citizenship is a thorny one with many factors at play. It is tempting, then, to narrow the question. After all, it is not difficult to set forth a list of "obligations of citizenship." Citizens who fulfill those obligations would be "ethical," and those who do not would be "unethical." However, this approach has three flaws.

First, it presupposes that it is possible to set forth a complete list of civic obligations—a task whose success is doubtful. Second, it assumes that if such a list were developed, constituting the totality of issues that make up citizenship, it would be appropriate for it to have a sanctioning mechanism attached. But such a mechanism neglects a key component of the American experiment in self-governance: Good citizenship cannot be mandated, and each citizen has the perfect right to ignore entirely his or her civic obligations. Third, this approach does not take into account a case in which one civic obligation may be in conflict with another. As will be discussed below, this is in fact the key area in which we find ethical dilemmas for citizens. In other words, it is unlikely that a "rulebook" for citizenship will be forthcoming. A guidebook, perhaps, but not a rulebook.

Needed is a way of discussing the moral obligations of citizens in a way that is neither overly academic nor too simplistic, that is neither too Victorian in its outlook nor so ethically relativistic that all a citizen need do is stay home on Election Day claiming "disgusted disinterest."

Toward an Ethics of Citizenship

How, then, is it possible to discuss civic ethics in a pluralistic, rights-based democracy in which nonparticipation is allowed? If, on the one hand, it is impossible to create a "law of citizenship," while admitting, on the other hand, that a merely mechanistic description of how citizens behave holds no normative value, what is left? Let me expand on the definition of *ethics* given by Dale Miller and Stephen Medvic in chapter 2. They outline a common usage of the term *ethics* that relates to people's actions insofar as they are fulfilling a particular role—where *business ethics,* for example, covers the moral rules surrounding conduct in business by business actors. But there is a broader conception of ethics that extends beyond such roles. We expect people *as people* to behave morally. When a person's actions in business, for example, are unethical, we do not believe the person is behaving in a "business-unethical" fashion but simply "unethically." If I have been cheated, it was not by a "business cheat" but by a cheat. By the same token, the role of "citizen," unlike the role of "businessperson" or "political consultant," is not a separate one. In a self-governing society, the role of citizen is an inextricable facet of a person's existence as a member of the society. It is ontological. The role can be played poorly, or not played at all. But it cannot be removed.

Rather than develop a code of "citizenship ethics," then, our task is to develop a code of ethics for citizens, the *civic expression* of generally ethical behavior. The distinction is subtle but crucial. A code of ethics for people in their role as citizens will have different elements from a code of ethics for people in their role as, for example, parents. But it will not have an internal logic that is divergent—unlike, for example, a code of "legal ethics," which bases its internal logic on the Hegelian approach to truth seeking, the need for strong advocacy, and the presence of a judge.[6]

In a society in which there can be no law requiring good citizenship, can there be an ethics of citizenship? Yes, because ethics and the law differ in a key respect: enforceability. In *The Concept of Law,* H. L. A. Hart lays out four areas in which moral rules differ from laws: importance, immunity from deliberate change, voluntary character of moral offenses, and the form of moral pressure.[7] For our purposes, the last two areas are the most significant: ethics requires that actions be voluntary, and that the pressure to behave rightly not derive exclusively from the threat of physical punishment.

Rushworth M. Kidder, in *How Good People Make Tough Choices*, offers a concise definition of ethics from John Fletcher Moulton: "What he [Moulton] called 'manners' we would call 'ethics.' His phrase for it remains one of the more useful and astute definitions of ethics ever devised: 'obedience to the unenforceable.'"[8] The duties and obligations of citizenship, then, demand obedience to a set of norms that, in a democracy, is fundamentally unenforceable.

On what will such a code of ethics be based, if it is not to be simply a listing of the set of all obligations of citizenship? It will be based on the moral values that underlie those obligations. Our work at the Institute for Global Ethics, based on qualitative research and development in seminars and focus groups, has found strong consensus—around the country and around the world—on the following set of shared values: respect, responsibility, fairness, compassion, and honesty.[9] This list can help us in defining the parameters of ethical citizenship. Because such a list is widely shared and internalized, citizens have a basis for judging departures from an accepted ethical standard. When civic behavior is measured against such values, it is not difficult to spot that which is short of the mark. The beginnings of an outline of the "code of ethics for citizens" might look like this:

Respect
—Respect all candidates, officeholders, and others in positions of public trust
—Respect the validity of other citizens' viewpoints
—Respect the integrity of democratic institutions
Responsibility
—Vote in all elections for which eligible
—Communicate clearly, directly, and regularly with elected officials, candidates, and the media
—Advocate for own views in a civil fashion
—Do not tolerate unethical behavior by candidates
Fairness
—Moderate one's own demands, keeping in mind that others share resources and also have rights to their use
Compassion
—Facilitate all citizens' opportunity for meaningful participation

—Educate fellow citizens on process as well as issues
Honesty
—Demand honesty from candidates and elected representatives, even at the cost of beneficial programs
—In interactions with the government, portray positions with sincerity rather than "gaming the system"

Obviously, this is by no means a complete list, nor is it necessarily meant to be fully normative. It is one thing to say that we share a certain set of core values, and quite another to "operationalize" those values and claim their universality. Moreover, such a list of "operationalized values" is meant simply to illustrate principles that ought to guide our actions. The point: it is not impossible to develop a set of civic norms that would have a high degree of legitimacy across populations.

Ethical Dilemmas of Citizenship

Like ethical problems in other areas of behavior, the ethical dilemmas of citizenship come in two broad varieties: *right versus wrong* and *right versus right*. In most popular discussions of ethics, attention is focused on questions of right versus wrong. We are concerned with how best to avoid being unethical or how best to be ethical. We wonder, *what is the right thing to do?* hoping to avoid doing the wrong thing. However, this is perhaps the least interesting of the two areas. Once the right and the wrong have been determined, the decision is not a hard one: Do the right thing. It may be difficult to implement; there may be temptations that draw one away from doing the right thing. But it is not a hard thing to know what one *ought* to do when the choice is between a right and a wrong.[10]

On the other hand, right versus right dilemmas can be quite difficult. They occur when it is possible to make a strong moral case for pursuing either of the two options presented. Neither is "wrong"; they are both right because each reflects one of the core values outlined above. These are the real ethical dilemmas faced by ordinary citizens every day.

But are there moral wrongs when it comes to citizenship? Certainly. Voting more than once or giving money to a candidate improperly are two obvious ones, and the code outlined above suggests further possibilities. Uncivilly or inappropriately advocating for my own views might be seen as wrong, as might be purposefully lying to my fellow citizens about the likely impact of a particular ballot proposal.

The issue of participation itself is also in some ways a right versus wrong issue. One underlying assumption in the litany of woes so poignantly expressed on the Ohio hotline is a lack of *agency* on the part of citizens. Citizens are pushed out of the democratic process because they are disgusted by a set of unethical actors that includes officeholders, the political establishment, and the media. It would almost seem a wonder that anyone votes at all, let alone participates in other ways. However, this cannot be a very accurate picture, or else there would be *no* voter turnout. Experience and research leads us to believe that in many cases citizens know that they have in some sense abrogated responsibility and are prepared at least to talk about taking it back. Here, for many citizens, is the crux of the question of ethics in civic life: How can I be a good citizen? It is fundamentally a right versus wrong question.

Seeking the answer to this question, the Institute for Global Ethics examined the relationship between political conduct and citizens' attitudes toward politics.[11] The study consisted of a series of forums where citizens, officeholders, and members of the media were brought together to discuss and deliberate about ethics in politics. They discussed a variety of approaches to solving the issue raised by the problem statement, "Political campaigns do not foster citizen participation, nor do they result in the kind of leaders we want." The approaches were:

—Address structural barriers to citizen participation. The system just is not fair. Certain laws and processes provide some people with more than their fair share of influence and keep others from participating.

—Increase accountability. The "system" is not the problem, but rather what people do within it. We need to find ways to increase the accountability of everyone involved.

—Equip and motivate citizens to participate more fully. People seem to behave as if they lack the capacity to be good citizens. We need to focus our energies on educating citizens about how and why to participate more fully.

While these three approaches to the issue are not completely exclusive of one another (that is, there is no inherent contradiction in subscribing to both, say, the first and third), they do tend to pull in three very different directions. They each illustrate three divergent areas of concern in civic reform today: structure, accountability, and capacity.

From the point of view of a citizen, the structure and accountability approaches assume that the problem rests on someone else's shoulders. The system is configured so as to keep people out, or people in official capacities are behaving badly, and this is why things are so bad. The third approach, on the other hand, is inward-looking. It assumes that the problem, and the solution, lies with citizens.

The majority of participants, 55.8 percent across all locations, expressed a preference for the third, "civic capacity," approach to the question, compared to 26.4 percent for structure and 10.1 percent for accountability.[12] Rather than wait for everyone else to shape up before getting involved, these citizens see themselves as having an obligation to do a better job— and to help others do a better job—of citizenship. As one Columbus participant said, "I don't know if you can make politicians accountable, but you can help people demand it." This comment provides some basis for optimism, as it indicates that, at least to an extent, citizens see themselves as able to have an effect on campaign ethics, without reliance on a legislative deus ex machina.

Right and wrong in civic life, therefore, relates to two things: whether and in what way to participate in political life. What about right versus right questions? Right versus right dilemmas typically fall into four paradigms: truth versus loyalty, justice versus mercy, individual versus community, and short term versus long term. These sorts of dilemmas are susceptible to the following shorthand analysis: "On the one hand, it is right to do A because of B, but on the other hand, it is right to do C because of D." (In right versus wrong questions, by contrast, it will be difficult to fill in the moral reason for the "wrong" option.) Examples include:

Truth versus Loyalty: Do I donate money or time to, say, an environmental interest group that advocates for issues I support but does so using untruthful tactics?

Justice versus Mercy: Do I support extending equal social services to everyone regardless of race or ethnic origin, or do I instead support paying special attention to those whose cultural backgrounds may have deprived them of past opportunities?

Individual versus Community: Do I vote for candidate Jones, who promises to lower my taxes and so allow me more take-home pay, or do I vote for Smith, who promises more government services to those in need?

Short Term versus Long Term: Do I support using Social Security funds to pay for needed programs (some of which I benefit from), or do I support keeping Americans' retirement money in a "lockbox?"

For the purpose of illustration, the exact circumstances of each dilemma are not as important as the underlying idea: that, as a consequence of a citizen's role as a part of government, she or he faces right versus right dilemmas that go beyond voting-booth behavior.

But is not enough to simply say that ethical dilemmas come in four basic flavors. There must be a way to resolve them once they are analyzed. Philosophy gives us three such ways: ends-based, rule-based, and care-based.

An ends-based approach to resolving an ethical dilemma is essentially consequentialist, or utilitarian. It asks, what is the greatest good for the greatest number (or, conversely, what is the least bad for the smallest number)? A great deal of public policy is made by asking this question, as it lends itself to quantification. Jeremy Bentham was perhaps its most famous proponent, though, as Paul Taylor reminds us in chapter 12, John Stuart Mill is also closely associated with it.

Rule-based decisionmaking, on the other hand, is nonconsequentialist. The key question in this approach is: What is the applicable rule in this situation? The test is to universalize the decision; the decisionmaker acts as if he or she were setting precedent for all who follow in the same situation, imagining what one would want everyone to be required to do in like circumstances. This is Immanuel Kant's categorical imperative: "Act so that the maxim of your action could become, by your will, a universal law of nature."[13] In other words, imagine the world if everybody in the future were required to behave as you are about to.

The third ethical decisionmaking approach is one that receives less attention from the philosophers but remains the one that most ordinary people try to use as their yardstick. This is the "Golden Rule," or the doctrine that one ought not to do to others what one would not want done to oneself. Though associated with the teachings of Jesus, the "Golden Rule" moniker in fact comes from Confucius. Some version of this approach can be found in every major world religion.[14]

Conclusion: From the Least to the Most

The first right versus right example above—that of the environmental group using underhanded tactics—deserves highlighting here for two reasons. First, it is illustrative of what is probably the most common way citizens can promote more ethical campaigning: by refusing to support unethical campaigning. This point relates to the nonparticipation argument made earlier: to act ethically, citizens must, as a matter of principle, see themselves as moral agents in civic life rather than passive reactors. Second, the environmental example makes it plain that there are places other than the voting booth where citizens face ethical dilemmas and have the obligation of ethical action.

This last point may be the most important. In most of the informed activists' thinking about the citizen's role in political ethics, the discussion typically turns to lower voter turnout rates. That trend is often taken as a measure of the civic disengagement that appears most powerful in preventing people from behaving as robust citizens. The questions are framed in one of two ways: (1) How do we get more people to vote? and (2) How do we help people make informed decisions in the voting booth? In both cases, the exercise of the franchise is seen not as the *sine qua non* of a democracy but rather as the *ne plus ultra*. Even among the advocates of a strong civil society, citizens are frequently seen as having only one "job" in the political process: to vote. Thankfully, most academic thinkers do not believe this; however, the academic world is not one with which most citizens, even engaged ones, have much contact. Sadly, the rhetoric of civic reform most often heard reflects this bias toward asking citizens simply to vote. Rarely are citizens referred to as anything other than "voters"— even by many of the civic groups that seek to promote a robust citizenry.

What is needed, instead of the outcomes-based approach to citizenship that seeks only to drive up turnout, is a broad-based and thoughtful approach to civic education in general. Children and adults ought to be encouraged to view voting as but one of many obligations of citizenship. This movement needs to start in school, and government classes must contain a moral as well as an informational content. Appeals to the so-called "benefits" obtained from voting are disingenuous and misguided and enhance the consumerist ("what can I get out of it?") approach to the government that many Americans hold.

If citizens can be encouraged to become comfortable with the idea that it is appropriate to discuss morality in the public sphere, perhaps they can also be helped to use a method of analyzing and discussing ethical dilemmas that allows for difference, and makes possible a civil deliberation of policy options. Only then might we begin to develop the type of citizenry that is as robust as we want, and that an effective democracy requires.

Notes

1. The Institute for Global Ethics (www.globalethics.org) is a nonprofit organization promoting ethics through public discourse and practical action. The in-

stitute, with offices in Camden, Maine; Toronto, Canada; and London, England, was founded in 1990 and is supported by The Pew Charitable Trusts, the Rockefeller Brothers Foundation, other foundations, and members throughout the world. It publishes a weekly online newsletter, *Ethics Newsline* (www.globalethics.org/newsline/) and occasional reports, consults with organizations and educational institutions in the United States and overseas, and conducts frequent ethics seminars.

2. A national survey of eight hundred U.S. adults aged eighteen and older, including five hundred people who identified themselves as likely voters in the November 2000 elections and three hundred people who said they were unlikely to vote in the November 2000 elections, was conducted by telephone November 4–9, 1999. In addition to this national survey, similar surveys in Ohio and Washington State were done in June 1998 and November 2000. All are available at www.campaignconduct.org/.

3. Jack C. Doppelt and Ellen Shearer, *Nonvoters: America's No-Shows* (Thousand Oaks, Calif.: Sage, 1999), p. 11. This work, which focused on the nonvoters of the 1996 presidential election campaigns, was updated recently with data from the 2000 election, with no substantive change in outlook. George Will, "Who Votes? Who Cares?" *Washington Post,* October 31, 1996, p. A21.

4. See the March 2000 *Civic Values Survey* of 600 political donors (www.campaignconduct.org) and the survey of 505 political consultants commissioned by American University and carried out by Yankelovich Partners, April–May 1999 (www.american.edu/academic.depts/spa/acps/pdffiles/political_campaign _consultants.pdf [March 19, 2002]).

5. John Boiney, "Who Cares about Campaign Conduct? Discussing the Consequences of Misleading Political Advertising" (paper presented at the Improving Campaign Conduct conference, sponsored by American University, Washington, April 17, 1998).

6. Does this mean that lawyers are a different breed from other people, and so have a totally different code of ethics? No. But there *is* a professional code of legal ethics which, while fundamentally basing itself on a set of core values not unlike those of ordinary people, takes as its starting point a set of assumptions about the lawyer's role and relies on that. A lawyer is more likely to find a divergence between the dictates of her or his code of lawyerly ethics and code of personal ethics. See John Lewis, *Ethics of Professions: A White Paper* (Camden, Maine: Institute for Global Ethics, forthcoming) for a deeper discussion of this.

7. H. L. A. Hart, *The Concept of Law* (Oxford University Press, 1961), pp. 169–76.

8. Rushworth M. Kidder, *How Good People Make Tough Choices* (William Morrow, 1995), p. 60.

9. Ibid., pp. 77–92.

10. Further encouraging the typical sense of ethics as fundamentally a question of right versus wrong, citizens frequently approach civic involvement itself as a right versus wrong exercise. Those citizens who do vote are anxious to make the "right" decision in the voting booth, as if one choice must be wrong if the other is right. This is rarely the case in election campaigns, however. It is not often

that the electorate comes across a candidate who is actually unqualified for the office she or he seeks. So the dialectic structure does not work. Citizens, when they vote, more often make trade-offs between candidates than decide which of them is morally "right." Yet the rhetoric of campaigning, as well as the language of the press, would make it appear that the loser of the election must be morally repugnant and the winner a hero.

11. Under contract with the Kettering Foundation, deliberative forums were held in February, March, and April 2001 in Irvine, California; Columbus, Akron, and Cleveland, Ohio; and Seattle, Washington. In each case, two meetings were held in the evening, except in Akron, where only one meeting was held. In all, 137 citizens, journalists, and officeholders participated. They were asked to fill out pre- and postdeliberation questionnaires. After the deliberations were concluded, all journalists and officeholders and some citizens were interviewed.

12. Postdeliberation results (predeliberation numbers were different but not substantially so). Numbers do not add to 100 percent because some participants chose more than one approach.

13. Immanuel Kant, *Grounding of the Metaphysics of Morals* (Harper & Row, 1964), p. 70.

14. The right versus right paradigms and dilemma resolution principles are laid out more fully in Kidder's *How Good People Make Tough Choices*.

Contributors

Robert E. Denton Jr. holds the W. Thomas Rice Chair of Leadership Studies and serves as director of the Center for Leader Development at Virginia Tech University.

David A. Dulio is assistant professor of political science at Oakland University. During 2001–02 he served as a congressional fellow in the American Political Science Association Congressional Fellowship Program.

Robin Kolodny is associate professor of political science at Temple University.

L. Dale Lawton is director of the Project on Campaign Conduct at the Institute for Global Ethics in Camden, Maine, and formerly served as the director of the Sorensen Institute for Political Leadership's candidate-training program at the University of Virginia.

L. Sandy Maisel is the William R. Kenan Jr. Professor of Government and director of Colby College's Washington Semester Program.

Larry Makinson is a senior fellow at the Center for Responsive Politics, Washington.

Stephen K. Medvic is assistant professor of government at Franklin & Marshall College.

Dale E. Miller is assistant professor of philosophy at Old Dominion University.

Candice J. Nelson is associate professor of government and academic director of the Campaign Management Institute at the Center for Congressional and Presidential Studies at American University.

Brad Rourke is vice president of public policy at the Institute for Global Ethics, Camden, Maine.

Mark A. Siegel is chief of staff to Congressman Steve Israel (D-N.Y.); he served as the executive director of the Democratic National Committee from 1974 to 1977.

Paul Taylor is founder and director of the Alliance for Better Campaigns, Washington, D.C.

James A. Thurber is professor of government at American University and, as director of the Center for Congressional and Presidential Studies, is the principal investigator for the center's "Improving Campaign Conduct" project.

Michael W. Traugott is professor and chair of the Department of Communication Studies at the University of Michigan as well as a senior research scientist with the Center for Political Studies at the university's Institute for Social Research.

Carol Whitney is president of Whitney and Associates, a political consulting firm; she also serves as an adjunct professor in the Center for Congressional and Presidential Studies at American University and coprogram director of the center's Campaign Management Institute.

William H. Wood is the executive director of the Sorensen Institute for Political Leadership at the University of Virginia.

Index

255